FAITH IN THE R

FAITH IN THE REVOLUTION

THE POLITICAL THEOLOGIES
OF MÜNTZER
AND WINSTANLEY

——

Andrew Bradstock

First published in Great Britain 1997
Society for Promoting Christian Knowledge
Holy Trinity Church
Marylebone Road
London NW1 4DU

British Library Cataloguing-in-Publication Data
A catalogue record of this book is available from the British Library

ISBN 0-281-05067-8

Typeset by The Midlands Book Typesetting Company, Loughborough
Printed in Great Britain by Arrowsmiths, Bristol

CONTENTS

Acknowledgements   vi
Abbreviations   viii
Introduction   ix

Part One: Thomas Müntzer

1   Thomas Müntzer: an introduction to his life and work   3

2   'Suffering the sharp edge of the plough-share':
    Müntzer's theology and politics   13

3   'A servant of God against the godless': Müntzer as
    Christian revolutionary   32

Part Two: Gerrard Winstanley

4   Gerrard Winstanley: an introduction to his life and work   69

5   'To make the Earth a Common Treasury': Winstanley's
    theology and politics   82

6   'Christ rising in sons and daughters': Winstanley as
    Christian revolutionary   108

Part Three: Conclusion

7   Building the kingdom: towards a Christian
    contribution to revolutionary praxis   139

Notes   176
Further reading   202
Index   204
Bible references   210

v

Acknowledgements

I should like to thank a number of people who have helped and inspired me with this book and who, in their several ways, have tried to make it much better than it might otherwise have been. That it has turned out as it has is not in any way their fault.

The basic research was undertaken at the University of Kent at Canterbury and the University of Otago, and I owe an enormous debt to my supervisors, David McLellan in Canterbury and Peter Matheson in Dunedin, who both shared with me their specialist insights and gave me much wise counsel and encouragement. At Canterbury I was also stimulated by conversations with David Ormrod and John Marsden, and at Otago with John Evans. In Dunedin I received invaluable help in understanding some untranslated German scholarship on Müntzer from Ina Elliott, Bruce Hamill and Stephanie Howard, and should also like to thank Madeline Sim, Secretary to the Theology Faculty, for all her help, advice and friendship. More recently Matthew Barton has given me some much-valued help with the Müntzer section, and I have benefited from discussing specific themes in the conclusion with Pat Logan, Tim Gorringe and my colleagues Rachel Moriarty and Joe Cassidy. Conversations with Claire Jowitt have greatly expanded my knowledge of the seventeenth-century radicals, and I am also grateful to Claire, and to Sue Morgan, for sending me some material on Winstanley which I might otherwise have missed. I must also mention three other friends who continually stretch my thinking in the areas of politics and religion, Roger Vince, Philip Lyons, and Francis Davis.

Since being at LSU I have enjoyed the friendship, support and stimulation of many colleagues in my own and other departments, but particularly that of Andrée Heaton and Mary Grey. Both have helped and encouraged me enormously with this project, and that it was finally completed was in no small part due to them. I should also like to thank my past and present students in Southampton (especially Ceri Werren and Julie Hammond), and postgraduate colleagues at Kent and Otago, who, in formal and informal settings, listened patiently to some of the ideas in this book; their feedback has been much appreciated. Special thanks also to my students Diana

Jurd, Gemma Owen and Louise Welcome, for help with the preparation of the final manuscript; to Esther Egea Sánchez and Julie Hammond for assistance with the index; and to David Mackinder for his patience and understanding at the copy-editing stage. Financial support from various institutions is also very gratefully acknowledged, including LSU, who generously part-funded a return visit to Nicaragua I made in 1994–95; the ESRC, who funded my research at Kent; and the University of Otago, who honoured me with the award of a post-doctoral fellowship to undertake the work on Müntzer. I should also like to thank the editor of *The Seventeenth Century*, Richard Maber, for permission to include, in chapter 5, material which first appeared in an article published in that journal in 1991.

Lastly (though Luke 13.30a could be taken literally here) I want to acknowledge the special help of the following: Simon Barrow and James Penney, two friends with whom I have discussed the ideas in this book over a long period, and whose comments and criticisms have been invaluable; Denys Turner, who first introduced me to Winstanley during one of his undergraduate courses, and who has remained a much-valued mentor; Chris Rowland, whose suggestions to improve this book, and encouragement, advice and support, have meant so much; and Alex Wright, formerly Senior Editor at SPCK, for his ongoing faith in this project, much-valued advice, and patient understanding of the pressures of academic life. I'm not quite sure what it means to 'dedicate' a book, but if I were to do so it would be to those closest to me: Frannie Symonds and Christine and Richard Stainer, for their encouragement and understanding over the years; my mother, whose support and love I could never sum up in one line or, indeed, one hundred; and my late father, who, among other things, taught me the essence of nonconformity. He would not have approved of much in this book, but he knew about radical religion and, like me, certainly thought it should make a difference in the world.

Abbreviations

CW   Peter Matheson, tr. & ed., *The Collected Works of Thomas Müntzer*, Edinburgh, T. & T. Clark, 1988.

F   Günther Franz, ed., in collaboration with Paul Kirn, *Thomas Müntzer: Schriften und Briefe, Kritische Gesamtausgabe*, Quellen und Forschungen zur Reformationsgeschichte, 33, Gütersloh, Gerd Mohn, 1968.

W   George H. Sabine, ed., *The Works of Gerrard Winstanley*, New York, Russell & Russell, 1965.

Explanatory notes

All the quotations from Müntzer's writings have been taken from Peter Matheson's translation verbatim, with the exception that I have given a capital 'S' to the word 'spirit' where the reference appears to be to the Holy Spirit. The Winstanley extracts have similarly been reproduced unchanged from the G. H. Sabine collection, which retains the writer's original spelling, punctuation and capitalization.

Biblical references, other than those which appear in quoted material, are taken from *The New Revised Standard Version* (Iowa Falls: World Bible Publishers, Inc. 1989).

INTRODUCTION

There has long been a strand within the Christian tradition which
has argued that, when confronted with injustice and oppression, the
reign of God will not be extended solely through gradual reform or
the conversion of individuals. In some contexts human relationships
will appear so fractured that it will hardly be possible to fulfil the
Christian imperative to love one's neighbour in any piecemeal or
individual fashion; what will be required, rather, will be the revolutionary transformation of those socio-economic structures which make
Christian charity ineffective, which, by institutionalizing poverty
and powerlessness, deny the possibility of truly human relationships.
Fidelity to the vision of the kingdom of God as an order in which
the lowly are exalted and the mighty and powerful brought low can
thus entail, in some circumstances, a preparedness to embrace the
revolutionary option.

This position has not been a popular, let alone mainstream, one
within the Christian tradition: while church leaders have often given
their blessing all too readily to bloodshed in defence of 'national
sovereignty' or 'the *status quo*', few have been quick to own sacrifices
made in the cause of social transformation or human liberation;
while army chaplains get decorated and promoted, priest-guerrillas
receive only excommunication and censure. Nevertheless, voices
echoing a revolutionary position have been audible on the margins
of the Christian Church in every generation, and the aim of this
book is to recall them once more from the shadows, listen to what
they have to say, and do so with an ear tuned particularly to whether
they are saying anything *distinctive*. What, if anything, makes Christian
revolutionary politics *Christian*? Is there any singular contribution
which Christianity can offer to revolutionary theory and practice?
These will be our guiding questions.

The discussion focuses, therefore, not on the principle of Christian
participation in revolution, nor on specific issues such as the ethics
of the use of violence in political struggle, though such themes necessarily receive some treatment. Rather it takes as its point of departure
the fact of Christian involvement in revolutionary activity, and goes

on to ask whether beyond that, once an initial revolutionary commitment has been made, Christians are to be found saying or doing anything not already being said or done by other revolutionaries or movements. The aim is to construct a response to a question often implicit in analyses of, and apologias for, Christian revolutionary praxis, but seldom directly addressed in them, namely that of the 'specifically Christian contribution'.

We proceed by means of an analysis of the life and testimony of two revolutionaries who operated within a Christian frame of reference: Thomas Müntzer, a preacher and pastor of the early Reformation period in Germany who became embroiled in the Peasants' War of 1525; and Gerrard Winstanley, leader and main theorist of the Digger movement in England in the 1640s. Other suitable subjects for study could no doubt have been found – and some will appear from time to time in the discussion – but in the end a preference has been made for detailed analysis over general survey. What should be said, though, is that the choice of these two figures does not limit the possibility of a response being made to the question in a general way, given the quite different historical, cultural and religious milieux from which they are drawn; indeed, this diversity constitutes an important justification for the selection which has been made.

The discussion falls into three main sections: one devoted to an attempt to answer the preoccupying question with respect to Müntzer; one to a similar project with respect to Winstanley; and a conclusion which, in drawing together and developing the main points raised in the earlier sections, engages with contemporary theological reflection, particularly from the two-thirds world. Each of the two 'case studies' begins with a short biographical and literary introduction, and while one purpose of these is to provide a background for the analyses which follow, it also seems important, since the book aims to explore the possibility of a Christian contribution to revolutionary praxis, to include some discussion of this in respect of both figures.

The theme to which most attention is paid in this study is the *eschatological*, since it is in so far as Christians can hold before political struggles the horizon of the 'kingdom' or 'reign' of God as a perpetual critique of all earthly achievements that they can offer a valid and singular contribution to such projects. Every revolutionary project needs a guiding utopia, an overarching vision of the new order it desires to create from the rubble of the old; and it is at the level of giving content to such visions that the category of the kingdom can play an important role.[1]

The significance and implications of this are worked out in the conclusion to the book, though the studies of both Müntzer and Winstanley explore first the close interweaving of theological and political ideas in their writings, and the extent to which both placed their own revolutionary praxes within an eschatological perspective. In considering Müntzer, particular attention is paid to the mystical and apocalyptic dimensions of his thought, and to the way in which, as they fuse together, they impel him towards a revolutionary (and in the end disturbingly violent) onslaught against the godless. For Müntzer, the time of the harvest, of the final rooting out of the tares from the wheat, has come, and he himself has an important prophetic role in the drama. A utopian strand in Müntzer's work is also identified, one which anticipates that a feature of the new age – of which the harvest is a harbinger – will be the restoration of the perfect pattern of relationships between God, humankind and the creatures established by God at the creation and damaged subsequently by the fall. A not dissimilar utopian vision – the recapturing of a past 'Golden Age' – also surfaces in Winstanley's writings, and this, together with the millennial hopes which underpinned and inspired his programme, are discussed and evaluated. For Winstanley, we shall note, the second coming is no sudden, supernatural event, but the gradual 'rising up' of Christ in men and women, to draw them together into true community and so make the earth, as it was originally created, a 'common treasury' for all.

One conclusion drawn from these discussions is that, not only were millenarian, apocalyptic and utopian concerns central to the thinking of both Müntzer and Winstanley, both appeared to go so far as to hinge the realization of their respective projects on the imminent – and in Winstanley's case *immanent* – return of Jesus Christ and the restoration of the world to something like a state of prelapsarian perfection. It is therefore straightforward enough to argue that, for both, the eschatological dimension of their programmes owed its shape and content to the Christian framework within which they operated, though not that its *effect* as a contribution was wholly positive. Clearly, in so far as Müntzer drew from the apocalyptic interpretation he placed on events around him a profound insight into the drift of those events, a perception that he and the saints were encountering a propitious, God-given opportunity to act, its contribution was both constructive and powerful; and much the same must be said of Winstanley's millenarianism, which provided him with an interpretative framework against which to read developments in the last years of Charles I's reign and the significance of his 'digging'. Yet if, as seems to be the case, both men placed too heavy a demand on their eschatologies, in the form of an insistence that the millennium or reign of God be fully realized as a consequence of the specific struggles in which they were both engaged, questions must be asked about the extent to which those eschatologies contributed positively to their respective programmes. Reductionism in eschatology can give rise to false hopes about the potential of a particular project, specifically because it bypasses the necessity to make any realistic, empirically based analysis of the concrete possibilities of the given historical moment. Whether its eschatological dimension renders Christianity *per se* chronically incapable of offering to politics anything other than fantastic, ahistorical visions, or whether a more nuanced interpretation of the kingdom might point towards the identification of a distinctive and constructive Christian contribution, is explored in the concluding chapter.

This chapter also picks up and examines in a more general way additional themes which emerged in the preceding discussion. One is the extent to which a Christian's commitment to see revolution move in the direction of the reign of God can enable him or her to say something about the way in which the struggle is prosecuted, about revolutionary *ethics*. If the kingdom is understood as both a future event and an intrahistorical reality, what demands does it make for a consistency to be maintained between 'means' and 'ends' in political engagement? Another area considered is the vital role that revolutionary Christians have played, in cultures where religion helps to inform popular perceptions of the world, in rescuing Christian symbols from the ideological use to which they are often put by oppressing elites and hierarchies, the more easily to free them for a revolutionary reinterpretation. Exploding the reactionary instrumentalizing of Christianity in this way has, it will be argued, played an indispensable role in unblocking the Christian conscience for genuine and committed participation in revolutionary struggle. A closing reflection considers how far Christian 'hope', specifically in the ultimate conquest of death and the final resurrection, allows for a deeper interpretation to be placed on political projects. With their belief that the ultimate significance of the struggle to which they are committed does not lie without reserve in the here-and-now, is there a unique space which Christians can occupy in that struggle? The thesis of this book is that there is a significant contribution which Christianity can offer to revolutionary politics, and that it is long overdue for re-examination – and not least in the light of the role played by church-people (and even the institutional Church) in the recent transformations which have occurred in, for example, Nicaragua, the former East Germany, the Philippines, Haiti and South Africa. Of course, it may be argued that Christianity occupies few *unique* spaces within revolutionary struggles – there are other utopias, other bases for ethics, other perceptions of the 'deeper significance' of political struggle; yet even so, it is important that its contribution be recognized, identified and evaluated.

On one level an exercise such as this might seem to typify the armchair militancy for which Western scholars are all too often criticized, and it is, of course, one which those actually involved in transforming the world often have neither the time nor inclination to pursue. Yet precisely for that reason it behoves those of us who do have the opportunity and some measure of detachment to offer our contribution, though not, it must be said, for purely theoretical purposes. Events since 1989 – including the collapse of 'really existing socialism' and the seemingly inexorable forward march of (neo-) liberal capitalism – may have made revolutions even less likely to occur, let alone succeed, than before; but the situations which spawned revolutionary movements in the past not only still remain largely unchanged but are, in many cases, more combustible than ever before. Thus for many visionaries, both within and without the Church, when faced with social and economic structures which bind people to seemingly endless cycles of poverty, marginalization, meaninglessness and disempowerment, projects which encompass the hopes so beautifully expressed in Mary's song to the Lord in Luke 1 – that the lowly be lifted up, the hungry filled with good things, and the powerful brought down from their thrones – still seem to be the only bases for hope for a better world. And in so far as Christianity can help to keep hope alive and give it focus, direction and content, its 'contribution' to transforming projects will never be insignificant.

PART ONE

THOMAS MÜNTZER

1

THOMAS MÜNTZER: AN INTRODUCTION TO HIS LIFE AND WORK

F ew figures in the early Reformation period have attracted as much scholarly interest, or been the centre of so much debate, as Thomas Müntzer. For the past two hundred years, since the publication of Georg Strobel's *Leben, Schriften und Lehren Thomae Müntzers* in 1795, a stream – one might be inclined to say nowadays a torrent – of books and articles about him have rolled off the presses of Europe, the United States, the former Soviet Union and elsewhere.[1] For despite the shortness of his days – he died in all probability before reaching his thirty-seventh birthday – and the paucity of his writings (at any rate when placed alongside the outpourings of a Luther or Calvin), Müntzer continues, as he did in his own day, to fascinate, inspire, and antagonize all who take the trouble to read him (and some who don't!). There is a depth, a complexity, and an originality about his writings which seems continually to prompt new questions about who he was, what he believed, and what he achieved: '[t]hrough the thickets of Reformation controversy', as Tom Scott has rather poetically written, 'Thomas Müntzer has commonly been stalked as dangerous yet exhilarating prey, arousing in the hunter dread and fascination in equal measure'.[2] The purpose of this chapter is not to attempt another assessment of Müntzer's life, but simply to draw the broad contours of it, in the hope of offering a rudimentary background against which the main study itself may be read. Some attempt will be made to describe the situations from which Müntzer's writings emerged, though little by way of comment will be offered on them or on the writings themselves; that will be left for the subsequent discussion.

Despite the depth of feeling which Müntzer's name evokes, very little is actually known about his life. As Hans-Jürgen Goertz has put it, all that seems to confront the historian hoping to uncover something of Müntzer's early years are *verwehte Spuren*, 'blurred tracks'.[3] We know from the opening words of the 'Prague Manifesto' (Larger German Version) that he was born in the quiet German hillside town of Stolberg,[4] but it has been notoriously difficult to find any documentary evidence of his date of birth. Although Ulrich Bubenheimer, an authority on Müntzer's early years, has suggested 1482 as a likely year of birth, the most commonly accepted dates are 1488 or 1489, on the assumption that Müntzer began his studies at Leipzig University in 1506 (a date about which we can be a little more certain) at the conventional age of seventeen.[5]

Lack of certainty about the details of Müntzer's birth means that we are also in the dark regarding his social background. At one time the view prevailed that his origins were humble and that he knew from an early age 'all the bitterness of disgrace and injustice', but this may have been little more than romantic speculation.[6] On the evidence of what remains of a letter Müntzer wrote to his father around 1521, it appears that the family had some means: Müntzer refers to some sort of inheritance which was originally part of his mother's estate (perhaps the fruits of her labours), and which, following her death, his father is not allowing to pass to him (CW 22). The inheritance was probably not insubstantial, for Müntzer later notes, after the dispute with his father had (presumably) fallen out in his favour, that 'I have much household goods left after the mother's death . . .' (CW 31). If his father had fallen on hard times, as Müntzer's letter appears to indicate, this was in all probability a recent development, and not necessarily an indication that the family had always known poverty. Neither the occupation nor even the identity of Müntzer's father is known for certain, though the etymology of the family name suggests that his forebears might have been minters or goldsmiths. Until any further discoveries are made, however, it is probably best to refrain from trying to fashion too bold a picture of Müntzer's early life with so few solid materials.

Between 1506 and 1512 Müntzer appears to have studied at Leipzig (if the 'Thomas Müntzer de Quedlinburgk' in the university register for winter 1506 is in fact our man),[7] and then at Frankfurt an der Oder, gaining, or so it would seem, degrees in the arts and divinity. No extant graduation list for these years for any German university records Müntzer obtaining any degrees, but he himself claimed both a 'master of arts' and a 'bachelor of holy scripture'

(CW 406). What *effect* Müntzer's study had on his theological development is an interesting point, since the faculties at both Leipzig and Frankfurt would have been firmly in the scholastic tradition, committed to the pursuit of rational explanations for religious belief, and therefore far removed in their ideas from the mystical, experimental theology Müntzer was subsequently to embrace. Müntzer in any case seems to dismiss any learning he may have enjoyed as of no consequence: 'I can testify with Christ and all the elect who have known me from my youth up, to having shown all possible diligence . . . in pursuing better instruction about the holy and invincible Christian faith', he writes, but 'instruction' here is the kind directly mediated by God: 'For at no time in my life (God knows I am not lying) did I learn anything about the true exercise of the faith from any monk or priest . . . I have not heard from a single scholar about the order of God implanted in all creatures, not the tiniest word about it . . .' (CW 357).

This passage might be taken as implying that, from his earliest days, Müntzer intended to enter the Church, though we cannot be certain of this. At any rate, he was ordained in 1514, and though he undertook teaching and tutoring from time to time to supplement his income, it was the only career he pursued. His first appointment was as a chantry priest at St Michael's, Brunswick, a post he held until 1522 (though he cannot have spent much time in the parish after 1517). Some impression of the high esteem in which he was held at Brunswick may be gained from a letter of the time addressed to him as a 'most learned, worthy, beloved lord', castigator of unrighteousness', and containing a wish that he may 'live in health and holiness before God Almighty in the fiery love of purity' (CW 6–7).[8]

The autumn and winter of 1517 saw Müntzer at Wittenberg, attending lectures given by Johannes Rhagius Aesticampianus, and he may have stayed in the town for a period of some eighteen months, albeit interrupted by brief visits to other cities. This would have been a formative time for Müntzer, for we know that he spent some of his time there studying Plato – particularly the writings on asceticism which echoed Müntzer's own developing concern with the mystical path of suffering; Quintilian, who deals in his *Institutio oratoria* with the concept of a natural order of creation (ordo rerum); and, most likely, the *Theologia Deutsch*, an edition of which was prepared and published by Luther in 1518. Müntzer would also have come into contact with Luther himself at a crucial moment – the Ninety-five Theses were posted in November 1517 – though it is not unlikely that Müntzer had become embroiled in the controversy over indulgences before that time.[9] Also at Wittenberg at that time would have been Melanchthon and Karlstadt, and the latter may have stimulated in Müntzer an interest in Augustine.

Müntzer's whereabouts in 1519 cannot be stated with absolute certainty. He appears to have spent a month or so in Orlamünde, almost certainly at the invitation of Karlstadt (who was rector of that parish), and while there to have immersed himself in some writings which were to influence him greatly, those of the mystic Johannes Tauler. He was also in Jüterbog over Easter, standing in for the preacher, Franz Günther. Müntzer's teaching at this time – at least to judge from a report by a friar who had heard him and taken offence – seems to have been close to Luther's, and he was clearly very outspoken in his criticisms of the Pope, the bishops, and some local priests.[10] A third port-of-call for Müntzer in 1519 was Leipzig, where he attended the public disputation between Eck and the Wittenberg reformers, an experience which may have helped Müntzer to put his disquiet about the present wretched state of the Church in a historical perspective, and prompted him to read the classical accounts of the Church's origins and discover from what heights she had since fallen. Certainly he lost no time after Leipzig in rereading Augustine and acquiring copies of Eusebius, Hegesippus and Jerome, and would have had plenty of time to get to grips with this reading when he took up an appointment in December as confessor to a house of Cistercian nuns at Beuditz; indeed, he makes mention himself of the 'ample time' the post afforded for his studies (CW 14–15). His time there ended in April of the following year, however, when he was appointed preacher at St Mary's, Zwickau.

In Zwickau Müntzer continued to denounce and harangue the Church and its priests, and something of the flavour of his sermons may be inferred from some comments he makes in a letter to Luther in July 1520. The monks and priests have 'seduced the church of God', he writes, and the laity are little better, having failed to pray for better leaders. Müntzer castigates all the hypocrites who promote not faith, 'but their own insatiable avarice', and pledges himself to undertake God's work and 'combat them with unceasing groans and with the trumpet of the word of God' (CW 18, 21). Zwickau was already a tense place when Müntzer arrived, and his sermons can hardly have helped to ease things. Through his meeting with Nicholas Storch, a leader of the so-called 'Zwickau prophets', Müntzer also learned something of the resentment felt by local working people, notably the clothmakers, about their conditions; he may have seen, too, how they stood to gain from a reformation of the Church. Storch's mysticism would also have impressed Müntzer, perhaps underlining for him the antithesis that existed between the elect, who relied on direct revelation from God, and the 'bookish' priests with their theology gained from learning rather than experience.

In April 1521, amid considerable uproar, Müntzer was dismissed from Zwickau, and from June until the end of that year he resided in the Bohemian capital of Prague, a well-known centre of radicalism and unrest where the ideas of Hus and Wyclif were still strongly felt. Initially he was well received, but as differences of opinion began to emerge between him and various sectors of the population his position there became less comfortable. While in the city, he compiled what has become known as his 'Prague Manifesto', of which four versions are extant.[11] Provoked, perhaps, by his unpleasant experiences in the city, but also by a desire to turn his audience to the right paths, Müntzer uses the manifesto to launch into a sustained attack on the 'hell-grounded priests' of the Church, who know nothing of the true path to faith which begins with the fear of God and so deceive those who are placed in their charge. Their days, though, are numbered, for God will shortly call on his servants to sift out the wheat from the tares; and Müntzer himself has his sickle ready sharpened in anticipation of his call. Müntzer's appeal, however, never reached its intended audience, for he was moved on from the city before he had a chance to nail up the manifesto: indeed the Czech translation was never actually completed.

After a year spent going from pillar to post and being ejected from virtually every town he set foot in, Müntzer arrived in Allstedt in March 1523 to take up the pastorate of St John's Church. Here he seems to have made an immediate impact, for within weeks of his arrival in the town, which had a population of perhaps only 600, reports were circulating that up to 2,000 people were flocking in from the surrounding countryside to hear him preach. Müntzer's stay in Allstedt, which was to last until August the following year, was undoubtedly the most settled period of his adult life. In June he married a former nun, Ottilie von Gersen, and a son was born to them the following Easter. He had the time to give full rein to his not inconsiderable pastoral gifts, and the most striking of the many fruits of his ministry in Allstedt must surely be the new liturgy he fashioned for his flock to enjoy in their own language, the first of its kind in the German tongue. Something of Müntzer's general concern for his people comes through in a rather touching sentence in a letter to a friend: 'Dealing with people these days means the sort of work which a mother has when her children have dirtied themselves' (CW 104).

It should not be thought that his sojourn in this quiet backwater dampened Müntzer's zeal for reform within the Church, or his hostility to those who were part of it. One particular focus of his anger was Count Ernst of Mansfeld, who was doing everything within his power to suppress the new doctrines of the reformers and ensure that the traditional teachings of the Catholic Church were upheld. Count Ernst declined an invitation from Müntzer to come to Allstedt to debate the question of heresy, and instead appealed to the elector Frederick to take steps to bring Müntzer to order. Müntzer also wrote to Frederick, requesting the opportunity to explain himself, and took the opportunity to remind the elector of the teaching of Daniel 7, that rulers may only expect to hold power so long as they take a stand against the godless: should they default in their duties, 'the sword will be taken from them and will be given to the people who burn with zeal so that the godless can be defeated' (CW 69). Frederick did not immediately respond to Müntzer's request for a hearing, but in November he spent a week in Allstedt with his court preacher Spalatin, and while there summoned Müntzer and his fellow preacher Haferitz to a disputation. In the wake of this, and in response to some questions directed to him by Spalatin, Müntzer published his *Protestation or Proposition* and *On Counterfeit Faith*, both of which were printed around New Year 1524. In both tracts Müntzer addresses the question of faith, pointing out that it is a gift from God and cannot be acquired through human effort. Of the two, *On Counterfeit Faith* is more directly a reply to Spalatin.

Müntzer's preaching against the Catholic Church excited some sections of the community in Allstedt, and matters came to a head around Easter 1524 when a small chapel at Mallerbach, just outside of the town, was razed to the ground by fire. The chapel had become a popular place of pilgrimage following a miraculous appearance there by the Virgin Mary, though shortly before its destruction it had been closed by the nuns at Naundorf in whose charge it lay.

Although Müntzer's teaching must have been indirectly responsible for the attack, and he in no way dissociated himself from it, there is no evidence that he was directly involved. Attempts by the authorities to apprehend the perpetrators of the crime proved fruitless, and following the wrongful arrest of one of the town council members on suspicion of arson, civil war almost broke out in the town between the citizenry and the authorities. Müntzer played a prominent role in urging the people to defend themselves.

Not long after this episode, in July 1524, Müntzer had opportunity to preach before John, Duke of Saxony (brother of the elector Frederick), and his son Prince John Frederick. With considerable boldness he reiterated his views on the decline of the Church from her original virginal purity, lambasted the false teachers responsible for her present adulterous state, and demonstrated how God is now revealing to the elect, through dreams and visions, 'the great need for a full and final reformation in the near future' (CW 244). Müntzer took as his text Daniel 2, the account of King Nebuchadnezzar's dream of a multi-layered statue fashioned of different metals, which only the prophet himself was able to interpret. Müntzer strove to present himself to the princes as a 'new Daniel', one able to interpret the signs of the times for them; and the signs were that the final layer of the statue, the Holy Roman Empire of which they were part, was very shortly to be destroyed by 'the stone dislodged from the mountain', namely Christ himself (CW 245). The princes must obey the injunction of Romans 13 and 'sweep aside' all those who obstruct the gospel (CW 246). That they did not respond to this appeal appears to have convinced Müntzer that the way forward to a reformation must lie in the creation of a new league or covenant between God and humankind, after the manner of the Old Testament king Josiah. Müntzer actually formed two leagues during his time in Allstedt, with the intention of bringing the people together with a common purpose of overthrowing the wicked and preparing the way for God's final transformation of the world.

Not for the first time was pressure building up against Müntzer. In July Luther wrote his famous *Letter to the Princes of Saxony concerning the Rebellious Spirit*, denouncing Müntzer – whom he had earlier called 'that satan in Allstedt' – in the strongest terms for being guided by an evil spirit, preaching a false gospel, and inciting the people into violence. In order to fulfil their God-given mandate to preserve the peace and punish the wrongdoer, Luther exhorted the princes to lose no time in banishing Müntzer and his followers from the country – an interpretation of the Romans 13 passage somewhat at variance from the one they had earlier received at Allstedt! The princes, for their part, though proceeding more cautiously than Luther had exhorted them, also felt driven to examine Müntzer more closely, and on 31 July he, and two councillors of the town of Allstedt, were interrogated at Weimar, the residence of Duke John. Müntzer came off badly, and was instructed to disband his league and refrain from preaching and publishing. Rather than obey these injunctions, however, he left Allstedt secretly on the night of 7 August.

He arrived shortly afterwards in the Reichstadt of Mühlhausen, where he quickly teamed up with the radical priest Heinrich Schwertfeger, known as Pfeiffer. Pfeiffer had already attracted quite a following – and some official opposition – as a result of his anti-clerical stand, and the two men began to draw up a programme of reform. They failed to win over enough of the people to their side, however, and in September, following a week of unrest, both were expelled from the city. Müntzer then seems to have gravitated towards Nuremberg, where he managed to secure the services of a printer and published *A Manifest Exposé* (of which a shorter and somewhat milder version exists entitled *The Testimony of the First Chapter of the Gospel of Luke*) and *A Highly Provoked Vindication and a Refutation of the Unspiritual Soft-Living Flesh in Wittenberg*. Both of these he had begun to draft out shortly before his departure from Allstedt. The *Exposé* is the longest of his writings, and treats, in a rather haphazard fashion (which possibly reflects the speed at which it was written) the main themes found in his earlier writings, including the nature of true faith, the deceitfulness and arrogance of the priests and scholars who teach the people error, and the anticipated separation of the elect and the godless. The *Vindication and Refutation* is a savage and unrestrained attack on Luther, clearly intended as a riposte to the *Letter to the Princes*.

If Müntzer regarded his first stay in Mühlhausen as something of an anti-climax, his return to the imperial city in late February 1525 might have seemed more promising. The city had undergone a political change in the intervening months, and Müntzer was able to assume the post of rector of St Mary's with a degree of popular approval. The region of Thuringia, in which Mühlhausen was situated, had also become one of the main centres of what we now refer to as the Peasants' War, the wave of uprisings that occurred in many

10

parts of central Germany in 1524–25 as the peasantry and artisans responded to the hardship and oppression they had long been forced to endure. In Mühlhausen Müntzer formed another covenant, the Eternal League of God, but this time it had an offensive rather than purely defensive purpose, and an unambiguously military structure. This act, and Müntzer's writings during this period, point unmistakably to the conclusion that he saw the peasants' revolt as a sign that the world had come to the last days, and that he was determined himself to be involved in the action. Filled with confidence that he was engaged in 'the Lord's fight', Müntzer set out on 26 April to travel to Langensalza, accompanied by Pfeiffer and some 400 followers, under the banner of the Eternal League. In due course the party was joined by some peasants at Gormar to form a Mühlhausen-Thuringian army, and a further 700 people joined up at Ebeleben. *En route* a number of abbeys and nunneries were looted and pillaged by the troop, and in early May they indulged in a week of plunder and destruction, laying waste large numbers of castles, monasteries and other civic and religious buildings in the region of Eichsfeld in the west.

Following this campaign Müntzer and Pfeiffer headed back to Mühlhausen, while a smaller detachment went to Frankenhausen, where the dukes of Mansfeld were preparing to do battle with the peasants. Realizing the vulnerability of their situation, the Frankenhausen contingent appealed to Mühlhausen for support, but inexplicably Müntzer waited several days before responding, and then set off on the two-day march with just 300 men. Perhaps Müntzer's supreme confidence in the success of the campaign he was about to mount – clearly demonstrated in his letters of the time – could account for the delay; in any case, it put the Frankenhausen army at a disadvantage, and lost them any tactical advantage they may have earlier held. In fact, however, their whole campaign seems to have been doomed from the start, for in addition to being heavily outnumbered by Count Ernst's troops, and pathetically ill-equipped, the camp to which they had withdrawn on the night before the battle, far from being a stronghold, actually left them in an extremely exposed position. Undeterred, Müntzer, on arrival, assumed command of the troops, dismissed with contempt a conciliatory letter from one of the counts, issued a threatening and abusive letter to Count Ernst, and continued to encourage his followers to see victory as theirs through the power of God. Somehow a plea for

11

mercy from the peasants did find its way to the princes the next morning, eliciting from them in response an offer that if the 'false prophet Thomas Müntzer' were handed over, alive, they might yet be spared. However tempted they might have been to take this escape route, Müntzer in the end prevailed, aided by the fortuitous appearance of a halo around the sun, which seemed, in view of its similarity to a rainbow emblazoned on the flag of the Eternal League, to be an unmistakable sign that God was indeed with them.

This notwithstanding, the inevitable happened shortly afterwards, and within moments the motley peasant band was routed and massacred. Some 6,000 died in the onslaught, and a further 600 were captured. Müntzer was one of the few who managed to escape, but he was soon picked up in a house in Frankenhausen where he had been hiding, together with his 'sack' of papers. He was kept imprisoned in Heldrungen for a week, during which time he wrote a last letter to the community at Mühlhausen and was subjected to interrogation and torture. A 'recantation' was published on 17 May, though its authenticity may be doubted.[12] Finally, on 27 May, both Müntzer and Pfeiffer (who had been captured fleeing as the princes attempted to overrun Mühlhausen) were beheaded, their heads and bodies being stuck up on pikestaffs for public edification. Müntzer's widow Ottilie later petitioned the council of Mühlhausen and Duke George for custody of her husband's belongings, but apparently without success.

Thus we have retraced, albeit with haste, the milestones in Müntzer's life, or at least the ones that history has allowed us to find; it is time now to begin to narrow our focus more closely towards our chosen theme. We shall begin by looking at the general outline of Müntzer's theology, in so far as it is possible to do this in any systematic way, before exploring the extent to which his writing and experience can help in the quest for a 'distinctive Christian contribution' to revolutionary politics.

2

'SUFFERING THE SHARP EDGE OF THE PLOUGH-SHARE': MÜNTZER'S THEOLOGY AND POLITICS

Müntzer's indebtedness to the German mystical tradition is a commonplace of Reformation scholarship. Whatever other dimensions there were to his thinking – revolutionary, apocalyptic, prophetic – all were rooted deeply in a *Weltanschauung* informed by the great mystical thinkers of the medieval age. Not all scholars would go so far as Hans-Jürgen Goertz in arguing that Müntzer's concern to rid the world of evil constituted an outward expression of a no less intense preoccupation with inner purgation,[1] but few can avoid the conclusion that he looked to the practical mystics of the Middle Ages, to Tauler, to Suso, to the author(s) of the *Theologia Deutsch*, for answers to the existential questions he confronted. Clearly there were some strands of his thought which he could not have gleaned from this tradition – not least, of course, his commitment to a transformation of the world and an amelioration of the economic position of the common people – but even here can be heard echoes of the contempt which that tradition held for the material; Müntzer takes up the cause of the poor and oppressed as much from a concern about the *spiritual* consequences of such oppression as anything else. Indeed, his main worry is that, because the people have to work day in and day out to survive, they have no time to attend to the health of their souls, and are forced to rely for spiritual guidance upon the learned scholars and priests; and thus they never get to hear about the possibility of receiving a revelation from God.[2]

What does it mean to say that mysticism was the foundation of Müntzer's theology? The origins of the word 'mysticism' can be traced to the Greek adjective *mu* (meaning 'closed'), and the related verb *muo* (to shut or close (the lips or eyes)), from which emerged a group of terms associated with the Greek mystery religions like *mystikon, mysterion,* and *mystes.* There is an important distinction, however, between the way these terms were defined in traditional Greek thought, and their usage in early Christian writings. In the former, such language conveyed more the idea that truth was not always easy to access, that it was to be discovered by human effort rather than disclosed by divine revelation; in the New Testament, however, the emphasis is on the revelation of the mystery of God's love for humankind in the life, death and resurrection of Christ. However, because it is *God's love* which is being made known, the revelation of it can only be partial and not fully comprehended or appropriated by human experience; and hence the element of 'mystery' remains.

From this central concern with the love of God and its (albeit restricted) accessibility to the believer, three main strands of meaning of the term *mysterion* emerged. These are set out particularly clearly in the sixth-century writings of Denys the Areopagite (sometimes known as Pseudo-Dionysius), who was largely responsible for the introduction of the term 'mystical' into the Christian tradition. First was the deeper or 'mystical' meaning of the Scriptures, the locus of the revelation by God of the mystery of God's love; second was the 'mystical' significance of the sacraments, which are the means by which Christians enter into, and participate in, the mystery of divine love; and thirdly came 'mystical theology' which focused, unlike the preceding two, not on the ways in which God may be known, but on the effect such knowledge has on the life and soul of the believer. Here the emphasis was on the surrender of the soul to God, and the outworking of a participation in the mystery of God in Christ in a life characterized by faith, hope and love. At the heart of Denys' teaching, and that of many subsequent mystical writers, is also an emphasis on the 'three ways' or 'moments' of engagement with God: *via purgativa*, purification (from sin and ignorance inherited from the fall); *via illuminativa*, illumination (or restoration to the 'life of grace'); and *via unitiva*, union, in which humankind regains the state of paradise lost by Adam at the fall.

We can be certain from what we know of Müntzer's life that he was familiar with the mystical tradition which developed from Denys and the patristic writers. We know, for example, that he read the treatise *Theologia Germanica*, which takes for granted the threefold path towards union with God of purification, illumination and union. This work, which Müntzer knew in the version prepared by Luther in 1518, was originally compiled around 1350 by a German group known as 'The Friends of God', with whom was associated Johann Tauler, whose influence on Müntzer was strong. Luther, in fact, attributed authorship of the *Theologia Germanica* to Tauler himself. Given Luther's very high opinion of Tauler's sermons and writings, it is possible that Müntzer first encountered them during his visit to Wittenberg in late 1517, though we know with much greater certainty that he devoted much of his month-long stay in Orlamünde in the spring of 1519 to immersing himself in those works. Georg Strobel, in his study of Müntzer first published in 1795, mentions that Müntzer carried around with him Tauler's sermons in two volumes, which, if true, gives some indication of their importance to him.[3] Gordon Rupp even suggests that Müntzer might have used Tauler's sermons as a '*vade mecum*'![4]

A number of central themes in Tauler are echoed in Müntzer, particularly those dealing with the relationship of the soul to Christ. Tauler stressed, as did Müntzer, that true faith is attained only as the believer seeks conformity with Christ: 'no one can believe in CHRIST until he has first conformed himself to him', Müntzer writes in *On Counterfeit Faith* (CW 223). To conform to Christ, to follow in his steps, means nothing less than to enter with him into his sufferings and tribulation. It is the 'bitter Christ' of the cross who is to be followed, not the 'honey-sweet' version preached by Luther and the scholars (CW 220, 366). In following the suffering Christ the soul gradually renounces all earthly desires, seeking instead to obey only the will of God until it finally reaches a state where the flesh is fully overcome. This state is called by Tauler, Müntzer and many others in the mystical tradition *Gelassenheit* – yieldedness, or complete surrender to the will of God. For both Tauler and Müntzer this path of renunciation and suffering was not an option for the particularly 'spiritually minded' Christian, but the only way that true faith and knowledge of God could be experienced. It is, in fact, on the basis of a distinction between experienced and inexperienced faith, between true and counterfeit faith, that Müntzer distinguishes the elect from the damned. A person 'must have the Spirit seven-fold', he writes in his 'Prague Manifesto', echoing Tauler's doctrine of the seven stages of salvation, otherwise he or she 'cannot hear or understand the living God' (CW 363).

Tauler and the author(s) of the *Theologia Germanica* were not the only mystical writers with whose work Müntzer was familiar. We infer from a rather jaunty letter to him from a nun called Ursula that he had read some Henry Suso (a contemporary of Tauler and a fellow Dominican), and there is a possibility that he came across some of Eckhart's sermons in works ascribed to Tauler.[5] Some scholars have also detected in Müntzer the possible influences of the *Book of Spiritual Poverty*, a very influential fourteenth-century mystical work assumed in Müntzer's day to be a work of Tauler, but emanating almost certainly, like the *Theologia Germanica*, from the Dominican 'Friends of God' in the Rhineland. However, useful though it is to locate Müntzer within the broader mystical tradition, and to note themes within it upon which he drew, it is only by taking a step further and examining the particular emphases and interpretations he placed upon some of these themes, notably what constitutes true faith and how it is obtained, that a proper understanding of Müntzer's theology may be formed. In fact, Müntzer has only a limited interest in the illuminative aspect of the classical mystical division, and almost none at all in the unitive: his concern is largely with the purgative.

It would be helpful at this point to insert a word of caution against an expectation of finding in Müntzer too highly a developed or systematized theology. Unlike Luther or Calvin, beside whose volumes of collected works his own appear very slender indeed, Müntzer's life was summarily extinguished at an early stage, with the consequence that his extant writings span a period of somewhat less than six years. They consist, moreover, mostly of correspondence, tracts, sermons and liturgies written largely in response to the pressing issues of the day; and while a good deal of Reformation literature which has come down to us was doubtless conceived under similar constraints, an understanding of the circumstances in which Müntzer produced his work should warn us against combing through them too closely in search of some preconceived ideological pattern. Nowhere does Müntzer attempt to set out a coherent exposition of his doctrines.

In seeking to make his theological position understood, Müntzer frequently chose to contrast it with what he termed the 'fraudulent' and 'perverse' teaching of his one-time mentor and later archenemy Martin Luther; thus an examination of the major differences between the two would be a useful way forward towards an understanding of Müntzer's teaching. We should note, however, that the Luther whom Müntzer persistently and vigorously denigrated is little more than a caricature of the reformer of Wittenberg whom historians and theologians have reconstructed for us from his copious writings and numerous contemporary references. One factor holding Müntzer back from attempting to engage seriously with Luther's thinking was the extreme animosity each felt, after about 1523, towards each other, and which each vocalized in the most vitriolic terms imaginable whenever the opportunity arose. (The graphic and often colourful imagery each uses to denounce the other is a highly entertaining feature of their writings.) In addition, Müntzer notoriously misunderstood, or chose to misunderstand and therefore parodied, certain of Luther's key themes, notably *solafideism* and his strong emphasis on the authority of the Word. Walter Elliger has argued that Müntzer had a 'misunderstanding which prevented approach to the kernel of Luther's view', though as James M. Stayer points out, 'no one in the Reformation era worked particularly hard to win a "fair" and "balanced" understanding of the theology of an opposing camp'.[6] Peter Matheson is inclined to think that 'Müntzer read Luther's writings once and once only, and then proceeded to write a vindication of his own position, making no attempt at a systematic answer to Luther's provocative questions and arguments'.[7] All of which suggests that we should approach some of the stark antitheses Müntzer liked to draw between his own religion of experience, and the 'easily come by' faith of 'Brother Soft-Life', with a little caution; it does not, however, render invalid a comparative approach as a way in to Müntzer's theology.

The key issue for Müntzer is what constitutes 'authentic' faith in Christ and how it is to be appropriated by the individual believer. The qualification 'authentic' or 'real' is vital here, because there was, for Müntzer, another type of faith abroad, preached by the biblical scholars with their 'stubborn and ignorant minds' (CW 196), which he labels *geticht* – 'false', 'counterfeit', or 'imaginary'.[8] This was nothing but 'the most potent poison', lulling those to whom it was preached into a false sense of security (CW 220). Unlike true faith, which could be known only through testing and suffering, this other faith could be simply and painlessly appropriated by following the direction of 'pleasure-loving, ambitious' preachers who have no awareness of that 'pure fear of God' of which the Bible speaks (CW 308, 270; cf. 284). They offer merely a 'speculative' faith, because they know nothing of that faith borne of tribulation to which the entire Scriptures and the lives of the patriarchs, prophets and the apostles bear eloquent testimony (CW 270, 217).

17

The faith which *did* know about distress, toil and 'the pure fear of God' was for Müntzer the only true faith. Persistently and aggressively he expounded the necessity of an *experimental* faith, contrasting it with the 'untested faith' of the biblical scholars. Drawing on a rich supply of original and often vivid metaphors, and an even more impressive range of biblical texts, Müntzer castigated the perpetrators of the easily-come-by faith, and argued that God can only be known through a long and painful process of extreme testing and inner turmoil (*Anfechtung*), self-emptying, and discipline; of conformity, in other words, to Christ and his anguish and death.

> ...a man can no more claim that he is a Christian before his cross has made him receptive to God's work and word than a field can produce a heavy crop of wheat until it has been ploughed. The elect friend of God who yearns for and endures the word is no counterfeit hearer, but a diligent pupil of his master, constantly and ardently watching all that he does, seeking to be found conformable to him in every respect, to the best of his ability,

Müntzer writes at the beginning of his essay *On Counterfeit Faith* (CW 214; cf. 223). 'No one is a son of God unless he suffers with him', Müntzer tells Luther in 1523 (CW 57), and no one can teach about conformity with God, he writes elsewhere, unless they are in conformity with Christ (CW 396). Conformity with Christ (*Christformige*) and with God (*Gotformige*) was certainly an important teaching for Müntzer, as it was, for example, for Staupitz. Perhaps it could be argued that for Müntzer the second stage in the mystical path, after purgation, is more accurately to be understood as 'conformity' rather than 'illumination'.

Müntzer's debt to the mystical tradition in which he steeped himself is further exemplified in the above passage from *On Counterfeit Faith* – and not just inasmuch as the term *der ausserwelte freundt Gottis*, which Müntzer uses very frequently, appears there. The metaphor of the soul as a ploughed field is a commonplace of mystical literature, and Müntzer draws upon it often. The picture is of God as a farmer who desires to see each field producing a good harvest. In its natural state, however, the field or soul is barren, full of 'weeds, thistles and thorns', and a fit breeding ground only for 'the raging devil in the guise of light, and showy corn-cockles, etc.' If it is to produce anything good, it 'must suffer the sharp edge of the plough-share' (CW 199).

True faith, then, cannot be produced other than by God working in the believer, fashioning that person, through much distress and tribulation (*Anfechtung*), into the likeness of God's Son. The profound contrast between this experimental faith, and the untried, untested version preached by the 'faithless, abandoned biblical scholars', could not be clearer (CW 270). They 'blether on non-stop' about faith, but have no experience of that whereof they speak (CW 270); they get it all from books, and then 'vomit it out undigested like a stork [disgorging] frogs to her young ones in the nest' (CW 358–9). The true believers, however, feel the cutting edge of the Spirit at work in their hearts, purging them of all desires and lusts of the flesh. Like Christ himself, the corner-stone, to change metaphors, they 'have to be knocked into shape by the master-mason if [they] are to grow into a true living building' (CW 220–1).

Müntzer employs a quite distinctive mystical vocabulary when he speaks of this process of the soul breaking free from the lusts and desires of the flesh. A not uncommon literary device among the mystics was to add the prefix 'ent-' to many ordinary verbs to stress, as it were, the negating of all bad influences and evil desires, and Müntzer also engages in this practice. Reinhard Schwarz[9] quotes some examples of this mystical vocabulary – *entblößen* (to reveal, to lay bare), *entfremden* (to estrange, to place at a distance), *entgroben* (to purge), *entsetzen* (to alarm) and *entwerden* (to 'get away from' one's self, to 'dis-become') – before highlighting the one occasion on which Müntzer uses this latter term (in his undated letter to one 'George'). Müntzer here contrasts the pious person with the 'mad biblical scholars': these latter like to 'display their wares', to make a public exhibition of their religion, whereas the followers of Christ can echo the words of the psalmist as he speaks of being 'reduced to nothing'. 'How can I know what is of God or the devil', Müntzer asks rhetorically, ' . . . unless I have got away from myself' (. . . *das ich myr entworden byn*) (CW 106; F 426). The term *entsetzen* appears rather more frequently in Müntzer, usually to describe the 'alarm' that the fear of man causes an individual before she or he is aware of the fear of God which can overcome it. 'Why be alarmed (*entsetzen*) by the phantom powers of men?' Müntzer asks the Princes during his sermon on Daniel, when 'God is at your side, closer at hand than you can credit . . . If we fear God, why should we be alarmed (*entsetzen*) by rootless, feckless men?' (CW 245, 251; F 257, 263). Abraham is an example for Müntzer of *ein entsetzter Mensch*, one who is freed

19

from those desires which hold back the fear of God. When God appeared to him in a vision he was 'terribly alarmed' (*entsetzt*), but because he knew what it was to be 'caught up (in the fear of God)' (*ein entsetzter Mensch*), he was able 'to draw the line between the impossible and the possible' (CW 286, 284; F 287). Luther, of course, treated with contempt the usage of these terms by those he dismissed as *die Schwärmer* (the enthusiasts), though Müntzer refuted his allegations that they were neologisms, claiming that his use of them was warranted by Scripture.[10]

In classic mystical style Müntzer stresses that it is only through direct encounter with God that the individual receives faith: 'you will never have faith', he writes, 'unless God himself gives it you, and instructs you in it' (CW 199). He posits the need for a personally revealed faith over against the sort which blind guides like Luther imagine can be acquired through Scripture alone: 'If someone had never had sight or sound of the Bible at any time in his life he could still hold the one true Christian faith because of the true teaching of the Spirit, just like all those who composed the holy Scripture without any books at all' (CW 274).

It is not that Müntzer wants to minimize the value of the Scriptures, for those who have access to them, as a source of testimony about God: indeed, his quite overpowering array of quotations from across the whole spectrum of the Bible (he directly quotes from all but nine of its sixty-six books, as well as from four in the Apocrypha) testifies to the central place it held in his thinking. As Christopher Rowland has written, Müntzer 'did not despise the Scriptures. What he inveighed against was book religion.'[11] A mere reading of the Scriptures alone was no substitute for experience in matters of faith: the Bible did not have the mediatory function it had for Luther. 'Even if you have already devoured all the books of the Bible,' Müntzer can claim, 'you must still suffer the sharp edge of the plough-share' (CW 199). Indeed, even if a person has 'devoured a hundred thousand Bibles . . . he can say nothing about God which has any validity': that person must experience 'the inward word which is to be heard in the abyss of the soul (*Seelengrund*) through the revelation of God' (CW 240).

Thus the gravest distorters of the truth were the so-called scholars of the Bible – among them Luther – who through their blindness missed the whole point of Scripture. Part of their problem was that they read the Scriptures selectively, drawing proof-texts from here and there to support a particular position, but ignoring the whole thrust of the book: 'They purloin one or two little texts but fail to integrate them with the teaching which gushes forth from the genuine source' (CW 73). Müntzer's own hermeneutic, by implication, attempted to see Scripture as one, as a whole. And for him, not only did the scholars miss the whole point of Scripture, they even had the gall to suggest that listening to them expound it was all that was necessary for the procurement of faith. In their self-sufficiency they decried the possibility of direct revelation from God which, for Müntzer, was indispensable for true faith: 'Scripture amply stills our needs, thank you,' they say, 'we don't believe in any revelation; God no longer speaks like that.' Müntzer could not rebuke them too strongly: 'they tap around in Holy Scripture so blindly', he writes, 'that they refuse to open their eyes and ears to the way in which it exhorts us in the most emphatic manner possible that it is by God alone that we should, and indeed must, be taught' (CW 298). They conveniently ignored the fact that the prophets always referred to God speaking in the present tense – 'Thus says the Lord' – and not the past – 'Thus said the Lord' (CW 359–60). They needed reminding, too, of the Scripture which says that we do not live by bread alone, but by every word which proceeds from the mouth of God, noting, Müntzer adds, that this word 'proceeds from the mouth of God and not from books' (CW 44).

This whole question of revelation is crucial for Müntzer. The biblical scholars deny that God any longer 'reveals his divine mysteries to his dear friends through genuine visions or direct words', and prefer to 'adhere to their bookish ways' (*unerfarnen Weyse*: literally 'without experience'); they even 'make a laughing stock of those who have experience of the revelation of God' (CW 235–6). Yet for Müntzer it is axiomatic that the God who spoke to men and women in biblical times through dreams and visions should continue to do so today. A leitmotif of the Sermon to the Princes, for example, is not only the God-given ability of Daniel to interpret Nebuchadnezzar's dream aright, but the significance of *gesichten* and *trewmen* in general as channels through which God communicates to God's people. Müntzer presents in this sermon a catalogue of biblical figures to whom God spoke in visions – the patriarchs Abraham, Jacob and Joseph, and, from the New Testament, Peter, Paul and Joseph the father of Jesus – noting that in almost all cases they received a divine message during a time of great tribulation (*betrubnis*). And this, of course, is why the 'pleasure-loving pigs, the smart-alecs who have never been put to the test' (including Brother Fatted Pig and Brother Soft-Life himself) reject the whole idea of revelation. Yet to expect visions, Müntzer continues, 'and to receive them while in tribulation and suffering, is in the true spirit of the apostles', into which the elect are now entering (CW 242). Of what use, anyway, would all these biblical references to visions be if we were not to expect them in our own day, Müntzer asks. Thus it should not surprise anyone if the elect do receive direct messages from God, particularly in these last days when the prophecy of Joel – 'our sons and daughters will prophesy and have dreams and visions, etc.' – is beginning to come to pass. Indeed, God is already making God's purposes known: 'I know it for a fact . . . that the Spirit of God is revealing to many elect and pious men at this time the great need for a full and final reformation in the near future' (CW 244).

Another experience at which the godless scoff in their ignorance is the first movement (*bewegung*) of the Spirit in the soul, which clears the ground, as it were, for God to work; and they do this, Müntzer writes in *A Manifest Exposé*, 'because they have never tasted the patient endurance (*langweyl*) which is the only way to discover the work of God' (CW 300/2). Experience of *langweyl*, a period of waiting, repentance, rejection of sin, and anticipation of the Spirit, is another crucial distinguishing mark of the true child of God over against the false. It is not an option for the believer, for there are no two ways to faith, and no short cuts ('one does not sneak into a house by the window') (CW 220). Thus the scholar will never be able to grasp the meaning of Scripture, even if 'the whole of it has been expounded to him in a human way', until 'he has been trodden underfoot with all his habitual ways in the wine-press. There he will attain such poverty of spirit as to acknowledge that there is no faith in him at all; only the desire to learn true faith' (CW 224).

The metaphor here is typical of those Müntzer employs to demonstrate how tortuous and humbling is the path of true faith. It is indeed the narrow way. Yet Müntzer is clear from his reading of the Scriptures that the elect have to come to God in this way, and in no other: if the soul 'is to be filled with the good things of God which never pass away', then first it must be emptied of all that pertains to self (CW 298), and this cannot be achieved by simply responding, at an intellectual level, to the exhortation, 'Believe! believe! Be firm, be firm with a strong, strong faith' (CW 220). To begin

22

with, there must be a movement of the Spirit of God in the abyss of the soul, leaving the stricken person trembling before the very name of God because of the worldly desires she or he has harboured there. This sense of awe and reverence as God's word comes into the heart Müntzer speaks of in terms of *Verwunderung*. With the apostle the stricken one cries out, 'O, what a wretched man I am', and, 'What on earth am I to do now? I am at my wits' end, and receive no comfort from God or man. For God is plaguing me with my conscience . . .' (CW 204). Then follows a process of self-emptying, of purging out all evil desires, which is characterized by continual trial, temptation and falling, supported by perseverance and discipline.

Müntzer often speaks of the soul's experience in the dramatic language of storms and billows: the believer will be buffeted by 'torrents of water' until the will to live is gone, but 'one should not flee these waves but negotiate them skilfully . . . for the Lord only gives his holy testimony to someone who has first made his way through perplexity' (CW 61). Those who adhere to the path of easy belief find all this unwholesome in the extreme, of course, but they are no better than 'mad, lecherous swine . . . who shrink back from the ferocity of the winds, the raging of the waves, and from all the great waters of wisdom' (CW 217). They have no inclination to abase themselves before God or lose their reputation. The true seekers after God, however, eventually find themselves emptied so completely of their 'creaturely lusts' that they 'must turn to God, for [their] natural self would collapse otherwise'. It is at this point that they will confess their unbelief and 'cry out for the doctor, whose boundless mercy is so great that he can never leave anyone in the lurch if he is poor in spirit like this' (CW 302). Like a person drowning, as Rupp graphically puts it, 'the believer comes gasping to the shore and there . . . rests'.[12] 'Hostile to his sins and embrac[ing] righteousness with all sincerity', it is only now, Müntzer concludes, that the follower of Christ is assured of salvation 'and comprehends properly that God has driven him from the evil to the good by his unchangeable love . . .' (CW 302). The soul has thus finally reached a state of complete renunciation of the world and commitment or *yielding* of itself to God (*Gelassenheit*), and God in turn supports and strengthens the soul in its dependent state. 'After the weakness experienced by the members of the elect in complete self-surrender (*gelassenheyt*) he [the Lord] supports and endows them with the strength which flows from him' (CW 60).

As one finds in Müntzer the soul pictured as a 'field' from which all worldly lusts and desires have to be rooted out, so it is possible to trace in his writings an apocalyptic which understands humanity to be composed of both 'wheat' and 'tares', the chosen and the lost, growing together until the divine harvester instructs his labourers to begin the work of separating them out. As we noted earlier, Goertz has suggested that there is a strong unity in Müntzer's thought here, and that his concern with both the 'inner order' and 'outer order' is rooted firmly in his mystical theology. In perhaps a rather over-schematic way, to which Müntzer's writing does not readily lend itself, Goertz has consistently argued that there are clear parallels between the work of God which takes place as the soul is purified, and God's (imminent) judgement and punishment of the godless in the world. 'The inner process of the birth of God is revolutionary,' Goertz writes: 'As sinful resistance in the soul is broken and destroyed under the revolutionary action of God in the dark night of despair and the destruction of the self-will, so also the same resistance in the "world" must be broken by the same action and the "world" itself destroyed. Only then will the Kingdom of God come into existence on earth.'[13]

The logic of Müntzer's thinking clearly demands that there be a concomitant transformation, as it were, on both the inner and outer levels. All the while the godless remain in the world, preaching their counterfeit false gospel, they hinder the work of the Spirit in bringing men and women into conformity with Christ. In his sermon on Daniel, Müntzer shows dramatically how the godless succeed in their aim, and prove themselves thereby to be the 'ravaging wolves' whom St Paul predicted would come on the heels of his departure, not sparing the flock (Acts 20.29). Not only do they lay the gospel open to ridicule, making Christ to appear as no more than 'a mere scarecrow or a painted puppet . . . compared with the great titles and names of this world', and a 'doormat for the whole world' whose suffering is 'nothing but a fairground spectacle' (CW 232, 234); they seduce the poor and uneducated masses into believing them by denying that God any longer reveals his divine mysteries in a direct way through visions. The scholars, in other words, teach that faith is only to be acquired through learning and not through experience, and thus, as Müntzer shows in a telling passage in *A Manifest Exposé*, have the people at every turn. They tell the people to search the Scriptures if they want to gain salvation, yet they know full well that poor ordinary folk have no time to learn to read because they are caught in an exploitative economic system – the fruits of which the scholars themselves enjoy – which makes the acquiring of their daily subsistence their main preoccupation. Thus, if they are to understand the Bible they have no alternative but to listen to the preaching of the scholars, and 'words cannot tell how cruelly this defrauds the poor and needy folk' (CW 272). The grounds for rooting out and destroying all who prevent the work of God, and for doing it without delay, are therefore plain for all to see.

Müntzer's politics are thus incorrigibly radical, though, as Eike Wolgast has recently reminded us, they do not become revolutionary, let alone violent, until the final weeks of his life. While for many years the view of Müntzer as a fully-fledged revolutionary by the early 1520s was seldom challenged, Wolgast carefully develops the argument that he embraced very late, and then only with reluctance, a *Widerstandslehre*, a teaching on resistance to the secular powers.[14] Not that the term 'teaching' should mislead us into thinking that Müntzer had a coherent political philosophy: as with his theology, Müntzer nowhere systematizes his political aspirations, and indeed, as Wolgast has argued, exact formulations and precise definitions would have seemed to him superfluous in view of his certainty about the imminent collapse of the hitherto-existing world with its power and social relations.[15] Nevertheless some sort of pattern does emerge from his writings.

For Müntzer, as we have already noted, it is essential that the true faith be preached in the world to counteract the spread of error and false faith, and responsibility for this task he assigns primarily to the secular rulers. In so doing he parts company from a number of his contemporaries, particularly Luther. Both Luther and Müntzer grounded their *Obrigkeitlehren*, their teaching on government, on Romans 13, but drew different conclusions from the text: while Luther placed the emphasis on verse 1, which treats of the duty of the subject *vis-à-vis* the ruler, Müntzer, by focusing particularly on verse 3, drew attention to the duties of governments towards their subjects, arguing that popular support was only warranted in so far as those duties were carried out. And what Müntzer understood as the duties of governments went beyond merely punishing those who stepped out of line: the ruler must actually further the work of God in the world. '[T]ake up your stance resolutely on the cornerstone', was Müntzer's appeal to the princes, 'and let God's true, unwavering purpose be yours . . . sweep aside those evil men who obstruct the gospel! Take them out of circulation! Otherwise you will be devils, not the servants of God which Paul calls you in Romans 13' (CW 245–6). For Müntzer, the authorities do not exist merely as a necessary evil to maintain peace and order, but have a positive role in the service of God for the protection and propagation of the faith.

The obedience due to rulers under the mandate of Romans 13.1 is conditional upon their fulfilling the duties laid down for them in verse 3; only in so far as they honour their responsibility to defend the faith are they justified in commanding the obedience of the people. Yet having exegeted the passage in this way, Müntzer does not derive from it any legitimation for resistance to governments. His position is rather – or so it would appear from his comments to Frederick the Wise – that, when rulers default in the execution of their duties, their obligations toward the godless will simply devolve to the people: the sword 'will be taken from them and will be given to the people who burn with zeal so that the godless can be defeated' (CW 69).

Biblical support for this assertion Müntzer draws from Daniel 7, one of literally only a handful of scriptures (including Romans 13) he uses in discussing questions of government and resistance. The key section in this chapter for Müntzer is verse 27, which speaks, in an apocalyptic context, of all the kingdoms of the world being given over to the saints of the Most High. Wolgast attempts a connection between this verse and the Romans 13 passage by suggesting that, in Müntzer's mind, Daniel 7.27 came into play when the requirements of Romans 13.3 were not followed, though, again, Müntzer does not establish from this scripture a right of revolt. Müntzer does not insist that Daniel 7.27 be 'implemented' immediately on the heels of any dereliction of duty by the rulers, neither does he clarify whether power is to devolve to the people as a result of a (legitimate) use of force by the elect, or through the direct intervention of God.[16] His position with regard to the latter point appears to be that God and humankind operate 'together' to bring about God's judgement on earth. The case of Joshua leading the people of Israel into the Promised Land demonstrates the point: 'they did not win the land by the sword, but by the power of God, but the sword was the means used . . . ' (CW 250). Müntzer's reference to the Daniel 7 passage in his letter to the Eisenach community of 9 May 1525 has a similar flavour: 'God has moved the whole world in a miraculous way towards a recognition of the divine truth, and [the world] is proving this by its great and earnest zeal against the tyrants, as Daniel 7 says clearly: that power should be given to the common folk' (CW 150). Almost every time Müntzer refers to this passage he does no more than recognize the inevitability – as with all God-given prophecies – of its fulfilment, albeit after the brief reign of Antichrist.

The dramatic events which he witnessed in the early months of 1525 finally convinced Müntzer of the necessity, indeed the *duty*, both of resistance to the rulers and action to establish a new socio-political order. Not only had the princes of Saxony resisted his admonition to them to take up the sword against God's enemies, they had gone out of their way to show their contempt for just and godly rule by proceeding to oppress the poor in a most violent way. The time for action against them and on behalf of the common people had arrived: indeed, that the people were now rising up against their rulers, provoked by the growing injustice, corruption and poverty with which they were daily confronted, was a clear sign from God that the Danielic prophecy about the fall of the last worldly kingdom was shortly to be fulfilled. In his Sermon to the Princes on Daniel 2 Müntzer had drawn his hearers' attention to the multi-layered statue in Nebuchadnezzar's dream, explaining that the layers represented the great historic empires and kingdoms of the world which had fallen; now the only one remaining, which represented the present Holy Roman Empire, would shortly be smashed by Jesus himself (CW 244). The spread of the peasants' action from south-west Germany to Hessen and Thuringia would have appeared to Müntzer, Siegfried Bräuer says, as a new and decisive phase in the harvest-time of God; 'surely God' Matheson imagines Müntzer musing, 'seeing the intolerable sufferings of his elect, was shortening the time?'[17] Yet it is only once he has established a theological justification for revolt that Müntzer begins to talk in such terms. 'What is the evil brew from which all usury, theft and robbery springs but the assumption of our lords and princes that all creatures are their property?' he writes in his *Vindication and Refutation*.

> The fish in the water, the birds in the air, the plants on the face of the earth – it all has to belong to them! . . . To add insult to injury, they have God's commandment proclaimed to the poor:

God has commanded that you should not steal. But it avails them nothing. For while they do violence to everyone, flay and fleece the poor farm worker, tradesman and everything that breathes . . . yet should any of the latter commit the pettiest crime, he must hang . . . It is the lords themselves who make the poor man their enemy. If they refuse to do away with the causes of insurrection how can trouble be avoided in the long run? If saying that makes me an inciter to insurrection, so be it! (CW 335)

Müntzer thus initially supports violence only as a defensive measure, against violation of common rights by the rulers, and to some extent his transformation from theological dissent to political opposition was forced upon him both by events and by the logic of his own position. The rulers, as a consequence of the violence they had perpetrated upon their subjects, had Christian blood on their hands, had forfeited their right to *be* rulers, and had brought down upon themselves the wrath of God. 'Just tell us, you miserable, wretched sack of worms,' Müntzer addresses Count Ernst, 'who made you a prince over the people whom God redeemed with his dear blood?' (CW 155). It is only now that Müntzer begins to compare the rulers to Nimrod, common shorthand at the time for tyrannical governors, and to speak approvingly of their downfall (CW 137, 142; cf. 43, n. 273).

Convinced, then, that the peasants' uprising was a sign from God that the overthrow of the godless would shortly be accomplished, Müntzer set about forming his *Ewiger Bund Gottes*, Eternal League of God. Whereas his earlier covenants had had a defensive purpose and no restrictions on membership, the Eternal League in Mühlhausen – whose very name was subversive, given that the city's ruling authority called itself the 'Eternal Council' – was established with the clear intent of carrying out the final overthrow of the godless. It was more militarist in its structure, and, perhaps to emphasize its role in the fulfilment of Daniel 7.27, its membership was limited to the saints. If these factors suggest Müntzer envisaged the battle against the godless being close at hand, the apology for his actions he prepared in the days leading up to the final battle at Frankenhausen leaves no room for doubting the apocalyptic significance he attached to the impending scenario. God is moving the whole world towards recognizing the 'truth', he wrote, and, in a conscious allusion to the Magnificat, Count Ernst was informed that the 'eternal, living God has commanded that you should be forcibly cast down from your seat' (CW 150, 156; cf. 151). Whatever motives drove the common people to revolt – and they were by no means entirely economic – their struggle became for Müntzer, as he made it his own, the one which would decisively clear the way for the kingdom of God, the reign of the elect.

One final point to be noted about Müntzer's political theology is that, aside from a somewhat detailed explanation of how the world will be reshaped in accordance with the order of things (*ordo rerum*) instituted by God at the creation of the world, it pays scant attention to the form society will take in the new age. It is true that, under torture a few days before his execution, Müntzer confessed 'he had launched the rising with the aim of making all Christians equal and of expelling and doing to death the princes and gentry who refused to support the Gospel', and that a common article of faith among those supporting the insurrection was that 'All things are to be held in common and distribution should be to each according to his need, as occasion arises' (CW 436–7). Caution needs to be exercised, of course, when evaluating statements made on the rack, though Rupp has argued, on the basis of Müntzer's familiarity with Plato and attachment to the term *Gemeinnutz*, 'common interest', that there are grounds for taking his communism seriously.[18] Günter Vogler has argued that by the late Middle Ages *Gemeinnutz* had come to characterize the ideal urban community, but that while Müntzer invested the term with religious meaning, and saw it as the basis of a new social order, he never spelled out precisely the form that new order would take.[19]

Müntzer also allegedly said under torture that, had events fallen out his way, he would have 'appropriate[d] all the land within a forty-six mile radius of Mühlhausen and the land in Hesse', and, after one warning, put to the sword any nobleman who refused to accept common ownership and distribution according to need (CW 437). It may also be inferred from Müntzer's confessions under interrogation that he harboured ideas of creating a 'theocratic republic', which, while having a communitarian framework, would not wholly discard differences of rank or even private property. (The 'Constitutional Draft', a peasant manifesto drawn up in south-west Germany in the winter of 1524–25, contained similar ideas, though whether Müntzer had a hand in its production is disputed.)[20] That the elect would rule in this new state was set out as early as 1521 in the 'Prague

Manifesto', and is echoed later in, for example, Müntzer's letter to the Stolberg community in 1523. Yet it is difficult to avoid Tom Scott's conclusion that Müntzer 'had no real "theory of society"', and that his blueprint, such as it was, was clearly intended as a provisional measure to cover an interim period during which 'the Elect would reign supreme before the ultimate true kingdom of God'.[21] Müntzer's theology, as Goertz has said, 'was really only a theology of revolutionary transformation and not a theology of the construction of a post-revolutionary state of affairs'.[22]

Müntzer does write with rather more certainty about his conviction that the world is shortly to be reshaped in accordance with the order of things (*ordo rerum*) instituted by God at the creation of the world (a theme to be explored more closely in the following chapter). Suffice to say, though, that what in the end is important for Müntzer is that the kingdom is for the elect, however he finally came to understand the term. His message about the mighty and the wise being brought low, and the poor uplifted, found a ready hearing among the common people, who rallied to his call for a transformation of both the Church and the world. To what extent his lack of success in leading their rebellion at Mühlhausen resulted from a refusal or inability to absorb the wider social, economic and political demands of the common people is a moot point; clearly they did misunderstand Müntzer's motives to some extent, as he himself acknowledged in his final letter, but neither they nor he would have drawn any sharp distinction between 'religious' and 'secular' goals. Thus, as Goertz writes, Müntzer's call for rule by, of and for the elect was also a demand, which the people were already articulating, for a better world, 'a world of neighbourly love and brotherhood nurtured from the depths of the divine gospel';[23] and it was a demand which, as both Müntzer and the people recognized, could not be accommodated within the existing socio-economic structures, but was achievable only after their revolutionary transformation. Müntzer does not therefore enter the peasants' struggle as a leader taking the people where otherwise they would not have gone, but neither is he deluded by any sort of false assumption that the peasants shared a common aim with him to introduce a 'kingdom of God' predicated on a conquering of all fleshly desires. What Müntzer did introduce to the uprising was a conviction that it was ultimately of eschatological significance, and could not therefore be in vain. This was a propitious moment, a *kairos*, in which God would act to avenge

God's people. 'Make a start and fight the fight of the Lord!', is Müntzer's appeal to the Allstedters in April 1525. If, in human terms, the odds against success were overwhelming, that was no reason to be deterred, for 'God is with you'; 'it is not your fight, but the Lord's' (CW 141–2).

In ultimate terms the success or failure of Müntzer's – and the peasants' – cause rested on the will of God: what the implications and consequences of that were must now be examined.

3

'A SERVANT OF GOD AGAINST THE GODLESS': MÜNTZER AS CHRISTIAN REVOLUTIONARY

M üntzer's politics were both incorrigibly revolutionary and rooted firmly in his mysticism; mysticism provided the framework for his ideas, and his sense of calling to wield the sword and purify the world of all who were hostile to God reflected a parallel concern to root out in his own soul the chaff that prevented him obtaining a true knowledge of God. Müntzer was clearly both a Christian and a revolutionary, but to what extent did his faith inform his politics? Did Müntzer's Christianity make any specific and distinctive contribution to his revolutionary programme?

It is doubtful, of course, whether Müntzer would have understood a question posed in this way, yet there are two features in particular which, for our purposes, may be highlighted and given closer attention: the apocalypticism which underpins his understanding of the social unrest he observed and later attempted to harness to fulfil his own vision; and the utopian nature of his ideas about the way the world would look once the peasants' struggle had achieved its aims. We shall look at each in turn.

Apocalypticism

While commentators on Müntzer acknowledge that apocalyptic ideas had an important role in shaping his ideas and actions, and in sharpening his polemic against those who peddled a 'counterfeit faith', some confusion as to what is actually conveyed by the term 'apocalyptic' still seems evident. The term – which can do service both as a noun and an adjective – may be understood to refer primarily, as its Greek root *apokalypsis* ('revelation') implies, to divine 'disclosure' or 'revelation' (and thus it is an alternative title for the final book of the New

Testament). More important than the actual content of any particular revelation or apocalypse is the fact of its being a disclosure of a heavenly mystery; an 'apocalyptic outlook' might be characterized by a quest for 'higher wisdom', for a direct and authoritative answer to the most pressing questions of the day. Apocalyptic writing, the setting down of these 'revelations', developed from the late Old Testament period, the best known example being the book of Daniel – 'the only true apocalypse in the Old Testament canon' according to Richard Bauckham[1] – on which, of course, Müntzer draws heavily. Although both Daniel and Revelation – like many writings of the genre – concern themselves also with events which are to come, a distinction should be maintained between 'eschatology' and 'apocalyptic'; as Christopher Rowland points out, the latter 'is as much involved in the attempt to understand things as they are now as to predict future events', and, indeed, the point of apocalyptic visions of a better world is often to show up the inadequacies of the present.[2] Eschatology has an important part to play in apocalyptic writings, but 'its presence in them is not their most distinctive feature'.[3]

Müntzer is clearly an apocalyptic thinker in the fullest sense, believing with the utmost conviction that only direct revelation from God can promote true faith and knowledge of God, and reveal authoritative insights into the meaning and potentiality of the present historical moment. The significance of this dimension of his thought will be examined shortly, but it would be useful first to explore its shape, beginning with the extent to which it may have been influenced by prevailing apocalyptic and eschatological ideas, in particular those of the twelfth-century prophet Joachim of Fiore and the later Taborite movement at Zwickau.

Some commentators have made much of apparent Joachite influences in Müntzer's writings, notwithstanding that Müntzer himself only refers once to this teaching, and then to disclaim any indebtedness to it! 'I have every respect for the testimony of the abbot Joachim', Müntzer writes in a letter to John Zeiss in December 1523, adding that he has 'only read his commentary on Jeremiah': 'but', he continues, 'my teaching is from on high; I do not have it from him but from utterances of God . . .' (CW 71–2). Furthermore, the book by Joachim which Müntzer claimed to have read, the *Super Hieremiam* published in Venice in 1516, was not, in fact, a genuine work, but a later fourteenth-century writing. This notwithstanding, Joachim's interpretation of history was still very influential in Müntzer's day, not least around Erfurt and Bohemia, and it would be surprising indeed if no traces of it had permeated his thinking.

Central to Joachim's philosophy was the idea that the meaning and destiny of history could only be understood by reference to the threefold work of the Trinity. Time, Joachim argued, must be understood as passing through three discernible, though not entirely discrete, ages (or *status*, stages): the first, that of the Father, was characterized by the giving of the law, and spanned the period from the Creation until the end of Old Testament times; the second, the age of grace represented by the Son, began with the appearance of Christ, and was still held to be subsisting in Joachim's own day; and the third, whose coming was widely believed to be not far hence, was to be the Age of the Spirit and the preaching of the 'Eternal Evangel', an age characterized, as Marjorie Reeves summarizes it, 'by fuller spiritual illumination, by Liberty and Love'.[4] Unlike some of his more radical followers, who missed the subtleties of his thinking, Joachim did not argue that the New Testament gospel of Christ or his Church would be superseded in the Age of the Spirit, nor, despite the apparent suggestion in his scheme to the contrary, that only one Person of the Trinity could be discerned at work in any one age. Rather, he considered that all three Persons operated in unity in every age, with the third of these ages being that in which people would know the 'full freedom of the Spirit' before history was finally brought to a close with the second advent and the last judgement. Significantly for those who see echoes of this eschatological scheme in Müntzer, Joachim held that the period of transition from the second age to the third would be marked by intense activity on the part of Antichrist, this activity clearly portending the dawning of the new age.

The extent to which Müntzer adopted a Joachite interpretation of history has considerably exercised a number of scholars, even prompting some to argue, on the basis of circumstantial evidence and a considerable amount of reading between the lines, that Joachim's Eternal Gospel played a determinative role in his interpretation of Scripture. We should note, though, that Müntzer only once makes reference to this 'everlasting gospel' – one of the teachings for which Joachim was posthumously condemned at the Fourth Lateran Council of 1215 – and that in his aforementioned letter to Zeiss, where he explicitly denies drawing on the abbot's work. Richard Bailey argues that this denial is actually a device which Müntzer adopted for self-preservation, official distaste for Joachim's teachings still being strong in his own day.[5] While recognizing that the evidence we have is far from irrefutable, and, indeed, mostly circumstantial, Abraham Friesen also attempts to build a case for Müntzer's reliance on Joachim's teaching. Rather inconclusively, he tries to develop an argument by piecing together known facts about Müntzer, such as his employment of the services of the printer Johann Herrgott for his *Hochverursachte Schutzrede* in 1524, and the publication two years later of a tract by this same printer with an opening paragraph which is 'a classic statement of the Joachist view of history'. Friesen also attempts to draw some inferences about Müntzer's relationship to Joachim from the fascination both had with the Old Testament.[6] Neither Friesen's nor Bailey's case, it seems to me, is well supported by the corpus of Müntzer's writings as we have it, and it would be safer simply to acknowledge that, while there may be traces of Joachite influence in Müntzer, no stronger connection than that is apparent.

Part of the problem, it would seem, is Müntzer's use of the multi-layered image of Daniel 2 as a key to understanding the process and destiny of history. Müntzer expounds this unambiguously apocalyptic passage in his Sermon to the Princes, taking the different sections of the image or statue and showing how each represents a particular historical empire or dynasty: the golden head the Babylonian, the silver breast and arms the Median/Persian, the bronze belly and thighs the Greek, and the legs of iron the Roman. Somewhat unusually – for some interpreters, including Daniel himself, had lumped the legs and feet of the statue together and projected a *fifth* kingdom as the coming reign of Christ – Müntzer defines the feet, composed of iron and clay, in terms of a further corrupt earthly power, the Holy Roman Empire of his own day, based on force (the iron) and patched with the 'dung' of hypocrisy. For Müntzer it is specifically this unholy alliance of the Saxon princes and the leaders of the Church – the 'eels and snakes coupling together immorally in one great heap' as he puts it in his sermon – which the stone in Nebuchadnezzar's vision, cut from the mountain by no human hand, has in its sights (CW 244). Müntzer is clearly prepared in this sense to adopt, with Joachim, a dispensationalist interpretation of history, though it would be difficult to find any further point of coincidence between his six-stage schema and Joachim's trinitarian one. G. H. Williams' typology of the differing eschatologies in circulation during the 'radical Reformation' is therefore particularly helpful, drawing as it does a clear distinction between 'the Trinitarian scheme of Joachim of Fiore' and that, 'conspicuous in the prophetic Spiritualist Thomas Müntzer, . . . based upon the Danielic-Hieronymic conception of four [sic] empires or monarchies . . .'[7]

If Müntzer does not embrace Joachim's trinitarian understanding of history, neither does he appear to have tied himself very securely to any one particular scheme of his own, even one based on the statue of Daniel 2. At the end of his letter to Nicholas Hausmann, for example, he includes a reference to the 'fourth beast' (CW 35), an image which Günther Franz quite plausibly suggests Müntzer drew from Daniel's vision recounted in chapter 7 of his prophecy.[8] In this vision four beasts appear, each representing kings or kingdoms which 'shall arise out of the earth' (v. 17), but the fourth is markedly more terrible than the others, and, in its day, will 'devour the whole earth' (v. 23). Müntzer's reference to this beast, in terms taken straight from Daniel, suggests that at this point he could have accommodated within his thinking a more traditional '*Fifth* Monarchy' position, though it might also suggest, and this would seem to be more likely, that any kind of rigorous interpretation of history into five, six, or however many stages, was considerably less important to him than a simple awareness that he was living at a crucial historical juncture. If this is the case, we would do well not to delve too deeply whenever Müntzer borrows apocalyptic imagery from the Scriptures – the fourth beast, the third angel, the Antichrist, and indeed the Danielic statue – recognizing that such imagery may be intended to serve no greater purpose than to underscore his general conviction that he was living at an apocalyptic moment.

Müntzer's concern not to tie himself rigidly to any one interpretative framework, in his approach to the prophetic scriptures, is highlighted in what is another significant difference between his writings and those of Joachim, namely the absence of any specific timescale concerning the end of the age. Joachim is noted for having calculated the approximate duration of each of the *status* of history in terms of 'generations', and for having placed enormous emphasis, in the light of this, on the *number*, if not exactly the *year*, 1260. Reeves assures us that Joachim 'took care to emphasize the uncertainty of all calculations of Last Things',[9] but he was certainly widely believed to have held that the age of the Son – comprising 42 generations each of

30 years – would end not many years after his death in 1202, following which Antichrist and then the third dispensation, that of 'the full freedom of the Spirit', would emerge. Müntzer, despite attempts by Bailey to prove the opposite, nowhere explicitly adopts any formula for estimating the time when the elect will conquer. He is not in any doubt that the time is imminent, but that is not a conviction reached on mathematical grounds.

The key numbers 42 and 1260, both widely employed by prophets and seers of the Middle Ages and later, are drawn from verses in Daniel and the Apocalypse. Both writings contain explicit references to the numbers themselves (42 months in Rev. 11.2 and 13.5; 1260 days in Rev. 11.3 and 12.6) and to the rather more cryptic period of 'a time, two times and half a time' (Dan. 7.25 and 12.7; Rev. 12.14), understood as three and a half years of 360 days each (= 1260 days). On the basis of Müntzer's letter to Hausmann, with its statement, 'The time of Antichrist is upon us', and the fact that Müntzer had read Daniel, Revelation and the *Super Hieremiam*, Bailey argues that 'we can speculate, with good reason, that Müntzer followed the basic biblical pattern of a seven-year tribulation divided into two three-and-one-half-year periods'. This seems hardly plausible when one considers Müntzer's writings as a whole, for it is only in extremely rare cases that he makes a specific prediction about a future event. Bailey latches on to one of these – Müntzer's warning in the shorter German version of the 'Prague Manifesto' that God will allow his Czech readers to be 'struck down by the Turks in the coming year' if they refuse God (CW 360) – to press the claim that Müntzer believed the Antichrist would be revealed, and the final and great tribulation commence, following the Turkish overthrow of Bohemia in 1522. Müntzer clearly *is* to be found here making a specific prediction, but it hardly seems a sound enough basis upon which to build an argument, as Bailey in fact does, that he held to a tribulation of 'two three-and-one-half-year periods', one stretching from mid-1518 to 1522 (when the Beast or Turk was established in the land), and the other from then until 1525 – a year which he would have expected to be significant even though he could not specifically have foreseen the decisive (not least for himself!) battle of Frankenhausen.[10] Rather, it seems more likely to be the case that the general turbulence created by the peasants' unrest brought Müntzer's apocalyptic hopes into much sharper focus, without his imposing on their protests and uprisings any rigid eschatological timetable.

If there is one area of overlap between Müntzer and the Joachites it is the central role that each assigns to Antichrist in the final drama. In the Joachite tradition the tribulation of the Church by Antichrist was an indispensable feature of that period of transition (through which many in the mid-thirteenth-century thought they were living) from the Age of the Son to the Age of the Spirit, and Müntzer, too, discerns that the time of Antichrist's raging is not far off. Writing to Hausmann in June 1521, for example, he expresses his conviction that the events foretold in Matthew 24 concerning the last days are being fulfilled: 'the time of Antichrist is upon us . . . the abomination of desolation is revealed'. Müntzer distances himself from the notion, popular in some circles, that Pope Julius II had fulfilled the prophecy concerning Antichrist; he was 'a true proclaimer of the same', but the real Antichrist will have power far in excess of any pope's: ' . . . the fourth beast will have dominion over the whole earth and his kingdom will be greater than all others' (CW 35). That Müntzer here speaks synonymously of Antichrist and the fourth beast of the dream in Daniel is interesting, suggesting again that he was tied to no one scheme for understanding the last times.

In his 'Prague Manifesto' written later that same year Müntzer returns to the apocalyptic theme, articulating again (particularly in the larger German version) his belief that momentous times are ahead. References to Antichrist and to other characters and scenes from the Apocalypse of John occur in this work, which Müntzer rounds off with a warning to his hearers that, if they do not join the fight against the 'high enemies of the faith', they will be 'doomed to fall into the hands of the Turk', who will be quickly followed by 'the real Antichrist . . . ' This latter figure, the 'real opponent of Christ', will 'reign in person', but Christ 'will soon afterwards give the kingdom of this world to his elect for all time' (CW 371).

Further references to Antichrist, which again suggest his regime to be imminent, appear in Müntzer's letter to Karlstadt of July 1523, in an earlier letter to Melanchthon, and in his marginalia on the pages of Tertullian. In the Melanchthon letter the reference is specifically to the work of Antichrist, 'the tribulation of Christians', and Müntzer rebukes the reformer for thinking that this was still to come when in fact it was 'already at the door'. 'The phial of the third angel has already been sprinkled on the fountains of the waters (I know this and tremble) and the outpouring of blood has been accomplished', Müntzer asserts in this letter, a direct reference to an episode in the apocalyptic destruction of the earth described in Revelation 16 (CW 45–6).

Antichrist is clearly a crucial figure for Müntzer, though it is a matter of debate whether any firm parallels may be drawn between his interpretation of it and that of Joachim. Antichrist, after all, was hardly the exclusive preserve of the Joachites, and Müntzer, with his thorough and comprehensive grasp of the Scriptures, would have been only too well aware of the prophetic warnings they contained about the last days, and well equipped to interpret them for himself – or rather, with the help of God. What one can say with certainty is that Müntzer shared with the followers of Joachim a conviction that the time of Antichrist's power had arrived, and that therefore, though they may still be some time off, the second advent of Christ and the reign of God were at least now on the eschatological horizon. But, and this is crucial for Müntzer, the elect cannot in the mean time sit back passively and await the unfolding of these events: Antichrist, and all who aid and abet him in his business of resisting the kingdom of God, must be destroyed by the elect, in order for the full salvation of God to be manifested.

Müntzer does not rely solely on the narrative in Daniel, or prophecies concerning Antichrist, to convey his conviction that the end of all things is at hand. In his letters and writings he draws on many other biblical images of the last days, reflecting both his command of this literature and his love of variety of metaphor and analogy to express his ideas and aspirations. One image upon which he often draws is that of the harvest, a particularly suggestive one in view of the emphasis it lays on the role of God's people, as wielders of the reaper's scythe, in the final sifting of the faithful and the reprobate. Two passages in Matthew's gospel and one in John's form the basis of Müntzer's thinking on the harvest: Jesus' brief reference to the harvest being plentiful but the labourers few in Matthew 9.37–8; a slightly longer narrative in John 4.35ff. where Jesus exhorts his hearers to see that the fields are already white for harvest, and that to reap them would be to gather fruit for eternal life; and the parable in Matthew 13.24–30 (upon which, of the three, Müntzer lays the most stress) of the wheat and the tares growing side-by-side in the farmer's field. We noted earlier how Müntzer uses this parable to illustrate the work of God in the individual Christian's life, rooting out the 'weeds, thistles and thorns from the rich soil which is [the] heart' so that true faith may grow there, and the necessity for the

Christian to 'suffer the sharp edge of the plough-share'. Now he goes on to show how, in accordance with the explanation given by Matthew himself in verses 36f., the parable also has apocalyptic overtones.

In the narrative, the tares, which are planted by an enemy of the farmer, spring up in the field at the same time as the intended crop, the wheat, but the farmer resists his servants' suggestion that the two be separated straightaway on the grounds that, in plucking the weeds, the fledgling wheat may thereby be dislodged as well. Both wheat and tares are to grow together until the harvest, when the reapers are to gather the latter first for binding and burning, and then the good crop for storing in barns. Müntzer follows Matthew in identifying the good seed as the children of God, the weeds as the children of the devil, the field as the world, and the harvest as the end of the age. Müntzer's 'field' includes (as Matthew's could not to the same extent) the Church, which has also been subject to a pernicious planting operation by the devil thanks to 'the idleness of the elect' (CW 166). The theme of the corruption of the Church is taken up again in the Sermon to the Princes, where Müntzer reiterates his demand that those opposed to God's revelation be strangled in the manner adopted by the Old Testament prophets in their dealings with the prophets of Baal: ' . . . the Christian church will never return to its origins', Müntzer declares; 'the tares have to be torn out of the vineyard of God' at harvest-time' (CW 250; cf. 190–1, 195, 171).

At the heart of all Müntzer's allusions to the harvest is a conviction that the time for it to be undertaken, for the sword to be put to the godless, has arrived. This is strongly expressed in the 'Prague Manifesto', for example, drafted in November 1521, where Müntzer speaks of the deeds of the 'elect' and the 'damned' 'flourish[ing] freely until *our time* when God will separate out the tares from the wheat . . . ' 'The time of the harvest has come', he concludes: 'I have sharpened my sickle . . . ' (CW 370–1, emphasis added). In the Latin version of the same tract Müntzer refers to 'the imminent harvest' when both the wheat and the tares will be 'winnowed out', to the 'slopes . . . whitening' with the harvest, and, again, to his own readiness to act as a reaper (CW 377). Interestingly, by March 1523, almost one-and-a-half years later, Müntzer has lost some of the sense of urgency about the need to begin harvesting. Writing to some fellow believers in Halle, Müntzer comments on the inevitability of the tares coming 'under the flail with the pure wheat', but asserts that 'the living God is sharpening his sickle in me so that I will *later* be able to cut down the red poppies and the little blue flowers' (CW 54, emphasis added; cf. 50). In his letter to Stolberg in July of that year Müntzer explicitly warns his followers against a cheap apocalyptic, the mistaken belief that by speeding ahead with a campaign to bring down the tyrants, without having first purged themselves of ungodly desires, they will induce God to 'rush to their aid'. God's prophecies cannot be short-circuited; 'where there is no poverty of the spirit, the kingdom of Christ cannot commence either' (CW 60).

One explanation for Müntzer's more measured tone at this time may be the somewhat more settled lifestyle he enjoyed during this period as pastor of the church of St John in Allstedt; perhaps the experience made him feel a little more at ease with the world and less driven to feelings that its demise at the hand of God could not be far off. Whatever the reason, Müntzer is found some sixteen months later making explicit again a conviction that work on rooting out the tares must begin now: 'the time of harvest is certainly with us', he writes in *A Manifest Exposé*. Müntzer's field of vision again includes the Church, 'a real old whore' now where once she was a pure virgin, though she 'can still be put right . . . by burning zeal'. 'A true Christianity for our days will soon be in full swing despite all the previous corruption' (CW 312).

One consistent feature of Müntzer's exegesis of the Matthean parable of the harvest is the particular role he discerns for himself as wielder of the heavenly sickle. Müntzer's understanding of his singular prophetic role in the forthcoming apocalyptic drama will be examined later, but it is worth noting at this point the strong calling he feels to act as a reaper on God's behalf in the final judgement: 'the living God is sharpening his sickle *in me* . . . ' we recall him writing to the group at Halle. In the 'Prague Manifesto' his sense of a divine calling to the task had been stated no less explicitly: '[God] himself has hired me for his harvest. I have sharpened my sickle . . . ' he writes in the larger German version (CW 371). The Latin version draws on the parable of the labourers who worked shifts of differing lengths in the field for the same pay: 'I am sharpening my sickle to put it into the harvest, having been hired by heaven for a penny a day', Müntzer writes (CW 377). The reference to 'sickle' is interesting because of its unambiguous apocalyptic connotations: in the book of Revelation (14.14f) the writer records how, in a vision, he hears the voice of an angel calling to 'one like a son of man' seated on a cloud, telling him that 'the hour to reap has come, for the harvest of the earth is fully ripe' and calling him to put in the 'sharp sickle' which is in his hand. Subsequently an angel appears also carrying a sickle, which he uses to reap the 'ripe grapes' of the earth. Müntzer may also have had in mind some words from two Old Testament prophets upon whom he draws in his writings – Joel: 'put in the sickle, for the harvest is ripe' (3.13); and Jeremiah: 'Cut off from Babylon the sower, and the wielder of the sickle in time of harvest' (50.16).[11]

It is, of course, implicit in Müntzer's comments that he is only fitted for the task of wielding the final sickle because he has suffered the harvesting work of God within his own soul, the sharp edge of the plough-share which roots out the fruit of the devil to make way for the growth of true faith. Others who have endured in this way will also be called as reapers in these last days (for Müntzer does not envisage carrying on the task alone), but only those. This is made clear in a passage in *A Manifest Exposé* where he speaks of those sent out to the harvest having been 'like a strong scythe or sickle . . . sharpened by God from the beginning of their lives';[12] '[n]ot everyone can execute this office', he continues, only those who 'have the assurance of faith possessed by those who wrote the Scriptures . . .' (CW 308, 310; cf. 199). In the Sermon to the Princes, however, where Müntzer is intent on persuading his noble hearers to take up the sword themselves in apocalyptic fashion, he is somewhat more ambiguous in his interpretation of the reapers. 'You are angels when you want to do what is right', he says at one point (CW 246). Later, in an even more explicit reference to the separation of the wheat and the tares, he speaks of 'the angels who sharpen their sickles for the harvest' as being 'the earnest servants of God who execute the zealous wisdom of God' (CW 250). The overriding point is clear, though; there can be no passive waiting on God to perform the reaping of the earth unaided. The faithful, with Müntzer to the fore, are those whom the divine householder entrusts with the work of rooting up and burning the weeds, so that the good crop may be gathered into his barn. And woe to 'the world and its scum, the biblical scholars, with their untested faith', who refuse to recognize that the faithful will be the angels of God to execute God's harvest, or even to take seriously the text in Matthew about the separation of the elect and the godless (CW 288).

Although this picture of the harvest of the wheat and the tares is the one Müntzer employs most frequently to depict the trauma the world will shortly have to endure, it is not the only one in his arsenal: the stone of Nebuchadnezzar's dream, which smashed the statue representing the four great kingdoms, is another whose significance should not be underestimated. We noted earlier that, in his exposition of Daniel 2, Müntzer warned that the stone cut from the mountain was on its way to annihilate the ruling powers of the present age, and that this stone he interpreted explicitly as Christ himself. 'Christ, the gentle son of God', Müntzer writes, 'is the true stone, hurled from the great mountain into the sea, into the pomp and affluence of this world' (CW 232).

Müntzer later developed the metaphor of the stone in more detail. Just as in Daniel's account it grows to become a mountain filling the whole earth, so, for Müntzer, the stone Jesus Christ increases in power over time. In Daniel the transformation of the stone takes place after it fulfils its function of destroying the statue, whereas for Müntzer it appears, almost snowball-like, to increase both in size and velocity as it rolls inexorably towards its ordained purpose. Of central importance for Müntzer is his belief that the time for it to fulfil its purpose, to usher in the new kingdom, has arrived: once the stone was small (though even then the world could not resist it), but now it has become 'so powerful, so unstoppable, striking and smashing the great statue right down to its old clay pots' (CW 245). Here the metaphors become mixed as Müntzer weaves into his discussion God's promise to the psalmist that the nations would be broken with a rod of iron and dashed in pieces like a potter's vessel (Ps. 2.9; cf. Rev. 19.15). But the warning to the princes of Saxony could not be clearer: know for sure that the stone is even now about its destructive work, he tells them, and in response 'take up your stance resolutely on the corner stone', the foundation stone of the new kingdom, and 'let God's true, unwavering purpose be yours'. Take the side of God's covenanted people and, on their behalf, destroy the powerful forces of the godless (CW 245).

Another biblical image which Müntzer employs is that of the approach of summer, and this he draws from references in Matthew (24.32-3) and Luke (21.29-31) to the use by Jesus himself of the flowering fig tree as a sign of the nearness of summer and a metaphor for the arrival of the kingdom. The litany of future events which provides the context for Jesus' remarks at this point – wars, famines, earthquakes and other tribulations – acts, like the leaves on the fig tree, as a sign or portent: just as certainly as the leaves announce the coming of the summer, so these catastrophes, when they begin to occur, will be a warning that the kingdom is 'at the very gates'. In one of his most apocalyptic letters, that to Philip Melanchthon dated 29 March 1522, Müntzer exhorts his reader to wake up to the fact that the tribulation (of Antichrist) is about to begin, and to delay no longer: 'the time has come . . . summer is at the door' (CW 46).

There are other apocalyptic images in Müntzer's writings. At the beginning of the larger German version of the 'Prague Manifesto', which has very clear apocalyptic overtones, Müntzer announces himself as one 'fill[ing] the sonorous marching trumpets with the new song of praise of the Holy Spirit' (CW 362). These words recall strikingly the ninety-eighth Psalm, in which the poet announces the coming judgement of the Lord (v. 9), and exhorts his or her readers to worship the Lord with a new song (v. 1) and the sound of trumpets (v. 6). Müntzer also employs the imagery of the trumpet in two of his letters – those to Luther and Duke Frederick – with the intent of demonstrating, on both occasions, that his message is to warn and alarm those who strive against the word of God or seek to blaspheme God's name (CW 21, 68).[13] Another image from the world of music appears in Müntzer's letter to the people at Erfurt, written a few days before the Frankenhausen engagement; if you long for the truth, he writes, 'come and join us in the dance, for we want to tread it out evenly' (CW 159).[14] Having two sentences earlier made a reference to the nineteenth chapter of the book of Revelation, Müntzer very likely had in mind the apocalyptic figure on the white horse described there (vv. 11–16), who represents the judgement of God on the nations and who treads the metaphorical 'winepress of the fury of the wrath of God the Almighty' (v. 15).

Some of the names Müntzer hurls at Luther also appear to have apocalyptic significance: 'virgin Martin . . . the chaste woman of Babylon' (CW 341) is taken from Revelation 18, and perhaps the letter of Jude provided the source for the expression 'the unspiritual soft-living Flesh in Wittenberg', Müntzer's first reference to Luther in the *Schutzrede* which the latter provoked him into writing (CW 327).[15] '"In the last time"', says this short epistle, quoting an unknown saying of the apostles, '"there will be scoffers, indulging their own ungodly lusts" . . . worldly people, devoid of the Spirit, who are causing divisions' (vv. 18–19). Matheson has argued that one of

Müntzer's names for Luther, 'Dr Liar' – which worked as a pun in the German (*doctor lügner*) – has eschatological overtones (CW 328, n. 22; F 323). Müntzer clearly saw in Luther's antagonism towards the 'true faith' signs that he was among those enemies of God whose appearance in the last days was predicted in the Scriptures.

In the days leading up to Frankenhausen, Müntzer's sense of urgency about the situation oozes from nearly every line he writes. 'It is high time' he writes to the people of Allstedt at the end of April 1525; 'make a start and fight the fight of the Lord!' 'The master wants to set the game in motion', he continues, employing one of his original metaphors; 'the evil-doers are for it.' 'Go to it, go to it', he implores on three separate occasions in this one letter, 'while the fire is hot', 'while it is day' (CW 141–2).[16] Two weeks later a rather more sober letter is dispatched to the folk at Eisenach, but the message is essentially the same: 'Now . . . God has moved the whole world in a miraculous way towards a recognition of the divine truth, and [the world] is proving this by its great and earnest zeal against the tyrants' (CW 150). As always Müntzer's case is supported by appeals to Scripture, particularly prophecies about the end time which are about to be fulfilled; his readers in Allstedt are referred to a number of biblical references – including the wholly apocalyptic twenty-fourth chapter of Matthew – where 'the whole business can be read up' (CW 142). The strongly apocalyptic thirty-fourth and thirty-ninth chapters of Ezekiel also feature prominently in Müntzer's writing – the former recording a divine promise that God's flock will be protected from corrupt and self-interested shepherds – as does Mary's Magnificat (Luke 1.46f), which also treats of the liberation of the oppressed from the hands of the mighty. In two letters to the counts of Mansfeld in 1525, Müntzer warns his noble readers that God is about the business of casting down the mighty from their seats, adding a comment to Count Albert that 'the lowly (whom you despise) he has raised' (CW 157).[17]

If Müntzer identified the unrest building up around him, the inchoate resistance of the peasants to the tyranny of their rulers, with the apocalyptic drama foretold in Revelation, Daniel and other scriptures, he also discerned for himself a particular role in the unfolding of that drama; or rather *roles*, for he cast himself, over time, as a latter-day reincarnation of a number of different biblical heroes of the faith. There is a parallel here with his approach to prophecy and history. In that area, we noted, rather than commit himself to any one particular scheme for interpreting the past and projecting the future, Müntzer employed all prophetic models loosely to convey the general point that history was indeed approaching a climax; and with regard to his own prophetic role *vis-à-vis* that climax Müntzer similarly eschewed identification with any one particular apocalyptic figure. Indeed, as if to demonstrate unequivocally the seal of divine approval he felt on his own mission, he took the mantle of a number of prophets who each, in their own lives, showed clear signs of a calling by God.

In a number of places Müntzer testifies in a general way to his having been called by God. 'It is not my work I am doing, but that of the Lord', he writes to Luther in 1520 (CW 21). Perhaps the most explicit of his claims to special status as an agent of God appears at the beginning of the 'Prague Manifesto'; by 'special diligence' and 'the utmost industry', he claims, he has reached a better understanding of the basis upon which ongoing Christian faith is built than anyone else (CW 362; cf. 357, 372). In his comments on Joachim, Müntzer reminds us that he owes nothing of his learning to any human agency, and in his Prague statement he affirms that 'no tar-salved priest, no spirit dissimulating monk was able to tell [me] anything about the ground of faith, not the tiniest point'. Nor could these types help him with the *ordo rerum*: 'I have never heard any donkey-farting doctor whisper the tiniest fraction or slightest point about the order [established in God and all creatures] . . . ' (CW 362-3).[18]

References to Müntzer's special call also appear in some of his later writings. In his letter to Frederick the Wise of October 1523, for example, he states that 'the almighty God made me an earnest preacher', and suggests that his name has a special significance for oppressed and oppressor alike: 'My name (as is proper) is bound to excite alarm, disgust and contempt among the worldly wise. To the little band of the poor and needy, however, it has the sweet savour of life, while to those who pursue the pleasures of the flesh it is a gruesome abomination presaging their speedy downfall' (CW 67-8).

In his letter of July 1524 to Duke John, Müntzer claims that he has a duty to teach the faith to the people of his day just as Paul did to the first-century community at Rome, 'following the unambiguous directions given me by the testimony of God' (CW 82). Eric Gritsch argues, on the basis of texts such as these, that Müntzer portrayed himself as a prophet in the tradition of Jeremiah and Ezekiel, with a mission to save Christianity, and even, in the light of the remarks at the beginning of the 'Prague Manifesto', that he saw himself 'as the last of God's prophets . . . initiating the final age of the world'. This is perhaps to read rather too much into the text, though it is true that Müntzer saw himself as a John the Baptist figure.[19] Gordon Rupp makes the rather more measured judgement that Müntzer is less of a 'crackpot megalomaniac' than many of his contemporaries, and indeed, 'compared with some of Luther's claims about his own achievements (by the grace of God!), Müntzer is reserved about claims for his own prophetic mission'. Rupp notes, too, how soberly Müntzer makes his claim to direct inspiration in respect of his translations of the Psalms: 'in order to improve matters [for the poor people]', Müntzer writes, 'I have translated the Psalms in accordance with German style and form but under the intimate and direct leading of the Holy Spirit' (CW 168). Yet Rupp concludes that 'it is part of Müntzer's apocalyptic view to be conscious of his own prophetic vocation', as evidenced by his references to 'sharpening his sickle', being hired by God for the harvest, and to himself as 'the Servant of God' ('sometimes in the history of the Church the most arrogant of titles!').[20]

Other of Müntzer's self-designations throw light on the developing nature of the role he saw himself called upon to play as the end drew near. Under letters written in 1522 and early 1523 he signs himself a 'messenger of Christ' or 'a willing courier of God' (CW 46, 54). By September of 1523, having got into a dispute with Count Ernst, he becomes 'Thomas Müntzer, a disturber of the unbelievers' (CW 67). In the *Manifest Exposé* of mid-1524 he is 'Thomas Müntzer, with the hammer' (CW 260), which, like Jeremiah (23.29), he will use against those so-called prophets who treat dishonourably the Word of God. In the days preceding the 'final battle' he is 'a servant of God against the godless' (CW 142). Finally, for the battle itself, he takes the sword of Gideon.

Gideon is one of the key biblical figures upon whom Müntzer models himself, indeed, whom he *becomes*, for the wielding of his sword was certainly no symbolic or rhetorical gesture. Just as Gideon, with a mere three hundred men, took on the vast armies of the Midianites, so Müntzer leads his followers, outnumbered and inadequately armed, against the mighty forces of the princes at Frankenhausen. 'A hundred thousand people will not make me afraid, even if they are camped all around me', Müntzer writes to the community at Schmalkalden in early May 1525 (CW 149); the words echo some of the psalmist David (Ps. 3.6), but have clear Gideon-esque overtones. Müntzer identifies with the slayer of Midian in three further letters he pens that week, signing off in each case, 'Thomas Müntzer with the sword of Gideon' (CW 151, 156, 157). And as Gideon relied on God to give him the victory, so also does Müntzer. 'You need fear no one', he writes to the people of Frank-enhausen just days before the fighting begins: 'God . . . will endow your small band with more strength [than] you would ever believe' (CW 144).

If Müntzer was Gideon, the scourge of the armies of Midian, so also was he filled with the spirit of Elijah, another mighty man of God who once slew four hundred and fifty prophets of the false god Baal in a single day. The significance of Elijah for Müntzer is twofold. First, he is a model of a person called by God at a particular point in history to destroy those who oppose God, and Müntzer began to draw support for his position from Elijah as early as his letter to Hausmann and the shorter German version of the 'Prague Manifesto' in 1521 (CW 34, 360). He also speaks approvingly of Elijah's action in destroying the priests of Baal in his Sermon to the Princes in 1524 (CW 250), and calls in the *Manifest Exposé* for 'a servant of God . . . endowed with the spirit of Elijah' – implicitly himself – to step forward (CW 300).[21] Müntzer's *Vindication and Refutation*, provoked by Luther's vitriolic attack on him, is issued 'from the cave of Elijah, whose zeal spares no one' (CW 327) – Elijah having himself had occasion to steer clear of his persecutors. But Elijah is also an important messianic and apocalyptic figure. The gospel writers recall several times the prophecies concerning his role as the forerunner of the Son of Man, and Matthew, Mark and Luke each show these to have been fulfilled in the person of John the Baptist. In the Transfigura-tion narrative which follows in the accounts in Matthew and Mark, Elijah also represents the fulfilment in Jesus of Israelite prophecy concerning the Messiah. In his marginal comments on Tertullian's *De resurrectione carnis*, Müntzer notes Elijah's apocalyptic role as a forewarner of the coming day of judgement, his words clearly echo-ing the Lord's promise in Malachi 4.5 to send the people 'Elijah the prophet before the great and terrible day of the LORD comes' (CW 425). The case has often been made for identifying Elijah as one of the 'two witnesses' of Revelation 11: they are recorded as being able 'to shut the sky that no rain may fall during the days of their prophesy-ing', and to bring forth fire and consume their foes, and Elijah demonstrated both of these powers during his lifetime. Their responsibility is to effect the conversion of the world in the end time through their preaching, a task Müntzer, as one possessing the 'spirit of Elijah', clearly understood to have been entrusted to him in these last days.[22]

The close identification in the New Testament between John the Baptist and the prophet Elijah is noteworthy in so far as John is another figure whose mantle Müntzer is eager to claim. 'If . . . the Christian people is to be set on its feet again', he writes in *A Manifest Exposé*, these people 'must learn to sigh . . . to pray and long for a new John . . . someone must arise who will point men to the revelation of God's little lamb, who comes from the father as the judgement of the eternal word'. The clear implication, as with the references in this same document to Elijah, is that the someone is Müntzer himself: who else has a faith 'solidly based on the experience of his unbelief', or one which 'measures up to his passionate desires'? (CW 296).[23] Yet the work of John is not only linked with the final judgement of the world; he is also, in contrast to the 'pleasure-loving, ambitious types' who do not practise what they preach, 'an angel testifying to Christ, one mirrored in all true preachers' (CW 308). John, in other words, is a model for Müntzer of a preacher who, by his example, leads people into that true faith which comes through suffering and self-denial, and which knows the movement of the Spirit in the depth of the soul – though the task of such preachers today is even harder, thanks to the pernicious influence of the scholars and preachers of the false gospel (CW 296).

Other figures whose cause Müntzer sees himself taking up are Josiah; Daniel – to whom we have referred briefly already; and Jehu. Josiah is Müntzer's model as he forges his first alliance: in his letter to Zeiss in 1524 he makes a reference to the 'holy king' and the covenant the people made with God in his time (CW 100, 93). The king's attack on the idolatrous priests of his time also receives commendation from Müntzer twice in his Sermon to the Princes (CW 246, 250). The need for a new Daniel – the central theme of this sermon, of course – is vital, Müntzer argues, given the princes' failure to understand the significance of the events happening around them. As Nebuchadnezzar failed to grasp the significance of the statue in his vision, and its impending destruction, so the Saxon princes needed to see that the last of the kingdoms which the statue betokened was the one which they themselves served and was shortly to meet *its* end. Hence the need for a new interpreter both to explain the dream and to show them what their response must be, the annihilation of all who obstruct the coming of the new kingdom, the reign of God. Müntzer's attraction to the figure of Jehu is no surprise given the account in 2 Kings 9 of his obedience to the Lord's command to slay three of the Lord's enemies, Joram, Ahaziah and Jezebel. As Müntzer writes to Christopher Meinhard in 1524, the emergence of a new Jehu will be a sign to the godless, 'with their senseless violence, to shrink back before [such a] one' (CW 77), whose own use of force, as in the case of Elijah and Gideon, will be sanctioned by God as a final avenging blow to the adversaries of God's people.

'A new Jehu', 'a new Daniel', 'a new John', 'a servant of God . . . of the spirit of Elijah', 'Thomas Müntzer with the sword of Gideon' . . . Müntzer was the last in the line of an illustrious band of warriors renowned for their unflinching obedience to the Lord's command to disturb – and in most cases destroy – the faithless: and the military prowess of these men, at least those of the Old Testament, is crucial for Müntzer, given his deep conviction that the godless, the tares in the divine field, must in these last days be rooted out and destroyed. (In the guise of John, the voice of one crying in the wilderness, his duty was to arouse the elect and prepare them for their role in this work.) Thus as he takes on these roles, subsumed under the generic designation 'a servant of God against the godless', Müntzer makes it plain to his followers that theirs is not simply a human struggle against earthly powers, but, as Tom Scott puts it, 'a transcendent battle in the name of God, a holy war against the reprobate and obdurate'.[24] Müntzer's close identification with the apocalyptic figures of Daniel, Elijah and John bears clear testimony both to this and to the singular role which he, as a chosen vessel of God, had to play in the dismantling of the old order and the ushering in of the new.

Singular, we should note, but not solitary, for Müntzer never envisaged fighting the last battle alone; indeed, the part which those whom he termed *die Auserwelten* – 'the elect' – would play in the final drama is central to an understanding of his whole apocalyptic. The concept of a specially chosen or elect people of God derives from a doctrine of predestination, according to which humanity is held to be divided into two distinct groupings, those destined for eternal damnation and those saved from such a fate.[25] Such a doctrine clearly underpins biblical parables based on images of wheat and tares and sheep and goats,[26] but how is one to know to which camp someone belongs? Who are the sheep or wheat, and who the goats or tares? The key to such knowledge, for Müntzer, is to be found in the concept of *urteyl*, judgement, a gift of God to the elect by which they are enabled to know themselves to be among the chosen, and to recognize those who are the ungodly. This concept is essential for Müntzer, and vital for an understanding of his leagues, his apocalyptic, and his participation in the peasants' struggle.

If the centrality of the elect as a category in Müntzer's thinking can be clearly discerned in his writings, his definition of the term, whom he actually saw coming within its bounds, suffers from a considerable lack of clarity; were they a small persecuted minority, or the suffering and oppressed masses? The least contentious thing to say would be that Müntzer's position changed or developed over time. Essentially the elect were those who had been shaped by God into the image of God's Son, and who had experienced the painful and tortuous journey to true faith; and therefore what distinguished them from the ungodly was not so much their outward deeds – for they could still be tempted into sin – but their inner sensitivity to the movement of the Spirit in the ground of their soul. As Müntzer writes in *A Manifest Exposé*, making the contrast plain: 'however great a sinner he may be, the conscience of the elect man will direct him away from his sins, as long as he senses the movement of the Spirit during his time of tribulation, as Psalm 39 testifies. But the conscience of the godless does not do this, as Psalm 35 points out' (CW 290).

Only those who had experienced inner suffering and transforma-tion were worthy of the task of rooting out wickedness in the world. Yet Müntzer was not a sectary, in the sense that he gathered around him a small band of saints which he believed could single-handedly carry through God's will in the last days, nor did he propose something like a 'dictatorship of the spiritually illuminated'.[27] Like Luther, Müntzer recognized that 'Christians are not so many that they can get together in mobs', and so initially he allowed into his league both the pious and the evil-doers. Yet it is difficult to deny that at Mühlhausen, where he formed the Eternal League of God and where he rallied his troops for the battle at Frankenhausen, Müntzer implicitly equated the elect with the German *Volk*, the poor and materially oppressed common folk; that he made, in other words, the peasants' cause his own, a move which fits uncomfortably with the notion that the elect are only those who have known *Anfechtung* and *Gelassenheit*.

Stayer argues that Müntzer equated the revolutionary peasants with the elect because they responded to his correct doctrine, though as Bailey pertinently asks, 'How many of the peasants who took part in the rebellion and who had suffered a type of social *Anfechtung*, had truly experienced the birth of faith in their soul . . .?'[28] Whatever Müntzer's thinking at this time, he attributed both the collapse of his programme and his own demise to his misplaced faith in the peasant hordes, and came to regret it bitterly. The people did not understand me properly, he wrote from prison while awaiting his execution: 'they sought only their own interests and the divine truth was defeated as a result' (CW 160).

Before assessing the significance of this, more should be said about Müntzer's *Bünde*, his leagues or covenants of the elect which provided the whole dynamic of his apocalyptic.[29] Reduced to its essence Müntzer's view was that the Church, once pure and undefiled, had been corrupted by its faithless and godless clergy, but that a new age was dawning which would see their annihilation at the hands of the elect on the basis of their God-given capacity for judgement (*urteyl*). The elect would utterly destroy the enemies of God, and the sign of this would be the forging of a new covenant between God and humankind. The term *Bund* in Müntzer thus suggests not merely a league or pact made by men and women among themselves, but a covenant of the kind God made in Old Testament times with the chosen people of Israel. The significance of this is as follows: firstly, the task for which a *Bund* was brought into being was not of human origin, but divine; and, secondly, the elect do not expect to triumph through their own strength, but because of their obedience to God's calling. The implications of this will be assessed shortly.

So what significance did Müntzer's apocalyptic perspective have for his overall scheme? Firstly, it sharpened up his two-tier conception of humanity. Central to Müntzer's *Weltanschauung* is a dualism involving good and evil, godly and godless, and his employment of apocalyptic terminology as he sees the day of their final conflict approaching gives his message a much sharper and more pronounced emphasis. Müntzer's writings are full of opposites and polarizations. There is authentic faith, which he himself has experienced, and which has its beginning in the movement of the Holy Spirit; and counterfeit faith, peddled by those who originate from the devil and which has to be ruthlessly wiped out. There is the abyss of the soul in which the word of God is received, and the abyss of the pit or hell into which the teachers of the false faith should be propelled. There are authentic visions and dreams which are from God, and the false 'poisonous, accursed dreams of the monks' and 'deluded dreamers'. A person can know the fear of God, or the fear of men and of the devil. A person is either a servant of God, or among the servants of Antichrist.

Müntzer expresses his dualist conception of humanity in other ways. There is the separation we have already observed between the elect and the abandoned or damned, but Müntzer also talks frequently of 'the Christian people' (sometimes 'the poor Christian people'), 'the friends of God' and 'the servants of God', and of their adversaries 'the godless', 'the evil-doers' and 'the unbelievers'. Sometimes the terms are conjoined, as in 'the godless evil-doers', 'the elect friends of God' and 'the godless, abandoned men'. It is also worth noting, in passing, the sharp and often original invective Müntzer reserves for the learned scribes and false teachers, whom he sometimes gathers under the generic term *die Schriffgelerten*: they purport to teach the faith of Christ to the people, but in reality they have stolen from the Bible its real message and so only seduce their hearers into wandering farther away from the truth. In their attitude to the Bible they compare to confidence tricksters and cruel murderers, and are also blasphemers, abandoned scoundrels, beasts of the belly, swine, perverted phantasts and whore-riders. They have as much knowledge of God as the carved wooden idols they serve, and, most seriously of all, betray the people who look to them for counsel. Müntzer calls them traitors, criminals, turncoats and devils.

Müntzer's language, as he reflects on the treatment these blind teachers will shortly receive at the hands of the elect, is also unambiguously apocalyptic. The damned and the elect will ultimately be separated, of course, but that is to put it rather mildly: generally Müntzer's language is much more severe, uncompromising and ruthless. At one point he writes of the tares being 'torn out' of the ground at harvest-time, and the violent and bloody end of the godless, anticipated by the earnest servants of God as they sharpen their sickles in readiness, is a theme to which he returns frequently. The evil-doers are to be swept aside, driven away from the elect, and then strangled without mercy or eliminated by the sword. The counterfeit faith they peddle, too, must be ruthlessly wiped out. In the case of Count Ernst, whose heart (like Pharaoh's of old) God has hardened, he is to be handed over to destruction.[30]

Müntzer's terminology, like many another apocalyptic writer, has echoes of battle and of victory and defeat: his apocalyptic, in other words, furnished him with a grammar with which to frame his vision of the final triumph of the elect over the damned. The mighty, in fulfilment of Mary's song of praise, are being forcibly cast down from their seats, and the godless scholars go to their downfall; the elect, on the other hand, unless seduced into showing a fraudulent clemency, will surely prevail. Their cause, like that of the common folk, is spoken of in the language of power: the sword, punishment, vengeance, nullification and – one of Müntzer's favourite terms, this – *unüberwintlich*, best translated 'invincible', 'unconquerable' or 'unstoppable'. Müntzer uses this adjective in relation to a number of different themes in his writings, and his frequent use of it conveys much about the strength of his certainty that both his theological and political convictions enjoyed, as it were, divine sanction. Thus the holy Christian faith can be spoken of as 'invincible', as can the testimony of the elect given them by the Holy Spirit that they are the children of God. In contrast to the faith of the 'strawbrained little doctors', which is proved from books rather than experience, Müntzer's tried and tested faith stands on invincible (*unuberwyntlichen*) ground (CW 369; F 503). Importantly, the reformation which the world is shortly to experience will also be *unüberwintlich*. Müntzer's confidence spills over as he reflects on this in his sermon on Daniel: 'I know it for a fact', he announces, 'that the Spirit of God is revealing . . . the great need for a full and final reformation in the near future (*eine treffliche, unuberwintliche zukünfftige reformation*). This must be carried out' (CW 244; F 255).

Müntzer does not forget, of course, that the battle will not be won in his strength, nor that of the elect, but by the power of God. His letter to his followers in Allstedt in April 1525 bears the clearest testimony to this, though numerous references in others of his writings show that, while it is God's people who physically engage the enemy, the power upon which they depend for victory comes from on high. In his sermon on Daniel, Müntzer quotes the example of Joshua, who 'did not win the [promised] land by the sword, but by the power of God, but the sword was the means used . . . ' (CW 250). The militant dimension of Müntzer's mysticism again comes to the fore: both human instrumentality *and* divine endorsement are necessary if the people of God are to overcome their adversaries: 'don't let us have any of these hackneyed posturings about the power of God achieving everything without any resort to your sword', he had earlier written in the same sermon (CW 247–8). 'The very clearest wisdom of God . . . which can only spring from the pure unfeigned fear of God . . . alone can equip us with its mighty arm to exercise vengeance on the enemies of God' (CW 234). Count Ernst is reminded that he is to be 'handed over to destruction by God's mighty power': indeed, according to the Magnificat, it is the Lord who brings down the mighty from their thrones (Luke 1.52), as Müntzer of course recognizes (CW 156, 157; cf. 151). It is God, too, who separates out the tares from the wheat (CW 370), who pours out 'his invincible anger' (*seinen unuberwintlichen zcorn*) against the godless (CW 364; F 497), and who has 'moved the whole world . . . towards a recognition of the divine truth' (CW 150).

Müntzer's frequent usage of this expression 'the whole world' (*die gantze welt*) is also clearly apocalyptic. He speaks of 'the world' fifty-one times in the 'Prague Manifesto', the Sermon to the Princes and his last twenty letters, and on eighteen of these occasions qualifies it with the adjective 'whole'. What God is doing in Allstedt and in Mühlhausen has significance for all humankind everywhere. The whole world has been led astray and seduced by the biblical scholars and deaf priests, who 'set themselves up as instructors to the whole world' (CW 237) but who in fact are an affront to it. Therefore Müntzer must 'broadcast [the true] Christian faith to the whole world by word and writing' (CW 112); if it appears in print it will be 'for the whole world to see' (CW 133; cf. 362). He will lift up his voice against Count Ernst 'for all the world to hear' (CW 155). Now, in these last days, the tide is turning: 'the accursed monkish dreamers . . . are being exposed to the whole world for the idle good-for-nothings that they are' (CW 238; cf. 133). God is moving 'the whole world . . . towards a recognition of the divine truth' (CW 53). There is almost certainly a connection between Müntzer's emphasis on the 'whole world' and his concept of the *ordo dei*, discussed more fully below. Müntzer used the analogy of 'the parts' and 'the whole' to picture the relation of the created order to God; the fall destroyed the unity of the parts, but in Christ they become fully restored to 'the whole'.

Müntzer understands the events in which he is caught up to be of world-historical importance, and at times he specifically echoes biblical prophecies concerning the end time. When speaking of his message being preached to the whole world Müntzer harks back to some words of Jesus recorded by Matthew: 'This good news of the kingdom will be preached throughout the world . . . and then the end will come' (24.14). Müntzer had earlier referred to this passage in his letter to Hausmann in 1521, and suggested there that he thought the time for 'the preaching of the Gospel of the kingdom throughout the world' had begun (CW 35). In *A Manifest Exposé*, penned shortly after he delivered his Sermon to the Princes, Müntzer wrote that, in his day, 'the gospel will spread even more fully than in the time of the apostles' (CW 314). Müntzer's reference to Christ, the stone, filling the whole world, recalls the statement in Revelation 1.7 that 'every eye will see him' when he comes. A comment early in the larger German version of the 'Prague Manifesto' about the spirit of the fear of God, which the elect enjoy, being something which 'the world cannot abide' (CW 363), brings to mind Jesus' warning that his followers 'will be hated by all nations because of my name' (Matt. 24.9). Müntzer acknowledged later that the elect will be regarded as lunatics by the world (CW 47).

Perhaps, though, the most important consequence of Müntzer's 'apocalyptic' reading of his situation was the capacity it gave him to discern, in the drift of contemporary events, unmistakable signs that he was living at a momentous, decisive point in history, at a *kairos*; and these signs, generally speaking, were the fallen and adulterous condition of the Church, the degenerate state of the Holy Roman Empire, and the increasingly militant response of the poor people to the tyranny and injustice under which they were forced to live.

The first two signs came together for Müntzer in his interpretation of the statue in Nebuchadnezzar's dream. The fifth and bottom layer, the empire 'we see before us', is, like the fourth, made of iron, but is 'patched with dung . . . that is, with the vain schemings of hypocrisy, which swarms and slithers over the face of the whole earth'. In case we have any doubt as to Müntzer's train of thought here, he gives us the graphic image of 'all the eels and snakes coupling together immorally in one great heap', and the explanation that the former represent the secular lords and rulers, and the latter the priests and evil clerics (CW 244). From his reading of Eusebius and Hegessipus Müntzer learned that, very early in its history – in fact soon after the death of the apostles – the holy bride of Christ lost her pure virgin state by engaging adulterously with the rulers and kings of the world. Müntzer prophesied against manifestations of this adultery in his own day, but the stiff-necked nature of the Church's leaders, both in Rome and Wittenberg, seemed to him portents that the last struggle before the end time was near.

Yet there were other unmistakable signs that the Church would shortly be felled by the stone coming down from the mountain, and that a new one would emerge in its stead. The gospel, unlike in the days of the apostles, was being preached far and wide: 'from many lands and strange nations great numbers of the elect will appear . . .' (CW 314). Further, the faithful today are much more courageous and conscientious in attacking the idolatrous practices of the ungodly; the early Church was lax in this regard because St Peter was a 'timid man' who feared for his safety, 'dissembled when among the pagans', and set a bad example for all the apostles. Now the followers of Christ were beginning to follow the injunction of Deuteronomy 7 to break down and destroy the altars and images of the godless, which had always been God's command (CW 249). The obedience of the Church in this matter, its crusading and universal character, were conclusive proof that it *was* the Church of the last days.

The growing rebellion of the peasants against the corrupt and unjust form of government they had to suffer was another sign that God was moving the world towards a final transformation. Müntzer was impressed, both with the speed with which the resistance spread, and the form it took; it had both anti-clerical and communal dimensions, and furthermore the protagonists seemed open to the possibility that the end of their oppression might lie in the formation of a new Christian community. Müntzer was heartened as he heard of the activities of the peasants in the north, and of the spread of the revolt, in Holy Week 1525, to Fulda and towards Thuringia and Mühlhausen. With infectious enthusiasm he encouraged the Allstedters to participate: 'The whole of Germany, France, Italy is awake . . . At Fulda four abbeys were laid waste during Easter Week, the peasants in the Klettgau and the Hegau in the Black Forest have risen, three thousand strong, and the size of the peasant host is growing all the time', he wrote, following with the exhortations 'go to it', 'show no pity', 'don't let your sword grow cold', and so on. The basis of Müntzer's entreaty was that this was the fight of the Lord: God was giving the orders, as in the days of Moses, and God would give the victory. 'God goes before you . . . do not be deterred. God is with you.' Echoing the experience of Gideon, Müntzer encouraged his followers to believe that, even if there were only a handful of them, provided their trust in God were unperturbable they 'need have no fear of a hundred thousand' (CW 141–2).

The apparent success of the peasants' uprising only served to convince him further of the divinely ordained nature of the campaign. From Görmar near Mühlhausen he wrote to reassure the people in Frankenhausen that they need have fear of no one: 'The voice of the Lord says: Look, the strength of my needy people will be increased, who will dare attack them? So be bold and put your trust in God alone ...' (CW 144). In a similar vein he rallied the Christians at Schmalkalden preparing for battle: '... it is rather weak of you to be so very afraid, when it is plain as a pikestaff that God is standing by you. Be of good courage, and sing with us: "A hundred thousand people will not make me afraid, even if they are camped all around me"' (CW 148–9).

Müntzer's most dramatic display of confidence in the outcome of the struggle was at Frankenhausen itself. While some among the assembled bands of peasants prevaricated in the face of an offer from the princes of a peaceful end to the conflict (involving the handing over to them of Müntzer, alive), he reiterated his conviction that God would be their strength – a conviction made remarkably more plausible when, at the very time of its utterance, a corona or 'halo' appeared around the sun. The similarity of this heavenly sign to the rainbow emblem on the peasants' standards left Müntzer in no doubt it was a divinely given portent of success, and enabled him to carry the doubters with him too.

That literally within hours of this occurrence the peasants were routed in the most bloody fashion serves to highlight in a particularly stark fashion the consequences of making too close an identification between, as it were, one particular historical struggle and apocalyptic scenarios described in the Scriptures. Müntzer's confidence in the success of the peasants' uprising, it must be concluded, rested ultimately upon a misplaced belief that the end had come, that the eschatological promises of God concerning the overthrow of the mighty and the separation of the tares from the wheat were being fulfilled in his day in Europe and, indeed, throughout 'the whole world'. In this sense Müntzer's apocalyptic might be said to have impacted on his revolutionary agenda in a significant, dramatic and somewhat negative way.

Yet was it Müntzer's apocalyptic *per se*, or the demands he made upon it? Müntzer was clearly justified in drawing from his observations of the contemporary scene the conclusion that the transformation of the world was at hand. The signs he saw around him clearly *were* portents of a convulsion of continent-wide proportions, and, as Goertz has written, events at Frankenhausen in no way warrant the conclusion that Müntzer's 'instinct for necessary changes' misled him. 'There was too much amiss', as Goertz says, 'not only in the church, but also in the temporal jurisdictions and in social structures'.[31] Yet Müntzer's investment of his faith in the disorganized and inchoate peasants' movement, his equation of that movement with the elect and his confidence that God was shortening their time of suffering, led him to sadly naive conclusions about their prospects; specifically, his identification of their struggle with the last (apocalyptic) battle spared him from the necessary task of relating his (and their) political ambitions to the concrete process of history, and thus to a seriously misplaced confidence in the outcome of their struggle. All of which leads to a conclusion that an apocalyptic identification of the *kairos*, when freed from demands that it be given eschatological significance *now*, can, as Müntzer on one level powerfully demonstrates, profoundly sharpen one's focus on contemporary events; yet when, as ultimately happens in Müntzer's case, such reductionist demands *are* imposed, the result is a failure to take seriously the realistic possibilities of the given historical moment, and the still-birth of what, in principle, might be revolutionary ideas. It is a question to which we shall return in due course.

What, finally, are we to make of Müntzer's willingness to embrace violence as a means of bringing in the new order, and his implicit preparedness to risk his own life in the process? On the first point, it could hardly be argued that in adopting the violent option he was contributing anything new to revolutionary thought, let alone anything *Christian* (though it will be suggested later that a violent response to injustice might in some cases appear to require no more justification on theological grounds than a non-violent one); but how profitable might it be, in the spirit of our quest for a 'distinctive contribution', to reflect on Müntzer's apparent readiness, in the words of John 15.13, to 'lay down his life for his friends'? This is admittedly a difficult area, for we are not to suppose that it is only Christians who know anything about self-sacrifice. Examples of those who have demonstrated heroic and selfless devotion to a cause can be found in all political and religious traditions, and, indeed, Ernst Bloch has wondered whether the self-sacrifice of those who die with no hope of a resurrection or of having merited heaven – with no promise of an Easter Sunday to sweeten their Good Friday – might not be more pure than that of the Christian.[32] Yet the centrality of the resurrection hope in Christianity can introduce a new dynamic into revolutionary struggle, one that can arguably be perceived beneath what superficially appears to be the cavalier attitude to death demonstrated by Müntzer. A resurrection hope (strongly linked in Müntzer, of course, to utopian and apocalyptic expectations), can, as José Míguez Bonino has argued, give rise to an 'availability' for struggle 'which cannot be limited by the threat that otherwise seems insuperable – death'; and this is so because 'the Christian has left his death behind him [and] to that extent he does not need to make an effort to ensure his own life'.[33]

It would be unwise to claim too much for this suggestion, which is both highly subjective and of limited applicability; indeed, of itself it could only be considered a useful contribution to revolutionary theory were the concept of resurrection to find universal acceptance! Yet when considered within the wider context of Christian 'spirituality', understood as a total way of life borne of a deep commitment, the signs are somewhat more hopeful, prompted as we are in the direction of exploring the possibility that Christianity can provide a depth of meaning to revolutionary struggle which cannot be offered by materialistic ideologies. This is another theme to which we shall return at a later stage.

Utopianism

Tied closely to Müntzer's apocalyptic is a conviction, utopian in character, that the world is shortly to be reshaped in accordance with the order of things (*ordo rerum*) instituted by God at the creation of the world. For the framework of his ideas on the *ordo* Müntzer may have been indebted to Quintilian's *Institution oratoria*, though he infused the concept with his own theology to the extent that it constitutes arguably the most original part of his thinking. How Müntzer precisely understood the concept has been the subject of considerable debate, though in essence it assumes the establishment by God, at the creation, of a hierarchical pattern of relationships between Godself, humankind and the creatures, which, as a consequence of the fall, became grossly distorted, and would remain so until the world was transformed. One clue as to how Müntzer saw this 'order' appears in some sermon notes he penned in 1523: 'This is what is meant by contemplating and sorting out the order of things; first the four elements and the heavens, then the plants, then the animals, then man, then Christ, then God the Father Almighty, who is uncreated . . .' (CW 387).

Müntzer comes close at times to developing a natural theology: in the 'Prague Manifesto', for example, he suggests that the order of God is 'implanted in all creatures' (CW 357). Yet this order is not really to be comprehended without divine revelation: faith comes to a person, he writes elsewhere, 'because God discloses and reveals himself through the order established in him and in all the creatures' (CW 106).[34] Perhaps there are stronger hints of a *creation* theology in some of Müntzer's writings: the 'hierarchy' outlined in his sermon notes, at least from the elements to humankind, bears a striking similarity to the order of creation set out in Genesis 1.

Reinhold Schwarz, while stressing that Genesis 1 provides the 'key' to Müntzer's concept of the *ordo rerum*, also draws attention to the hint in the *Vindication and Refutation* of a connection in Müntzer's mind between that chapter, Psalm 19[35] (which stresses the purity of the law of God), and Isaiah 11 (on the basis of the knowledge and fear of the Lord).[36] This connection is not clearly spelled out, though Müntzer seems to have coupled the restoration of the *ordo* with the indwelling in humanity of the pure fear of God: the soul must ultimately be 'bound' to the pure law of God, not as at present to creaturely things. 'I strive for the purity of the divine law, Psalm 18', Müntzer writes, 'by pointing to the beginning of the Bible, to what its first chapter says about the ordering of creation, and explain how all the sayings of the Bible point to the fulfilment of the spirit of the fear of God, Isaiah 11' (CW 332).

Müntzer also draws on the early chapters of Genesis in *A Manifest Exposé* to explain, as he does with some emphasis, that God's 'ordering of things' – the nature of the relationship between God and humanity and between humanity and creation – is to be understood in terms of 'dominion' and 'possession' (CW 316). The word he uses in each case is *Besitzung*, implying possession or ownership: God is the 'owner' of men and women, with unrestricted power to control them, and humanity likewise owns and controls the creatures.[37] God's proprietorial rights over the creation are also discussed in some notes Müntzer added at the end of his sermon 'On Following Christ'; a number of scriptures are highlighted which treat of

God possessing us, God's people, even down to our own individual 'inmost being' (CW 398). The point is, though, as Müntzer explains elsewhere, that this hierarchy of relationships in the created order became distorted when Adam became entangled with creaturely things (CW 388): the intimate communication between God and humankind was lost, and fear of one another replaced fear of God. And this happened on a world-historical scale, for since the fall all the relationships which exist within and between humanity, nature and the divine — spiritual, social, natural, political, salvific — have become out of joint and in need of restoration to their rightful order. We long for a time when 'the voice of its true owner (*warhaftigen besitzers*) is heard in the soul' (CW 77; F 403).[38]

This complete restoration of the *ordo* will not be realized until evil is finally overcome in the world, but there is a sense in which Christ has already made good the damage caused by Adam's sin and repaired the corrupted order of things. 'The opposite to Adam is Christ', Müntzer writes, 'for just as [Ad]am distorts the order of things . . . so Christ held fast to the highest and despised creaturely things' (CW 388). Christ has fulfilled the law. The christological dimension in Müntzer's conception of the *ordo rerum* also emerges clearly in his marginal comments on Tertullian, and in a letter to John Zeiss in December 1523. 'The disobedience of the creatures is cancelled out by the obedience of the word which became flesh in nature', he writes in the latter; ' . . . Christ has atoned for all the damage done by Adam, so that the parts may hold together with the whole' (CW 70–1). In the approving comments he makes on his copies of Tertullian's *De carne Christi* and *De resurrectione carnis*, Müntzer is again concerned with the contrast between the first Adam and the second: he affirms that Christ has redressed Adam's sin by his innocence and restored the order of things, but — and this is crucial for his apocalyptic — *omnia propter hominem*, 'all for the sake of man'.[39] The re-creation of the *ordo rerum* is, for Müntzer, a *this*-worldly event, not to be postponed until after the second appearance of Christ and the inauguration of the reign of God. The dualism of the gnostics is rejected, and Tertullian himself also taken to task for 'let[ting] the coming of Antichrist coincide with the day of judgement like the monk Martin Luther'. It is the elect, the restored and renewed people of God, who exercise judgement on Antichrist and all his followers here and now. 'The judgement of Christ will be long in coming' (CW 428). Luther's and Tertullian's position — and this is of course one reason for Müntzer's jibe at them – allows a human passivity with regard to the last things: for Müntzer the elect are called to act in the intervening period.[40] Some remarks of Müntzer's in a letter to John Zeiss reveal another dimension to his conception of the reformation the world will undergo in the last days. Müntzer saw the relationship of the created order to God in terms of 'parts' to a 'whole', an understanding which he drew from passages like Psalm 118 and chapter 1 of Paul's letter to the Colossians (and, according to Rupp, probably from a reading of Nicholas of Cusa and Plato as well).[41] 'The will of God is that of the whole over all his members', he writes; 'the work of God flows out from the whole and from each of his members' (CW 97). In the 'Prague Manifesto' Müntzer berates the 'accursed priests' for not ever making known the 'tiniest fraction' about the order of God established in the creatures, or having understood in the slightest how 'the whole . . . [is] . . . a unity of all the parts' (CW 357, 363) – or rather, is greater than the sum of its parts. 'It is in its entirety that all knowledge of created things must be approached', Müntzer writes elsewhere (CW 403).[42] Yet, as his comments to Zeiss make clear, Adam's fall broke up the unity of the parts, which must now await their true restoration into the whole through the redemptive work of Christ.

Schwarz identifies two further terms Müntzer employs to convey the distinction between the unity or wholeness of Christ and the broken nature of humanity: *Einfältigkeit* and *Mannigfaltigkeit*.[43] The expression *eynfeltigkeyt Christi* (simple, undifferentiated Christ) occurs in the *Vindication*, and is drawn from 2 Corinthians 11.3, translated by Müntzer, 'See that your mind is not distracted from the simplicity of Christ' (CW 340; F 334). The contrast here is between the simplicity of Christ and the multifaceted nature of the created order. In *On Counterfeit Faith* Müntzer highlights 'the distinction between the directness (*einfeltigkayt*) of God and the deviousness of the creature laid down in the order between God and the creatures' (CW 217; F 219). Men and women have ignored God's command not to touch the tree of knowledge, and have been seduced by creaturely lusts and desires; they should therefore heed God's warning to Adam of the harm that would befall him if he allowed himself to be so distracted 'instead of finding his sole delight in God . . .' (CW 340; F 334).

In an earlier letter to Zeiss Müntzer suggests how the reconstitution of the parts into the whole, and the restoration of the *ordo rerum*, can proceed. The starting-point is the transformation of the elect: '. . . by the working of faith, our fleshly nature must partly fade away in us who are *part* of him, as was the case with the *whole* Christ, our head', he writes (CW 70, emphasis added). The relationship between humanity and the creatures can only be made right, in other words, once that between humanity and God has been restored; and *that* is only possible as people experience true faith, become conformed to Christ, and are 'possessed' by God instead of worldly lusts. 'One has to understand', Müntzer writes in *A Manifest Exposé*, 'how the heart of the elect is always moved by the power of the Most High to return to its origin' (CW 290). But this is only the start of what will become an apocalyptic scenario, for Müntzer effectively expands his mystical beliefs about the possession of the Spirit in the depths of the soul into a sort of cosmic theology; the movement of the heart towards God becomes a movement leading to the unity of all parts with the whole. The emptying of the soul of all creaturely desires, and its repossession by God, will bring about a new relationship of possession between humanity and the creatures.

Incorporated into Müntzer's vision of a universe of rightly-ordered relationships is a Church restored to the pure, unadulterated condition he believed it enjoyed at the time of the apostles. As already noted, Müntzer's reading of the Fathers led him to conclude that the Church, as originally established by Christ, was holy and undefiled, but continued in that state for only the shortest time due to the idleness of the elect in allowing the enemy to sow his wild oats (as Müntzer might well have put it!) among her wheat. 'The holy bride of Christ remained a virgin until after the death of the followers of the apostles, but . . . from that moment on became an immoral adulter-ess' (CW 167).[44] Müntzer sometimes referred to the Church of his day as the 'hangman's' or 'executioner's' Church, one well and truly in the pocket of the princes (whom he termed executioners on account of their 'right' (which he came to dispute) to bear the sword) (CW 405–6, 339). Yet it will not remain so forever, and Müntzer clearly envisaged that a restoration of the Church to its apostolic purity would be a feature of the new age, and a model for all social relationships in the new order.[45]

At times Müntzer seems to suggest that the renewed apostolic church will be the reconstitution of the present; in the Latin version of the 'Prague Manifesto', for example, he warns that 'the Lord will build up, console and reunite' the contemporary Roman Church in its 'fragmented, derelict and scattered' state, 'until it sees the God of gods dwell in Zion from eternity to eternity' (CW 378). But the end result will be a qualitatively different Church: the elect, including many drawn from among the heathen, will be 'far superior to us lazy, negligent Christians' (CW 314). Müntzer's aim, as Nipperdey writes, 'is not the restitution of the primitive church, but the real freedom of God's children, so that the "earthly life may be transformed into heaven"'.[46] 'We must believe that we fleshly, earthly men are to become gods', Müntzer writes in A Manifest Exposé: through Christ's incarnation we 'become God's pupils with him – to be taught by Christ himself, and become divine' (CW 278). Müntzer may be close to the ideal, popular in the late Middle Ages, of the viri spirituales, whose adherents expected, Marjorie Reeves tells us, 'not so much a recapturing of the life of the first Apostles . . . as the creating of the life of new apostles'.[47] Siegfried Bräuer has argued that even Müntzer's liturgical experiments can be seen in this light, as 'an important stage towards the anticipated lordship of Christ by means of a purified congregation of the truly faithful'.[48]

One clue to understanding the qualitatively new life which the elect might expect soon to enjoy may be found in the longer version of Müntzer's later letter to Zeiss. In a 'postscript' to this letter Müntzer briefly alludes to the mystical experience of having the heart wrenched away from the world, and then comments that the person who has achieved this state 'can choose good days (gute Tage) rather than bad with a good conscience, as is clearly indicated by the evangelist John and by Elijah [and] Enoch' (CW 98). Schwarz points out that, according to a medieval legend based on a reading of John 21.22–3, the apostle John did not die, but, like Elijah and Enoch, who were both transformed without seeing death, was called by Christ into his kingdom. For Müntzer, then, Schwarz suggests, the notion of gute Tage might be related to the experience of being swept into a paradise of the kind enjoyed by Enoch, Elijah and John; and if so, it is also linked to the concept of a restored prelapsarian state of innocence which the pious will enjoy as their reward. But the reference to Elijah and Enoch also has a more precise apocalyptic function for Müntzer since, as already noted, it is they who will assume the role of the 'two witnesses' spoken of in Revelation 11.3, and whose preaching will be instrumental in the eventual conversion of the whole world. Thus the 'good days' might also encompass that time when the world has been purged of all the godless and the *ordo* restored. There is a strong mystical element in Müntzer's thought here, for the elect cannot enjoy good days in the new age without first having their 'heart . . . torn away from clinging to this world by wretchedness and pain' (CW 98) and, indeed, without being prepared to step into the struggle against godless unbelief. This is a necessary part of the final purification process which the Church must experience at the hands of the Spirit if it is to return to its original state, and all the elect must come to true faith and learn the 'pure fear of God'. It is in this context, Schwarz concludes, that one should understand the good days signalled by Enoch, Elijah and John.[49]

Like all good utopias, Müntzer's picture of good days, a renewed Church and a restored natural order offers both a biting critique of the world as it is and a vision of a better one to pursue; using all the theological resources at his disposal, he draws the starkest of contrasts between the way the world is and the way it might be, and on that level exemplifies Christianity's potential to offer to politics what Míguez Bonino calls a 'mobilising dream', a stimulation to 'further adventure and discovery' in the pursuit of a better world.[50] What Müntzer conspicuously does not provide, of course, is any 'historical reference', an account of how the move from the present to the future might be begun; the new order is, as it were, guaranteed on the basis of its place within the divine eschatological timetable. To that extent, then, his 'specific contribution' might be considered incomplete, and Marxist jibes about revolutionary Christianity as 'the anticipation of communism nurtured by fantasy' depressingly correct. For the present we shall suspend judgement, and move to consider a visionary of a different hue; but it is a challenge to which we shall return in due course.

Part Two

—

Gerrard Winstanley

4

GERRARD WINSTANLEY:
AN INTRODUCTION TO HIS
LIFE AND WORK

—

Despite the considerable interest shown in Winstanley since his 'rediscovery' at the end of the nineteenth century, very little is known for certain about his life. In the title page of his first published work, *The Mysterie of God Concerning the Whole Creation, Mankinde*, the author makes reference to his Lancashire origins, and most commentators agree that an entry in the parish register of Wigan recording the baptism in 1609 of 'Garrard, son of Winstanlie' is the material one. If this is the case then the Digger leader's background might have been reasonably well-to-do; his father is described in the register as a mercer, and may also have been a burgess in Wigan for some years until his death in 1639.[1] In his entry in the church burial register Edward is described as 'Mr', suggesting that he had been a person of some considerable standing in the town. In any case, Winstanley himself tells us that he was 'never brought up to beg or work for day wages'.

Of the family's religious affiliation little is known, except that it was protestant in some form.[2] Christopher Hill has inferred from the fact that Gerrard 'did not follow the career traditionally marked out for the clever son of middle-class parents, going to a university and becoming a clergyman' that his parents were 'unfriendly to the church', though James Alsop has recently argued that commerce was a road to advancement very commonly travelled by young men of the time.[3] It is possible that Winstanley may at one time have belonged to the established church, since he refers in *The New Law of Righteousnes* to his having been 'a blind Professour and a strict goer to Church', believing 'as the learned Clergy (the Church) believed'; but by the time he wrote that work, however, he had lost the habit, recognizing that those still under it lived in 'confusion, ignorance and bondage . . . I look upon them with the eye of pitty and love, seeing them as yet to lie under those strong delusions, and powers of darknesse, which I my self did lie under . . . ' (W 243).[4] Yet Winstanley also appears to have followed his parents' example at some point in his life and become involved with nonconformists, since he mentions in *Truth Lifting up its Head above Scandals* that he had 'gon through the ordinance of dipping' (W 141), something commonly practised by the Baptists. G. H. Sabine wonders whether Winstanley was at one time also a lay preacher among the Baptists, since the skill of being able to vary one's arguments to suit one's audience, which Winstanley demonstrates in his writings, was one acquired by many who engaged in regular extempore preaching (W 7). It would appear, though, that by the time the digging commenced Winstanley had abandoned all formal church-going, having come to recognize the sufficiency of 'an inward light and power of life within' (W 243).

Of Winstanley's education nothing is known, though since his writings give little evidence of scholarship or learning it may well have been quite limited. Noting Winstanley's ability to quote Latin – the sentence 'Daemona non Armis, sed Morte subegit Iesus' appears toward the end of *A New-Yeers Gift for the Parliament and Armie* (W 373) – Hill has suggested that Winstanley may have enjoyed a grammar school education; but Winstanley himself gives few clues.[5] On many occasions, like Müntzer, he contrasts experimental knowledge with book-learning, seeing the latter as at best worthless and at worst (especially when employed by the clergy) dangerously delusive. About universities in particular Winstanley is similarly dismissive, accusing them on occasions of hindering the work of God and the return of Christ. He suggests in *The New Law Of Righteousnes* that preachers who buy their knowledge in universities may be compared with both Simon Magus and the money-lenders whom Christ whipped out of the temple (W 214, 238). One cannot be sure, however, whether these sentiments might be due to a sense of disillusionment borne of a first-hand experience of university education; frustration at having missed a higher education; or a straightforward feeling, as the text seems to imply, that such an education would simply have been a pointless exercise. It is certainly difficult to believe that Winstanley's tract *Truth Lifting up its Head*, dedicated to 'the scholars of Oxford and Cambridge', was written by someone who was, in fact, one of them.

The fact remains that of Winstanley's early development, and of the social, economic, religious or educational factors which may have helped to shape it, practically nothing can be said with any certainty. Perhaps his antipathy toward the established church was in part due to the influence of his family; perhaps his objection to the church's doctrine and the 'book-learning' of its clergy stemmed from an inability on his part to comprehend them fully, or to feelings of envy and disappointment at having missed the advantages of a formal education; perhaps, too, the originality of some of his work can be attributed in some measure to this incomplete formal education, to an unfamiliarity with the work of earlier and contemporary political theorists. But this is really no more than, at best, informed speculation.

In 1630, or shortly before, Winstanley moved to London, and on 10 April that year became apprenticed to Sarah Gater of Cornhill, the widow of William Gater, a merchant taylor. An entry in the manuscript records of the Merchant Taylors Company in London records that on 21 February 1637, barely seven years later, Winstanley himself became a freeman of the company. On 28 September 1640 he married Susan King at St Martin's Outwich, his residence at that time being in the parish of St Olaves in the Old Jewry. The marriage entry records his status as a Merchant Taylor.[6]

Becoming a freeman of the Merchant Taylors Company gave Winstanley the right legally to set up in business on his own, though we may infer from the details that are extant of a case brought against him in 1660 to recover a debt that his turnover was quite small. But then it was not a good time in which to try to establish oneself in a trade – the period was one of severe economic depression and political uncertainty – and within six years his business had been wound up. As Winstanley himself acknowledged in the transcripts of the 1660 lawsuit, 'in the year of the Lord 1643 when the late unhappie wars in England were violent, your oratour left off his trading . . . by reason of the badness of tymes'.[7] In some of his earlier writings Winstanley gives a more colourful account of his experiences: 'by thy cheating sons in the theeving art of buying and selling', he writes in *A Watchword to the City of London and the Armie* dated 26 August 1649, 'I was beaten out both of estate and trade, and forced to accept of the good will of friends crediting of me, to live a Countrey-life, and there likewise by the burthen of Taxes and much Free-quarter, my weak back found the burthen heavier than

I could bear . . . ' (W 315); and in *The New Law of Righteousnes*, penned the previous January, he reflected that 'though I was bred a tradesman, yet it is so hard a thing to pick out a poor living, that a man shall sooner be cheated of his bread, then get bread by trading among men, if by plain dealing he put trust in any' (W 188). Whether the attempt to sue him in 1660 was an isolated case, or whether such actions had been a feature of the previous seventeen years, Winstanley's failure as a businessman clearly haunted him for much of the rest of his life. What also undoubtedly left its mark on him – and what he may be harking back to in his reference to 'cheating sons' – was the experience of being defrauded in 1641. Winstanley appears to have invested several hundred pounds on the strength of what turned out to be fraudulent bonds, the losses he incurred as a consequence of this episode being sufficient to drive him, at one point, in search of parish charity.[8]

Following the closure of his business, then, in 1643, Winstanley moved, as the passage from the *Watchword* suggests, to live with friends, almost certainly at or near Cobham in Surrey. From the will left by Winstanley's father-in-law, William King, it is evident that the latter had property in Ham in the parish of Cobham, and it is therefore quite possible that Winstanley, not wanting to return to Wigan as a failure, and his own father being by now dead, turned for assistance to his wife's family, perhaps taking employment with them as a herdsman. Support for this assertion can be found in a passage in the *Watchword* where Winstanley refers to some opponents of the Diggers coming to his house and drawing away four cows that did not belong to him (CW 328).[9] Sabine considers that the move to Surrey was made with little delay, since Winstanley later described himself as having been in Kingston to see Francis Drake take the Covenant, believed to have been in 1643 (W 6, 325–6). That the digging venture began on St George's Hill, a few miles from Cobham, provides further evidence that Winstanley may have lived in that area, and it is also worth noting that at the time of the Diggers' arrest for trespass in 1649, Winstanley is described in the court papers as being from Walton-on-Thames, some five miles from Cobham.

Winstanley's first pamphlet appeared in 1648, but of the five years preceding its publication – like so many other chapters in his life – virtually nothing is known. That period was one of profound political and economic upheaval and, though his early writings give nothing away, Winstanley could scarcely have been unaffected by the civil war and the economic and political instability it left in its wake. The untimely end to his career as a merchant had been one consequence of the 'badness of tymes', and it is very unlikely that the quality of his life met with any improvement in the immediately succeeding years. In a passage in *The Saints Paradice*, probably written in 1648, Winstanley catalogues the economic disasters a person is liable to suffer – 'losses of his estate by fire, water, being cheated by false-spirited men, death of his cattle, or many such like casualties, whereby he becomes poor . . . and meets with hard language, hungry belly, to be despised, imprisoned' – and it is hard to avoid the conclusion that he may have experienced at least some of them himself.[10]

The period from about May 1648 to April 1650 would appear to have been Winstanley's busiest and most productive, and was to become, of course, the one upon which all subsequent interest in him principally centred. During this period he published no fewer than twenty tracts, and embarked with a group of others on the digging venture, firstly at St George's Hill near Kingston in Surrey (from 1 April 1649 to about August 1649), and then at Cobham Heath, a mile or two away, from where they were finally evicted in April 1650. Fifteen pamphlets were produced by Winstanley during the digging itself, all concerned to explain and defend the experiment, many taking the form of appeals and letters to prominent figures or groups whom Winstanley thought might come to the aid or defence of the Diggers. The other five all pre-date the digging, and may be divided loosely into the essentially mystical – *The Mysterie of God Concerning the Whole Creation, Mankinde* and *The Breaking of the Day of God*; those which, while demonstrating a continuing interest in matters spiritual, show their author developing a more rational approach to theology – *The Saints Paradice* and *Truth Lifting up its Head above Scandals*; and *The New Law of Righteousnes*, published in January 1649, which reveals Winstanley having a concern about the economic as well as the spiritual struggles facing humankind. In this latter work Winstanley observes that material poverty and social and economic inequality are linked to, and indeed arise from, the practice of 'buying and selling the earth from one particular hand to another' (W 158) and enunciates the view that the days of such practice are numbered – indeed they are due to end very shortly when Christ begins to rise in his people and lead them once more to act righteously towards one another. The first hint of the digging venture, eventually to commence three months later, also appears in this writing, Winstanley recording the instruction he received in a trance to 'Worke together. Eat bread together', and his intention, 'when the Lord doth shew unto me the place and manner', to join with others who are called 'common people, to manure and work upon the common Lands . . . to eat my bread with the sweat of my brows, without either giving or taking hire, looking upon the Land as freely mine as anothers' (W 190, 194).

By 1 April 1649 the 'place and manner' had been confirmed, and on that day, a Sunday, Winstanley and a group of others gathered on St George's Hill[11] in the parish of Walton-on-Thames and began to erect huts, dig over the land, and sow corn, parsnips and other vegetables. The Diggers welcomed any who wished to join them in their work, and after a short period their number had risen to around thirty or forty. Opposition to them, however, grew with similar rapidity, and on 16 April local property owners, apprehensive about the Diggers' increasing popularity, and fearful that 'that conflux of people may bee a beginning whence things of a greater and more dangerous consequence may grow to a disturbance of the peace and quiet of the Commonwealth', asked the Council of State to intervene militarily. The President of the Council contacted General Fairfax, asking him forcibly to disperse the community, but the general, after having the matter duly investigated, came to the conclusion that the Council's concern was misplaced. Captain John Gladman, who had been delegated the task of 'visiting' the Diggers, reported that he found their activities 'not worth the writing nor yet taking notiss of; I wonder the Council of State should be so abused with informations'.[12] Fairfax interviewed Winstanley and William Everard as leaders of the digging community on 20 April (the day the first digging manifesto, *The True Levellers Standard Advanced*, was sent to the printers), and to symbolize their view that the general was 'but their fellow creature' they both declined to remove their hats, the normal mark of respect when in the presence of one socially superior. In defence of their activities the Digger leaders told Fairfax that they wanted to cultivate communally the waste land which they now claimed rightfully belonged to the poor, and would not interfere with enclosed or privately owned land: they would 'meddle only with what was common and untilled'. They expressed their hope that many other people would shortly follow their example, and indeed that all who owned property would voluntarily give it up and join their communal enterprise. They also undertook not to use force, even in self-defence. Fairfax later visited the St George's Hill colony himself, but despite his continued belief that the Diggers posed no threat to the local populace, the latter maintained an aggressive posture towards the community, several times subjecting its members, their crops and houses to attack. On at least two occasions local people forcibly removed the Diggers from their colony, once to lock them up in Walton church, and another time to drag them into Kingston. On both occasions they were subsequently released. On 1 June the Diggers announced, in their manifesto *A Declaration from the Poor Oppresed People of England*, that they had a right not only to the common land but, on the same basis, to 'the Woods and Trees, that grow upon the Commons' (W 272), and declared their intention to cut down some of the trees and make a living from the sale of the wood until their crops were ready for consumption.

In the wake of this statement further violence was perpetrated against the Diggers. In early June some soldiers stationed at Walton supported the locals in an attack on the Diggers, during which a boy was seriously injured, and Winstanley was prompted to write a letter of complaint to Fairfax which apparently elicited a promise from the general that troops would no longer interfere with the colony. A few days later the local landowners staged another violent attack on the community – recorded by Winstanley in *A Declaration of the Bloudie and Unchristian Acting of William Star and John Taylor of Walton* – and on 23 June the Diggers were sued for trespass and a number of them arrested. Following their refusal to comply with the court's ruling that they could only plead through a hired attorney, Winstanley and the others were found guilty without making a defence and fined £10 each, with plaintiff's costs of 29s 1d. Winstanley records his views on this matter in two tracts, *An Appeal to the House of Commons* and *A Watch-word to the City of London and the Armie*, dated, respectively, 11 July and 26 August 1649. Unable to meet this bill, their property was sequestrated and, by August, having given up the struggle to survive at St George's Hill, they moved a short distance to Cobham Heath and once more began to erect some housing and plant some grain.

Here, however, the reception was no friendlier. Winstanley found himself facing charges of trespass – for which this time he was fined £4 – and in November, at the instigation of the lord of the manor of Cobham, Parson Platt, and his opposite number at St George's Hill, Francis Drake MP, local freeholders and gentry, with the support of some of the local soldiery, invaded the colony and attacked both property and people. The involvement of the soldiers again provoked Winstanley into addressing a complaint to General Fairfax (two letters were sent in December 1649), though he does note that Fairfax's promise to prevent further harassment of the Diggers by his troops had hitherto been kept. Once more the Diggers had no homes and no food, though the work of cultivating was apparently recommenced with renewed vigour on 1 January 1650, when Winstanley published one of his more lively and optimistic defences of the cause, *A New-Yeers Gift for the Parliament and Armie*. (Twelve days earlier, on 20 December, a reprint of Winstanley's first five tracts had been published under the title *Several Pieces Gathered into One Volume*, for which the author had written a short preface.)

In the following February or March Winstanley published a tract entitled *England's Spirit Unfoulded, or an Incouragment to take the 'Engagement'*, demonstrating his support for the new republican regime and his belief that it represented, as Aylmer puts it, 'a possible, perhaps indeed the only possible, basis for further social advance'.[13] This tract is unusual in that Winstanley on no other occasion comments publicly on a current political issue (other than, of course, the attacks by the army on his digging experiment). On 4 March Winstanley published another tract, *A Vindication of those whose Endeavours is only to make the Earth a Common Treasury, called Diggers*, seeking, among other things, to counter attempts by his opponents to identify his community with the Ranters; and this was followed on the nineteenth of the same month by *Fire in the Bush*,[14] which harked back in many ways to the more 'spiritual' writings of the pre-digging period. The following week a further manifesto was issued, *An Appeale to all Englishmen*, one of its aims being, apparently, to give encouragement to the other Digger communities that were springing up around the country. By April the Cobham community's new-found vigour appears to have resulted in the erection of six or seven houses and the cultivation of eleven acres of ground, not an inconsiderable area of land.

But Parson Platt and others hostile to the Diggers had not been idle either, and in March and/or April 1650, in a desperate effort to keep their venture – and themselves – alive, Winstanley's group sent out an appeal for help to some of the other communities in the Midlands and the South East. It was by then, however, too late, and before the end of April Winstanley's digging project was over. In the end the brutality and the violence of the local people, spurred on by the ever-active John Platt, which manifested itself in the trampling and destruction of their crops and houses, and enforced homelessness for the community, including their children, proved too much. In what was in effect an admission of defeat, Winstanley published his last tract as a Digger, *A Humble Request to the Ministers of both Universities and to all Lawyers in every Inns-a-court*, on 9 April.

In what turned out, perhaps, to be a symbolic winding up of the communistic venture, Winstanley and fourteen other Diggers were indicted at the Surrey Assizes later in 1650 for disorderly and unlawful assembly, a charge that related to the original setting-up of the community on 1 April 1649. Sabine notes that due to the non-survival of the relevant records we cannot be certain about the outcome of the case, though there is *prima facie* evidence that a prosecution followed. Perhaps also, Sabine suggests, 'if the authorities had thought it worth while to press the indictment returned against the Diggers, he [Winstanley] may have served a jail sentence' (W 58).

In the autumn following the collapse of the digging Winstanley and some of his companions left Cobham to take up temporary employment with a Lady Eleanor Douglas,[15] an apparently eccentric and perhaps mystic woman who owned an estate in Pirton, Hertfordshire. Soon, however, Winstanley was accused of mismanaging the property, and in December 1650 he wrote his employer a strongly worded letter complaining, *inter alia*, of her failure to pay him and certain other of her employees for their labours. Winstanley appears to have been owed as much as £20. Winstanley also explained his motive in coming to work for the lady: 'I came not under your rooffe to earne money like a slave. It is the convertion of your spirit to true Nobilitie, which is falne in the earth, not the weight of your purse that I looke after'.[16] The sometime Ranter Lawrence Clarkson, in one of the few contemporary references to Winstanley's post-digging activities which have been unearthed, refers, probably with this affair in mind, to Winstanley's 'most shameful retreat from Georges-Hill . . . to become a real Tithe-gatherer of propriety'.[17]

In 1651[18] Winstanley completed his last work, *The Law of Freedom in a Platform*, in which he set out for the first time a detailed blueprint of the communist society he desired to see established in England. The ideas it contained had clearly been concerning him for some years previously, for he states, in the Dedicatory Epistle to Cromwell, that 'It was intended for your view above two years ago, but the disorder of the Times caused me to lay it aside . . . ' (W 509). The decision to present it to the Protector at this time, Winstanley explained, arose from his having been moved 'to pick together as many of my scattered papers as I could finde, and to compile them into this method, which I do here present to you, and do quiet my own spirit' (W 510). The poor and illogical arrangement of the work certainly bears the hallmarks of a piece not completed at one stretch. *The Law of Freedom* contains no reference to the digging venture which had ended eighteen months before, and the rationale behind its dedication to Cromwell appears to be Winstanley's belief that Oliver, as he tells him, has the power 'to Act for Common Freedome if you will', whereas the writer himself is forced to admit, 'I have no power' (W 510).

Of Winstanley's career following the publication of *The Law of Freedom* not a great deal is known, though recent research by Richard Vann, James Alsop and R. J. Dalton allows us to be considerably more certain of some of its details than earlier students of the Diggers. Alsop notes, for example, that within six years of the collapse of the digging experiment Winstanley had acquired a certain social status, due largely to his father-in-law William King having turned over to him and his wife Susan his property in Cobham. Profits from this land were to continue to go to King and his wife, though Gerrard and Susan were to have the use of it. On King's death (which was to occur in April 1666) it was originally intended that the land should pass entirely to the Winstanleys and then their heirs, or, in the absence of the latter, to Winstanley's own heirs (presumably in the event of his remarriage); however, two years before his death, and in the light of the death of his daughter Susan, Winstanley's wife, King revoked his legacy in order to leave the land to another daughter, Sarah. Nevertheless the earlier arrangement conferred on Winstanley the title of gentleman, which is how he was described in the aforementioned Chancery case of 1660, and in King's will of 1664.

Winstanley's decision to take employment shortly after the end of the digging, and his 'promotion' a few years later to the ranks of minor landed gentry, point quite strongly to the conclusion that in his later years he gave up his practical commitment to make the earth a common treasury. Indeed his decision at some point to re-enter the commercial world as a corn-chandler (the occupation which appears in his burial entry) suggests some revisioning of his once strong theoretical commitment to communist ideas, a rethinking of some of the central tenets of his earlier philosophy; during the digging, for example, he had called the 'buying and selling of Land, and the Fruits of it, one to another . . . *The cursed thing*', and an 'Imaginary Art [that] breeds discontent, and divides the creation, and makes mankinde to imprison, enslave, and destroy one another' (W 269, 464).[19] Yet it does not appear that his decision once more to go into business improved Winstanley's economic position, and one of his perennial handicaps, according to writers like Alsop and Vann, was his lack of astuteness in financial affairs – a conclusion supported by such evidence as his bankruptcy in 1643, the charge of mismanagement made against him by Lady Eleanor Douglas, and the tangle into which he got himself in the last ten years of his life trying to recover a large sum of money owed to his second wife's late uncle, whose estate he was executing. (In view of the hostile and violent opposition the digging had to endure Alsop goes too far, however, in suggesting that perhaps Winstanley's management shortcomings contributed to the collapse of the digging projects at St George's Hill and Cobham Heath.)[20] Yet if Winstanley did not enjoy riches, neither was he uncomfortable, at least if Clarkson's reference to him becoming 'a real Tithe-gatherer of propriety' is to be believed.

Recently discovered evidence suggests that Winstanley also softened in his attitude to the legal system, perhaps even as early as 1652, the year in which *The Law of Freedom* was published. Although his writings contain numerous denunciations of 'Sessions, Lawyers, Bayliffs of Hundreds, Committees, Impropriators, Clerks of Peace, and Courts of Justice, so called' which 'whip the People by old Popish weather-beaten Laws' (W 264), it appears that in the autumn of 1652 he was prepared to assist, along with the sergeant of mace and another freeman of the City of London, in an 'apprayment' of the estate of his recently deceased brother-in-law Giles Hicks. At issue was a sum of money owed by Hicks at the time of his death to his (and Winstanley's) father-in-law William King, but what is remarkable, as Dalton points out, is that Winstanley should be prepared willingly to participate in a system which even at that time he was continuing to denounce in print.[21]

No less remarkable is the fact that he appears also to have taken something approaching a U-turn in his attitude towards established religion after the digging, the main exponents of which, the 'beneficed clergy', he had at one time denounced in the strongest terms. Recent research has established that at various times between 1659 and 1668 the former Digger was a parish way-warden, an overseer, and a churchwarden, and that in the early 1670s he was appointed one of the two chief constables of the Elmbridge Hundred; all of which suggests a considerable degree of conformity to the state church – including, after 1660, Anglicanism – during those years. Two children born to Winstanley and his second wife also appear to have been baptized at Cobham between 1667 and 1670.

Winstanley also appears to have had some connections with the Quakers both before and after this period. The similarities between Winstanley's philosophy and that of the Friends, and between the Diggers and the Quakers as movements, was long recognized by scholars; indeed, more than one writer in the seventeenth century considered Winstanley to have founded the Quakers.[22] Whether Winstanley had any formal links with Quakers was, however, long disputed, although it now appears safe, on the basis of Alsop's research, to infer that the Gerrard Winstanley who was given a Quaker burial in London in 1676 was the former Digger leader – though this is still not to say anything about the extent of his involvement with the Friends. Hayes has suggested that Winstanley never became a Quaker and that the funeral was arranged by his second wife in honour of his radical past;[23] and this would go some way towards explaining his apparently strong commitment to Anglicanism in his later years. Yet there is also *prima facie* evidence that Winstanley did have some involvement with the Quakers, at least in the 1650s; this evidence, uncovered by Reay in the late 1970s, takes the form of a letter written by a leading Quaker, Edward Burroughs, to Margaret Fell in 1654, in which Burroughs says, 'Wilstandley [sic] sayes he beleeves we are sent to perfect that worke which fell in their handes hee hath bene with us'.[24] Whether this suggests Winstanley thought that the Quakers were the natural successors to the Diggers – 'where else could he go after it became clear that Christ was not going to rise in Charles II's England?', asks Hill[25] – or that he embraced their doctrines, must remain an open question; the absence of any evidence that he was active in the movement in the 1660s and 1670s, when seen alongside that suggesting his readmittance to the Church of England, lends weight to the view that his commitment to the move-ment, if any, was transitory. If Winstanley did join the Quakers after

1660, however, it is hard to avoid Alsop's conclusion that this would have evidenced 'an abandonment of his most radical ideas and a return to a position close to the one he held before his conversion to the Digger movement'.[26]

The significance of Winstanley's apparently circular route back, following the failure of the digging, to political, economic and religious positions not dissimilar to those he held before the venture, will be explored in due course. We turn now to examine his theological and political ideas, and the extent to which the former can be said to make any singular contribution to the latter.

5

'TO MAKE THE EARTH A COMMON TREASURY': WINSTANLEY'S THEOLOGY AND POLITICS

Since Gerrard Winstanley's writings first became a subject for serious study at the end of the nineteenth century, much debate has centred on the extent to which he can be considered 'Christian' and 'revolutionary' within any meaningful definitions of those terms. His writings are littered with Bible quotations and religious terminology, but how far did his theology, which in any case was highly unorthodox, appear actually to inform his thinking? His tracts suggest he was committed to transforming society along some sort of communitarian model, but was the digging rather more of a symbolic gesture than a revolutionary tactic? If Winstanley is to contribute to a discussion about Christianity and revolution, it would seem vital first to establish his credentials in both areas, and then examine the dimensions of his religious and political thought; and that will be the purpose of this chapter.

Winstanley's interpreters divide broadly into two camps with regard to the significance of the religious terminology he employs in his writings, one holding that his theology provided the main conceptual framework for his understanding of the world and underpinned his political and economic programme, the other that the religious language he used was no more than a cosmetic flourish, a sop to the milieu in which he lived. Thus for some interpreters theology helps to shape Winstanley's political philosophy, while for others that philosophy could be restated, without alteration to its substance, in wholly secular language. Both groups are clear that Winstanley rejects much of the traditional theology of his day, but those who want to stress that he remained a fundamentally theological thinker caution against making an assumption that, in so doing, he gave up theology altogether: it was rather the case that he adopted an alternative theology.[1] Both schools recognize, too, that Winstanley's thought does not remain static, and that at times, not least during the period of the digging, it undergoes something of a transition; again, however, this does not imply for some an abandonment by Winstanley of the theological premises upon which his world-view was built, more a 'shift in emphasis' in his thinking.[2] George H. Sabine, who edited the first complete[3] collection of Winstanley's writings, considers Winstanley's train of thought to be complete before the digging even commences, and that *The Law of Freedom*, though different in focus and purpose from the earlier tracts, represents only a 'change of emphasis', not 'of the convictions that lay behind Winstanley's communism' (W 59, 36). Paul Elmen, who also argues that the transition in Winstanley's thought does not undermine the unity of his position, argues that the motivation behind the digging, and the degree of certainty Winstanley had about its ultimate success, cannot be understood apart from reference to his religious beliefs: 'Because his views were fundamentally theological', he writes, 'Winstanley hopefully undertook a task which economic considerations alone would have told him was impossible: the communization of the English land.'[4] For Timothy Kenyon, 'the case for identifying Winstanley's understanding of the "Fall of Man" as the fulcrum of his thought is compelling'.[5]

Scholars in this camp are united on two central assumptions: first, that Winstanley's theology played a central role in his thinking throughout his literary career; and secondly, that no *fundamental* shift in his thinking can be detected between the publication of his early 'mystical' writings in 1648, and that of the blueprint for his communist utopia, *The Law of Freedom in a Platform*, four years later. However, the approach more commonly adopted by writers who want to give less weight to Winstanley's theology is to delineate stages in his literary career during which his thinking underwent major transformation. Thus, while they might accept the first assumption above in respect of Winstanley's early tracts, they reach the virtually unanimous conclusion that by the time the digging began, and certainly by the time it was over, the theological impulses which might originally have prompted Winstanley into action could no longer be said to be a major motivating factor.

This line of reasoning has surfaced regularly in Winstanley scholarship ever since the rediscovery of his writings towards the end of the last century, with his last tract, *The Law of Freedom*, cited as proof positive of an abandonment by Winstanley of his earlier mystical position for a straightforwardly materialist one. Perez Zagorin, for example, argues that with this tract Winstanley's philosophy 'complete[s] the circuit along which its inner logic had impelled it. Inspired still by a deeply felt religion of conduct, he passed, nevertheless, to a substantially rationalist-materialist position'.[6] J. C. Davis suggests that the subtitle of *The Law of Freedom* – 'True Magistracy Restored' – indicates the true nature of the shift in his thinking: 'Winstanley drops both his millenarianism and his anarchism and concerns himself with the remodelling of the state by men; Cromwell, not Christ, is to be the agent of the change.'[7] A more extreme position is taken by George Juretic, for whom any talk of a mere shift in Winstanley's thinking, whether at the point of the digging or during the preparation of *The Law of Freedom*, is gross understatement. What was actually the case, Juretic argues, was that once the digging experiment got under way Winstanley's ideas became 'rapidly secularized', so that by the time the first Digger tract, *The True Levellers Standard Advanced*, was written, the millenarian underpinning of the earlier tracts began to disappear. Then, Juretic writes, 'it was only a matter of time for him to discard completely his mystical beliefs . . . Mysticism failed to provide him with solutions to the political problems Winstanley encountered while farming the commons'. The way to a correct understanding of Winstanley does not therefore lie in trying to find a link between the pre-Digger and the Digger, but in recognizing that the real concrete political experience he endured during the digging project transformed him to such an extent that it is possible to speak of 'two Winstanleys': the early mystical millenarian and the mature full-blown secularist.[8]

If this general thesis is accepted, that Winstanley at some point lost the religious impulses which originally motivated him, the question still remains how to account for his continued use of theological terminology and biblical idiom in his later writings. Strikingly, the conclusion reached by virtually all defenders of the thesis is that the inclusion of religious language in these writings can be explained simply by reference to the times in which he lived: it serves, in other words, either to lend added weight or authority to conclusions he reached on straightforwardly rational grounds; to make his arguments more comprehensible to his readers by using the popular idiom of the day; or, since he was writing under the shadow of the

Blasphemy Ordinance of 1648, to provide his subversive and heretical message with a cloak of respectability. Thus Eduard Bernstein, for example, writes of the Diggers' pamphlets being 'couched in somewhat mystical phraseology, which manifestly serves as a cloak to conceal the revolutionary designs of the authors',[9] and David Petegorsky notes the 'theological garb' in which so frequently Winstanley's ideas were clothed.[10] For Christopher Hill, 'Winstanley drew on Bible stories largely because he thought they would help his contemporaries to understand him: he used them as poetic imagery'. The Bible was used to illustrate 'conclusions at which [he] had arrived by rational means'.[11] This is not a view held only by Marxist critics, for Maurice Ashley suggests, during a discussion of the Fifth Monarchy movement, that if we 'ignore their biblical texts (as we are invited to ignore those of . . . Winstanley) . . . there are your seventeenth-century Jacobins or Bolsheviks'.[12]

What conclusions may be drawn from this discussion? Perhaps the first and most obvious point to make concerns the straightforward impossibility of being able to say with any certainty what the real source of Winstanley's inspiration was at any given time. Certain inferences may be drawn from both his language and his actions, but to establish a 'real' motivation behind them must of necessity be beyond the bounds of possibility. It must be acknowledged that the mere fact that Winstanley's use of religious terminology appears to diminish as he becomes more politically radicalized, and seems to look more and more like a convenient disguise for a materialist philosophy when it *is* employed, does not necessarily say anything about his 'subjective' assessment of himself as a Christian. It may also be the case that Winstanley's decision to republish his five earliest tracts while the digging was still in progress indicated that he saw his political position at that time as a 'logical development' of the ideas in those tracts, rather than a contradiction or rebuttal of them.[13]

A second point to note is the tendency among some interpreters of Winstanley to perceive his rejection of *traditional* Christianity as a rejection of Christianity altogether. The clearest statement of this position is made by Zagorin, who argues that, despite the presence of Christian terminology in *The Law of Freedom*, the religion expressed there is no longer Christian. Winstanley, he writes,

> had eliminated a transcendent God, an historic Christ, creed, dogma, and church, and retained naught but the ethical inspiration of the

gospel. And even this he did not allow to operate, in the traditional way, as the spirit of charity and love that was to be shown despite the existence of slavery and coercion which man's fall had made inevitable. Instead, the gospel ethic was for him the imperative compelling the remodelling of institutions in the image of reason.[14]

Hill also adopts a position close to this – though he stops short of actually saying Winstanley's theology was not Christian – when he points to Winstanley's thinking being 'in opposition to traditional Christianity' and to the 'profound difference between the content of his ideas and that of traditional Christianity' such that 'his thinking was struggling towards concepts which were to be more precisely if less poetically formulated by later, non-theological materialisms'.[15]

What such comments reveal are two false assumptions which seriously weaken the argument that Winstanley was (or became) a secular thinker. The first is that the particular interpretation of Christianity generally termed 'traditional' may serve as a yardstick against which to measure, and by implication reject, the claim of other formulations; and the second that Winstanley's tendency towards a more reductionist and pantheistic theological position amounts to a rejection of Christianity itself rather than one interpretation of it, that propounded by the Church of his day. Thus Winstanley's rejection of a transcendent God, historic Christ, and creed, dogma and Church, is, for Zagorin, a rejection of Christianity itself, whereas in fact Winstanley can be located in that small but vocal tradition which, albeit from its fringes but nevertheless from within the professing Christian Church itself, has continually set out to challenge perceived conservative and reactionary interpretations of the faith, and posit instead alternative readings of the gospel stressing themes of protest against injustice and hope for a radically new social order in the shape of the kingdom or reign of God. From Lollards to Hussites, through Müntzer and the 'radical Reformation' in Germany, and Quakers, Ranters and Fifth Monarchists in England, down to liberation theologians of the present day, voices echoing the self-same themes with which Zagorin and others have difficulty – divine immanence, universalism, iconoclasm, communitarianism and even revolution – have persistently been audible within the Christian Church.[16] These would hardly comprehend Zagorin's shock that Winstanley should find the 'ethical inspiration of the gospel' an 'imperative compelling the remodelling of institutions in the image of reason', nor for that matter his assumption that there is an apparent incompatibility between the 'blazing chiliastic expectancy of the religious radical who daily looks for Jesus' second coming to inaugurate a reign of righteousness' and hope for a 'rationalistic communism, abounding in plans and projects', let alone his contention that to move from the former to the latter is to pass beyond orthodoxy to heresy.[17] At the root of Zagorin's difficulty with Winstanley is a conception of Christianity as a static rather than developing faith, and a tendency to mistake one culturally related manifestation of it for its totality.

Another problem with Zagorin's position is that it does not fully appreciate Winstanley as a person of his time. Winstanley lived in an age in which religion permeated every area of life, the Bible shaped the way people thought, and the Church was central to the life of the community; and in such a climate most people, whether educated or not, would hold as self-evident many fundamental religious doctrines. So interwoven was religion into the fabric of society, and so intermixed with political, economic and social questions, that it would hardly have occurred to Winstanley or his contemporaries to wonder whether ownership of land, the central issue on the Diggers' agenda, was a *theological* issue. The Bible's relevance to all areas of life was accepted far more unproblematically then than is the case today such that, as Hill suggests, 'it is perhaps irrelevant to ask whether Winstanley "believed" the Christian myths, or whether he used them only as a convenient mode of expression, a metaphor. The question imposes twentieth-century assumptions on him. This was the idiom in which [people] thought'.[18] Yet to see Winstanley against the background of his own time is also to understand why he could not for *political* reasons accept what might to his critics appear a more conventional or traditional form of Christianity. For this was the Christianity preached by the clergy of the established Church, whose motives for so doing, Winstanley was clear, were both to promote support for the *status quo*, and their not uncomfortable position within it. The political task assigned to this theology in his own day gave Winstanley reason enough, quite apart from any misgivings he had on rational grounds, to reject it outright.

For Winstanley, the whole theological system of the Church was oppressive for the ordinary people to whom it was preached. The clergy encouraged belief in a God 'out there', beyond the creation, which, although Winstanley rejected on the grounds that knowledge about such entities was 'beyond the line, or capacity of man to attain to while he lives in his compounded body' (W 565), he did the more so because he saw how the clergy contrived to make God appear punitive and capricious; this was the God who approved the unfair distribution of the earth originally given as a common treasury, and, significantly, 'who appointed the people to pay Tythes to the Clergy' (W 532). Both God and Christ, Winstanley considered, were held by the priests 'at-a-distance' so that they could then be mediated to the people only through them. The clergy also preached a historic fall, through which all people individually are sinners, and by thus evoking feelings of insufficiency and fear in their hearers, who sought to restore their identity by relating to objects outside themselves, namely the God- and Christ-at-a-distance, the clergy made the people even more dependent upon them. With the addition of a heaven in the next life as a reward for subservience to them, or hell as a punishment for insubordination, the system by which the clergy reinforced their authority and power over the people was complete; 'by this divined Hell after death', wrote Winstanley, 'they preach to keep both King and people in aw to them' (W 523). The clergy persuaded the people to think 'That true Freedom lay in hearing them preach, and to enjoy that Heaven, which they say, every man who beleeves their doctrine, shall enjoy after he is dead: And so tell us of a Heaven and Hell after death, which neither they nor we know what wil be . . . ' (W 523).

For Winstanley these 'heavenly and spiritual things' served only to destroy the true knowledge of God and spoil the individual's peace. The clergy actually prevented Christ from rising in his people, and instead led them into what he called 'Imagination', a feeling of incompleteness, fear and uncertainty which kept them in subjection to the Church and the authorities. For Winstanley this was the antithesis of true religion, and he rejected it wholesale.

In place of this alienating form of religion Winstanley stressed the immanence of God, who could be known by all without the 'aid' of the professional beneficed clergy. Humankind, he taught, need not be bowed down by Imagination: 'Every single man, Male and Female, is a perfect Creature of himself', and has the creator dwelling in him 'to be his Teacher and Ruler within himself' (W 251). The individual can therefore judge all things by experience, which is more important than the whole edifice of doctrine and church government built up on biblical texts. Such line of thinking eliminated, too, any need for a learned clergy. Winstanley often preferred to use the word 'Reason' instead of 'God', because it emphasized God's immanence and stood in contrast to the Imagination from which God would redeem his sons and daughters as Christ rose in them and brought them together into community. The term may have signified for Winstanley something more akin to a 'spirit' or 'force' than a 'personal' God, but it removed the 'otherness' which the clergy had invested in it.[19] In fact, however, the question of an antithesis between immanence and transcendence appears never to have concerned Winstanley, and he could unproblematically hold in tension the notion that 'the same spirit that made the globe' is 'the indweller in the five senses of hearing, seeing, tasting, smelling and feeling'.[20] James Holstun employs the delightfully suggestive term 'Green Millennialism' to capture the essence of Winstanley's thinking, which he discerns as 'a pantheistic materialism that denies any radical distinction between spirit and matter, between God, humans and nature'.[21]

Christ, too, was no longer remote but within the individual, and Winstanley saw Christ in every person, and every person in Christ. As he says in *The Law of Freedom*, all who have shown themselves to be 'Promoters of Common Freedom, whether they be Members in Church fellowship, or not . . . all are one in Christ' (W 543). Heaven and hell are present states: heaven is humankind and hell describes the conditions men and women have created for themselves on earth. Winstanley left open the question whether there may be a physical heaven or hell, but did hold the highly unorthodox (and under the 1648 Blasphemy Act, illegal!) belief that all humanity would be saved. Sin, in Winstanley, is the whole system of buying and selling, with its resultant inequality and domination by landowners and priests. Antichrist, traditionally interpreted as the Pope or the Church, and the fall, are also to be understood in terms of property relations; the former is property itself, and the latter occurred once selfish desires began to manifest themselves, and not, as was usually held, the other way around: 'When Mankinde began to buy and sell, then did he fall from his Innocency' (W 511). Finally, Christ's second coming will be the establishment of a communitarian society on earth, and the entering into all men and women of Christ's spirit as they awaken to the rule of Reason within them and embrace the principle of community life lost since the fall. In summary, Winstanley rejects quite explicitly the whole theological system of the

Church, but not, *pace* Zagorin and others, Christianity itself; his own theological formulations are rather an attempt to keep the essentials of the faith and recast them in a non-alienating form, to recover what he believed to be the original message of Christianity which the Church, through time, had distorted and submerged.

There is yet another problem with attempts to see Winstanley as an essentially secular thinker, namely his continued adherence to some form of millennial hope, even, it would appear, up until and during the time of writing *The Law of Freedom*. Clearly there is little question that such a hope was influential in originally inspiring the digging venture. In *The True Levellers Standard Advanced* Winstanley suggests that an apocalyptic vision in the book of Daniel is to be realized in his own day, and two pages later[22] that 'all the Prophecies, Visions, and Revelations of Scriptures, of Prophets, and Apostles . . . doth all seat themselves in this Work of making the Earth a Common Treasury' (W 259–60), a work, as he was told in a trance, assigned to him and the diggers on St George's Hill. Thus 'all the Prophesies of Scriptures and Reason are Circled here in this Community' (W 253). His, he was clear, were the last days: 'the righteous Father suffered himself . . . to be suppressed for a time, times and dividing of time, or for 42 months, or for three dayes and half, which are all but one and the same term of time: And the world is now come to the half day' (W 261).

Winstanley's millennium, as we have observed, did not involve a literal physical return of Jesus Christ as King (as many believed the Bible taught), but rather the restoration of community as Christ began to rise in his sons and daughters. Nevertheless, it is not sufficient to say that his reformulation of the second coming in this way is an example of the use of biblical imagery to conceal an essentially political hope, for a belief that the millennium was now to begin appears, in fact, to have been the one single hope which sustained the digging project in the face of all opposition and hardship. 'We have another encouragement that this work shall prosper', Winstanley wrote at the outset, 'Because we see it to be the fulness of Time: For whereas the Son of Man, the *Lamb*, came in the Fulness of Time . . . Even so now in this Age of the World, that the Spirit is upon his Resurrection, it is likewise the Fulness of Time in a higher measure' (W 263).

We noted earlier Elmen's assertion that it was Winstanley's theological perspective which motivated him to undertake a task which purely economic considerations would have suggested was an impossibility. Sabine notes a reference in *The True Levellers Standard Advanced* where Winstanley appears to expect that, with the restoration of community life, barren commons and waste ground would once more become fertile, and comments that 'without such a belief, his communism was hardly workable, since it implied that a large part of the English population would be fed from the produce of land that had not previously been arable' (W 42).[23] Winstanley clearly saw the outbreak of digging in 1649, at St George's Hill and subsequently at a number of other locations, as a sign that the millennium was imminent, that Christ was beginning to rise in men and women; and this would have encouraged him to think that the venture must of necessity meet with success, and be taken up by more and more people until the transformation of the earth was complete. In practical terms this would most likely mean that, infilled with a renewed sense of community, the common people would revolt against property, refuse to sell their labour, and generate a situation in which no one would own more land than they could themselves cultivate, thus making most hitherto privately enclosed land the common possession of all.

Even more problematic for those who discern a rejection of theology in the 'later' Winstanley is the evidence from his last work, *The Law of Freedom in a Platform*, that his millenarianism sustained his political hopes beyond as well as during the digging venture. This writing, produced in the wake of the Diggers' enforced removal from Cobham Heath (whither they had resorted following their expulsion from St George's Hill), takes the form of a detailed outline of the radically new socio-economic order Winstanley hoped could be constructed on the ashes of the old 'kingly power'; and as such it stands apart from his earlier tracts in many respects, not least in so far as it recognizes that Christ's work of transforming people and drawing them together into community may be a somewhat more gradual process than anticipated in, say, *The New Law of Righteousnes*. In this last work Winstanley also goes to greater lengths to demonstrate how his new society may be implemented: Cromwell, to whom it is dedicated, not Christ, this time appears to hold the key. Yet millenarian hopes are not discarded: God, 'the Spirit of the whole Creation . . . is about the Reformation of the World', he writes in his foreword (W 502); or, we might say, is *still* about this reformation. 'This Kingly Power is the old Heaven, and the old Earth, that must pass away', he asserts in chapter 2, whereas the new 'Commonwealth's Government' will be 'Sion', 'Jerusalem', and the 'holy Mountain of the Lord God our Righteousness and Peace' (W 532, 534–5). These images Winstanley borrows from the unambiguously apocalyptic Old Testament prophet Micah, and they are joined by others from the Apocalypse and the book of Daniel. Kingly power and government is 'the great Man of Sin', 'the great Antichrist, and Mystery of Iniquity', 'the Devil', and 'the Power and Government of the Beast', soon to be cast down (W 530, 532); covetousness is 'the great red Dragon, the god of this world', from whom the groaning creation waits to be delivered (W 530); and the deceitful and oppressing 'Divinity' taught by the clergy 'is the language of the Mystery of Iniquity and Antichrist', and 'that great City Babylon . . . which hath filled the whole Earth with her sorcery, and deceived all people, so that the whole world wondered after this Beast'. 'How is it faln', Winstanley concludes, 'and how is her Judgment come upon her in one hour?' (W 570). Perhaps even more significantly, Winstanley still appears to believe that Christ is rising in his sons and daughters, if at a rather slower pace than he anticipated earlier: 'But surely Light is so broke out, that it will cover the Earth, so that the Divinity Charmers shall say, The people will not hear the voyce of our charming, charm we never so wisely,' he writes as he concludes his discourse on these false preachers (W 570). Indeed, the fact that a commonwealth has been declared in England, though the even greater work of establishing it upon right principles is still to be done, is a sign that 'the spirit of universal Righteousness' is rising up in women and men. 'We may hope' that 'these be the days of his resurrection to power', Winstanley writes, 'because the name of *Commonwealth* is risen and established in *England* by a Law' (W 534). The work of consolidating the Commonwealth's government is vital, Winstanley argues, not only because a failure in this regard will deny people the peace, plenty and freedom which they desire, but because it would 'shew our Government to be gone no further but to the half day of the Beast, or to the dividing of Time, of which there must be an over-turn' (W 535).[24]

Had Winstanley's millenarianism not been genuine – had he, in other words, truly been a secular thinker – it is at least arguable that he could have produced a more revolutionary programme than he did, since by interpreting the political struggle in which he was engaged *religiously* he failed to see it in a true historical perspective.

His millenarianism, in other words, made it 'unnecessary' for him to demonstrate how it was possible for his programme to be realized, and as a consequence that programme was destined to remain only as what it was, namely an idea superimposed on to his situation but not historically related to it. The significance of this should not be underrated, for although it is Winstanley's eschatology that forces us to classify his programme as in practice reactionary and not revolutionary, the line between the two definitions is thin: Winstanley's analysis was undoubtedly revolutionary in that it was rooted in the 'material activity and the material intercourse of men' in a way in which Marx would have recognized; yet his hopes for the fulfilment of his political programme were grounded, not in the real world, but in a belief that its time had come. Thus his ideas, as Denys Turner has written, 'fell stillborn from the womb, because they had not come historically to term'.[25]

One final weakness in the argument that Winstanley was essentially a secular thinker arises, particularly in the case of some of his Marxist interpreters, from an a priori understanding of religion as either, in John Maguire's words, 'a set of abstract platitudes, at best useless . . . [or] . . . in so far as it says anything about the social and political reality of its time', not religion at all.[26] For such thinkers – for whom perhaps the *locus classicus* is Engels' analysis of Müntzer in *The Peasant War in Germany* – even when one encounters a culture which is deeply religious (as in the case of Müntzer and Winstanley), and which gives rise to revolutionary programmes couched in language which reflects that culture, such language may be seen as at best superfluous and metaphorical, or, at worst, a means of misrepresenting political struggles in the guise of theological ones. Thus according to Engels, the class struggle in which Müntzer and Luther were engaged could be understood quite adequately without reference to the theological differences between them: 'Although the class struggles of that day were clothed in religious shibboleths, and though the interests, requirements, and demands of the various classes were concealed behind a religious screen, this changed nothing and is easily explained by the conditions of the time.'[27] Thus the presence of religious language in the revolutionary programme of a Müntzer or a Winstanley is politically insignificant: tautologous, abstract, metaphorical and non-cognitive; and this being the case, where such programmes *do* say something about reality, nothing is added by the use of theological terminology in the presentation.

Reasoning of this sort clearly lies behind some of the attempts to sift out the 'theological' from the 'political' in Winstanley, in order the more easily to play down the significance of the former. Petegorsky, as we have noted, refers to the 'theological garb' in which Winstanley's ideas were frequently clothed; C. H. George to 'the almost ornamental, certainly at best tangential, relation of the Bible' to his thought; and G. E. Aylmer to the way in which Winstanley 'uses millenarian images and scriptural texts to convey his sense of immediacy and crisis'.[28] Perhaps Christopher Hill pursues the point further than most. In his introduction to the volume of Winstanley's writings he edited in 1973, he begins by suggesting that, since Winstanley wrote before the industrial revolution, 'some of his insights may be of interest to those in the Third World today who face the transition from an agrarian to an industrial society'. Winstanley, in other words, may be read as a modern. If one were to raise the obvious objection that the situation in some parts of the developing world differs from the one Winstanley addressed in terms of religious culture, Hill would suggest that this may be got around by going behind the language Winstanley adopts to the essence of the message: 'We must make allowances for the Biblical idiom which Winstanley shared with almost all his contemporaries, and try to penetrate through to the thought beneath', he writes. 'It is worth taking a little trouble to break down the barriers of Winstanley's Biblical language . . .' All of which leads Hill to conclude, in an essay written five years later, that 'Winstanley's system of ideas could be rewritten in the language of rational deism; had he lived fifty years later he might have so expressed them'.[29]

The thesis that there has to be, as it were, a single unified discourse for revolutionary theory has to be seen as unhistorical. It is, on the one hand, another example of the failure of some modern-day interpreters to read Winstanley against the background of his own time, but, more profoundly, it attempts to suggest that the language in which he framed his ideas is somehow incidental to the ideas themselves: in other words, take up the 'religious screen', whose presence is required merely by 'the conditions of the time', and then, and only then, the real message of the writer can be properly understood. Yet the essence of Winstanley's politics cannot, as it were, be sifted out from the theological language in which it is presented, nor can it be argued that he used such language merely to help his contemporaries to understand him, or because it was the safest or most accessible way of expressing truths about humanity. There was a profound dialectical relationship between his theology and his political views. He saw the alienation of the poor oppressed people of England as at the same time political, economic and religious, and he sought, in working to overcome this alienation, not to abolish religion altogether but to recast it in an immanent and non-alienating form: to show, in fact, that the meek might inherit the earth now.

If there is apparently room for debate about how far Winstanley's philosophy may be considered 'Christian', it is a considerably more straightforward exercise to establish his credentials as a revolutionary, taking the term to be descriptive of one who initiates or supports action to overthrow a regime or political system of which she or he is a subject. In fact Winstanley's programme was more profound and far-reaching than many which would be encompassed within such a definition, seeking as it did, not the substitution of one ruler or system of government for another, but the 'turning upside down' of the whole structures of power themselves.[30] Certainly a far greater degree of unanimity may be observed among his interpreters on this question than on the nature of his theological position.[31] W. H. G. Armytage, for example, writes of Winstanley putting forward (in *The Law of Freedom*) a plan for the 'complete revolution' of society, and Petegorsky argues that, while some of the Diggers' contemporaries may have challenged points of detail of the radically new economic structure being shaped in England in the seventeenth century, 'none questioned as profoundly as Winstanley the foundations on which it was being erected'.[32] While Winstanley welcomed many of the changes which resulted from the upheavals of the late 1640s, they were, for him, really only a beginning; the execution of the king meant little if it left intact the oppressive system over which he had ruled. Thus Hill concludes that 'Winstanley wanted a far more complete break with the old order than had been achieved by the merely political changes of 1648–9'.[33]

Winstanley, of course, was not alone in expressing reservations about the achievements of the English revolution, though what distinguished him from most of his contemporaries was his profound conviction that, without a fundamental restructuring of the pattern of land-ownership in England, the political and social changes taking place would never be of even the slightest benefit to the poor and oppressed whom the Diggers represented. Whereas many other radicals were committed to pursuing limited *political* objectives, Winstanley emerges as the first to enunciate clearly and rationally the thesis that political liberty is essentially inseparable from economic equality. Merely overthrowing the king, he consistently argued, could not of itself be significant; the opportunity must be taken to dismantle the whole inequitable system of private land-ownership over which he presided, and which he had inherited from the bastard King William of Normandy, and the land restored to its rightful owners, the common people of England. It is essential to explore Winstanley's thinking on the land question, since it is at the core of his whole political and economic philosophy.[34]

We should note at the outset that for Winstanley the land has almost a sacred quality. This is of course implied in his immanentist understanding of God or Reason, though he also seems to imagine Christ to be still buried in the earth, working for its good while awaiting the opportunity to rise in his sons and daughters (which, as we have noted, is for Winstanley his 'second coming'). 'The body of Christ is where the Father is, in the earth, purifying the Earth', he writes in *Truth Lifting up its Head above Scandals* (W 114). Certainly for Winstanley the full return of Christ will herald what James Knott calls a 'miraculous greening' of the land.[35] The land is also crucial for Winstanley because it is the very source and sustainer of life: the Earth is our 'Mother ... that brought us all forth' and who, because of her love for us all, wants to give 'all her Children suck . . . that they starve not' – something she is hindered from doing all the while the landlords enclose off the land (W 265).[36]

Winstanley's critique of the system of private land-ownership starts from an assumption that the earth was originally created to be shared by all: 'In the beginning of Time, the great Creator Reason, made the Earth to be a Common Treasury . . . ' (W 251). The right to share the land on a communal basis was implied in the creation narratives in Genesis, though Winstanley thought communism was also the natural state because it allowed everybody the freedom to provide for themselves the necessities of life. It was the form of social organization, therefore, which people recognized as the most rational and the one most likely to guarantee their preservation. But it was not destined to survive, its collapse becoming inevitable once some of our forebears began to enclose the land for their own private possession. Winstanley outlines this process in *The Fire in the Bush*:

originally, when 'the whole Earth was common to all without exception', the stronger helped the weaker by working harder, but the 'singlenesse and simplicity' of this arrangement became corrupted once the stronger began to question why they should serve those who did less work, and argue their right to a larger share of the earth than the weaker. This, for Winstanley, was 'the first step of the fall', to be followed by the second, the 'outward action' of physically appropriating land for themselves: 'the elder brother moves him to set about, to inclose parcells of the Earth into severall divisions, and calls those inclosures proper or peculiar to himselfe, and that the younger, or weaker brother should lay no claime to it, and the younger brother lets it goe so . . . ' (W 489). Often this process is effected by the use of violence: as Winstanley tells the 'Lords of Manors, and Lords of the Land' in his *Declaration from the Poor Oppressed People of England*, their ancestors first acquired their land by the sword, and did first 'murther their fellow Creatures, Men, and after plunder or steal away their Land, and left this Land successively to you, their Children' (W 269; cf. 258). Although occasionally Winstanley can be somewhat ambiguous, he seems overall to have held the highly unconventional view that the emergence of private property was not a *consequence* of the fall, as traditionally believed, but constituted the fall itself. This is certainly clear from a passage in *A Humble Request*: 'when Mankind began to quarrell about the earth; and some would have all, and shut out others, forcing them to be servants; This was Mans fall . . . ' (W 424). All of which is highly significant, for it is this unorthodox view of the fall, and the assumptions implicit in it about human nature, which allow Winstanley to go on to make his claim that the earth will once more be restored to common ownership.

Conventional wisdom of the time was that, while a Golden 'propertyless' Age may once have existed, something innate in human nature, at least since the curse, prevented the realization of such a state again. Fallen humanity was now so subject to impulses of greed, fear, envy and lust, that for society to exist in any organized form accommodation had to be made to the need to own and protect private property. Human nature, in other words, was largely accepted as an unchanging and unchangeable phenomenon, and hence the concern of political philosophers since the Middle Ages had been to construct the most workable social structures permitted by humankind's limitations and weaknesses; in the case of Calvin, for

example, one with a strong emphasis on laws to check human sinfulness, or, for Thomas Hobbes, one where anarchy, the inevitable
consequence of unbridled competitiveness, was held at bay only by
a strong authoritative sovereign figure. Winstanley not only rejected
the position Hobbes was soon to articulate – 'this . . . power in man,
that causes divisions and war is called by some men the state of
nature, which every man brings into the world with him. But this
Law of darknesse in the members is not the state of Nature . . .' (W
493) – but in a passage which remarkably anticipates much later
thinking, actually suggests that human nature is largely shaped by
the prevailing social conditions: 'I am assured that if it be rightly
searched into, the inward bondages of the minde, as covetousness,
pride, hypocrisie, envy, sorrow, fears, desperation, and madness, are
all occasioned by the outward bondage, that one sort of people lay
upon another' (W 520).[37]

On the basis of his belief that self-interest is not innate to fallen
humanity, but generated and stimulated by the system of buying and
selling, Winstanley goes on to suggest, perhaps uniquely among
contemporary thinkers, that the prelapsarian community might be
once again attainable once private property is abolished and Reason
allowed to reign once more in the human heart. Whether human
regeneration had to precede the restoration of universal community,
or would result from it, did not concern Winstanley overmuch, since
both were effectively different sides of the same coin; as he argues
in the recently discovered tract *England's Spirit Unfoulded*, 'that enslaving covetous Kingly power, is corrupt bloud, that runs in every man,
and womans vaines, more or lesse, till reason the spirit of burning
cast him out. And as this Kingly power is cast out from within, so it
falls from without likewise.'[38]

Private property, then, was at the root of all the oppression and
suffering that beset men and women, and only its removal through
the earth becoming once again a common treasury could provide
the release for which they looked, and ensure true liberty and equality for all: 'so long as such are Rulers as cals the Land theirs, upholding this particular propriety of *Mine and Thine*', Winstanley wrote
in *The New Law of Righteousnes*, 'the common-people shall never
have their liberty . . .

But when the earth becomes a common treasury as it was in the
beginning, and the King of Righteousnesse comes to rule in every

ones heart, then he kils the first *Adam*; for covetousnesse thereby is killed. A man shall have meat, and drinke and clothes by his labour in freedome, and what can be desired more in earth. Pride and envy likewise is killed thereby, for every one shall look upon each other as equall in the Creation; every man indeed being a parfect Creation of himself. (W 159)

Not that Winstanley was the only one in his day concerned with questions of liberty and equality. Many of his contemporaries – most notably, perhaps, the Levellers – were championing, on the basis of the natural and God-ordained equality of all, the cause of individual rights. But few were willing to work through the inevitable contradiction that the individual right to property, if granted, could never be compatible with liberty and equality for all. Winstanley, almost uniquely, it would seem, was prepared to face the basic logic of this position – that only a society based on common ownership could guarantee true equality and liberty for all – and propose it as a serious alternative to the prevailing economic and social order. Not that the Levellers did not *recognize* the dilemma: 'I see that it is impossible to have liberty but all property must be taken away', their spokesperson Rainborough says at one point during the Putney Debates,[39] though neither he nor his colleagues appear to have wanted to pursue it. Indeed, they went to considerable lengths to deny that they had any 'levelling' instincts, outlawing explicitly in their last and most comprehensive manifesto, the third *Agreement of the People*, the right of any Representative to 'level mens Estates, destroy Propriety, or make all things Common'.[40] The most important concern of the Levellers was individual political rights: 'the poorest he that is in England hath a life to live, as the greatest he; and therefore . . . every man that is to live under a government ought first by his own consent to put himself under that government', as Rainborough put it in a famous speech at Putney.[41] For Winstanley, however, these were not the central issues; what mattered most was *economic* rights, the free access of all to the land and the sustenance it provided: 'True *Freedom* lies where a man receives his nourishment and preservation, and that is in the use of the Earth' (W 519). So while for the Leveller John Lilburne 'the poorest that lives hath as true a right to give a vote as well as the richest and greatest',[42] Winstanley's concern was that 'the poorest man hath as true a title and just right to the Land, as the richest man' (W 321). Commitments to extend the franchise to give the poorest the same political rights as the richest – which the Levellers, in any case, seem to have found far too all-embracing in practice[43] – held little interest for Winstanley, whose revolutionary programme would have abolished the concepts of 'rich' and 'poor' altogether. Political struggles, which Winstanley understood to be but manifestations of the struggle for land, would cease to exist once the earth became a universal community again.

Some of Winstanley's interpreters have discerned an inchoate form of 'class analysis' underpinning his programme.[44] Terminology of this sort has to be used with care, of course, and the temptation avoided to try to make him a 'modern' by imposing anachronistic labels on to his thinking; nevertheless, there are discernible signs of what we would today call 'class-consciousness' in Winstanley's analysis of the social and economic order he confronted.

The strongest hint of this is to be found in Winstanley's concept of 'kingly power', a collective term he employs for the landlords, priests and lawyers who together maintained the iniquitous economic system which so burdened the poor of his day. Winstanley saw, not only the self-evident division of society into the few who live by the labour of others, and the many forced to provide that labour as an alternative to starvation, but the way in which the entire English politico-legal superstructure served to legitimize and perpetuate such an inequitable system. '[D]o we not see', he wrote in *The Law of Freedom*, 'that all laws were made in the dayes of the Kings to ease the rich Landlord? but the poor laborers were left under bondage still . . . ' (W 586). 'Law is but the strength, life and marrow of the Kingly power', he had earlier written, 'upholding the conquest still, hedging some into the Earth, hedging out others . . . truly most Lawes are but to enslave the Poor to the Rich . . . ' (W 388). The English legal system, he was clear, was introduced by William the Conqueror to reinforce the division of land he effected in 1066 in the interest of his lieutenants, and had been used by successive monarchs to their benefit ever since. To ensure the enforcement of his laws the Conqueror appointed two 'national officers': the lawyer, whose 'work is conversant about nothing but the disposing of the earth'; and the clergy, whose duty 'was to perswade the multitude of people to let *William* the Conqueror alone with a quiet possession and government of the earth, and to call it his and not theirs, and so not to rebell against him' (W 522). For their efforts in 'preaching for him' and bewitching the people into 'receiv[ing] him to be Gods Anointed over them', William rewarded the clergy well, introducing a system of tithes requiring payment by the people of a tenth of their income to the Church. And not surprisingly, 'if the Clergie can get Tithes or Money, they will turn as the Ruling power turns, any way' (W 312, 357–8). It is the identification of the unholy trinity of landlords, priests and lawyers as a unified 'Kinglie power' that singles Winstanley out from other radicals of his time; many in the 1640s were attacking the monarchy, the legal profession and the Church as separate entities, but Winstanley stands virtually alone in presenting a coherent analysis of their interconnectedness and shared 'class' interests.

The concept of kingly power played a vital role in shaping Winstanley's response to the civil war. Like most radicals he welcomed (as we now know for sure with the discovery of *England's Spirit Unfoulded*) the removal of the monarchy and the Lords and the establishment of the Commonwealth, but he also recognized that in themselves these developments would not be sufficient to lift the people's burden, and *why*: kingly power was not in the hands of the king alone, but in those of the landlords, the lawyers and the 'Tything-priests'. The execution of Charles was therefore only a first step: the 'top-bow is lopped off the tree of Tyrannie, and Kingly power in that one particular is cast out; but alas oppression is a great tree still, and keeps off the sun of freedome from the poor Commons still, he hath many branches and great roots which must be grub'd up, before every one can sing Sions songs in peace' (W 357).

Winstanley was aware that the end of the monarchy actually served the interests of the gentry, whose aspirations had been frustrated by Charles; yet he persistently appealed for the interests of the poor majority also to be recognized, for Parliament to make the Commonwealth exactly that: 'You have taken away the King; you have taken away the House of Lords: Now step two steps further, and take away the power of Lords of Mannors, and of Tything Priests, and the intolerable oppressions of Judges, by whom Laws are corrupted; and your work will be honourable' (W 372–3).

This appeal to the Commons was based on three premises: first, Parliament had promised, on oath, that the common people would have their freedom in return for their support in fighting the king; second, the common people, 'especially they that bore the greatest heat of the day in casting out the oppressor', ought by virtue of their efforts to have earned a share of the land; and third, the landowners' claims to their property could no longer be upheld in law. Winstanley always held that the original parcelling up of the land was an act of robbery from the common people to whom it was given at creation, but since the execution of Charles even the tenuous right to land established at the time of the Conquest had lost its basis in law. The victory of the Parliamentary forces over the king had cleared the way for an end to land enclosure and all the evils it generated – the division of the people into rich and poor, an oppressive system of law, and a beneficed clergy – and for the restoration of the earth as a common treasury.

Winstanley's tactic of appealing to Parliament to carry through the revolutionary changes he desired – which finds its ultimate expression in the dedication of *The Law of Freedom* to Cromwell – together with his conviction that the reconstitution of the earth as a common treasury was tied in with biblical prophecies concerning the end time, have led some to question the extent of his revolutionary commitment. Walter F. Murphy, for example, has argued that there is a 'deterministic element' in Winstanley's writings in so far as he expected society to be transformed ultimately by God and not humanity. A certain amount of human participation would be necessary, but 'there should be no revolution. God was at hand and would himself destroy the city of man'. Winstanley might appeal to the property owners to give the earth back to the people, but in reality they had no choice; if they demurred they would be forced to let it go, not by the Diggers but by God.[45] Winthrop S. Hudson also considered ideas of revolution to be far from Winstanley's mind: before any of the social evils against which he railed could be overcome Satan must first be rooted out of people's hearts, and this was a work which only God could do. The logic of Winstanley's position was therefore that men and women could do nothing but wait; and the Diggers 'did not conceive of their venture as a means of effecting social change' but more 'as a "sign" demanding attention to a message from the Lord'.[46] Knott, too, understands the digging as a sign, a 'symbolic witness to the impending age of the Spirit', rather than a revolutionary act.[47]

The theme of waiting upon God for the ultimate success of his project is undoubtedly a recurring one in Winstanley, and is not limited to his earlier more mystical writings. It appears, for example, in *The New Law of Righteousnes*, written a few months before the commencement of the digging, in the *Watch-word to the City of London*, written as the project on St George's Hill was being abandoned, and in *A New-Yeers Gift*, written after the enforced move to Cobham. But if Winstanley does play down the importance of human agency in some of his early passages, the emphasis undoubtedly changes in the tracts written after the commitment to dig the commons was made. The context is all-important – both the immediate literary context within which his comments are set and the wider context of the activity in which Winstanley was engaged at the time of writing – and considering his apparently deterministic passages in *this* light suggests that it is somewhat to miss the point to ask whether he had ultimately to put his faith in *either* divine intervention *or* human action. For Winstanley both were important and interconnected: divine sanction assured him that his programme would ultimately be realized, but the means of that realization was the agency of himself and other enlightened men and women. Of themselves the Diggers could not hope to succeed with their mission, but their conviction that the final victory would be Christ's, far from absolving them of any responsibility to work, gave them an even greater impetus to continue. Thus whenever Winstanley expresses his conviction that God will ultimately bring about the restoration of the earth, there are almost invariably references alongside to the part he himself has tried to play in the process. In the *Watch-word*, for example, he recalls how he prayed, immediately after an unpleasant attack on the Diggers, 'O thou King of right-eousnesse shew thy power, and do thy work thy self, and free thy people now from under this heavy bondage of miserie', and then goes on in the very next paragraph to refer to his commission to make the earth a common treasury, and to the way he 'did obey thy voice, to speak and act this truth' (W 328–9). In *A New-Yeers Gift* Winstanley records how, on another occasion when the com-munity was attacked, the Diggers resolved 'to wait upon God, to see what he will do, and they have built them some few little hutches . . . and follow their work adayes still . . . And they have planted divers Acres of Wheat and Rye, which is come up, and promises a very hopefull crop, committing their cause to God, and wait upon him, saying, O thou King of righteousnesse, do thine own work' (W 368–9). And as he closes this tract he writes: 'And here I end, having put my Arm as far as my strength will go to advance Righteousness: I have Writ, I have Acted, I have Peace: and now I must wait to see the Spirit do his own work in the hearts of others . . . ' (W 395).

Winstanley's commitment to non-violent means to achieve his programme has also raised questions for some about the depth of his revolutionary commitment. Aylmer, for example, has argued that by January 1649 Winstanley had become a revolutionary in the sense that his ideas and policies were totally incompatible with the existing order, but 'not one in the sense of accepting the use of violence in order to attain these ends'.[48] A number of things can be said here. First, there is the obvious point that violence is not a necessary accompaniment to revolution, and, second, since the Diggers never represented more than a tiny minority of the common people of England, armed struggle was never a practical or sensible option. Yet there were also deeper reasons behind Winstanley's rejection of violence.

One, touched on above, was his belief in the legality of the claim of the common people to the land. The earth had originally been given for all to share, not for the few to enclose, and belonged therefore to the people by divine right; and even if this right had been disregarded by the bastard of Normandy and his man-made laws, the execution of Charles undermined whatever basis those laws had and restored again the people's right to the land. Furthermore, the common people, by 'adventuring their lives' against the king, had put the onus on Parliament to honour its side of the contract and give them their freedom – by which of course Winstanley meant the use of the earth: 'we claim this our bargain', he writes in *The Poor Oppressed People*, 'by the law of contract from them, to be a free people with them, and to have an equall priviledge of Common livelihood with them . . .' (W 276). Armed with such an incontrovertibly just case Winstanley believed he could succeed by reasoned argument alone, by what George M. Shulman terms 'a politics of dialogue';[49] and this is clear both from the volume of tracts he published and from the titles which some of them bore – *An Appeal . . .* , *A Humble Request*, and so on. Even after the defeat of the digging venture he did not immediately give up hope that he might persuade his fellow country-people with the reasonableness of his case, and in *The Law of Freedom*, entrusts responsibility for the realization of his blueprint for a new society to the Lord Protector himself: 'And now I have set the candle at your door', he tells Oliver, 'for you have power in your hand, in this other added opportunity, to Act for Common Freedome if you will; I have no power' (W 510).

Secondly, Winstanley held violence to be incompatible with the overall aim of his programme: universal freedom could not be achieved by means which actually ended up enslaving people. 'We abhor fighting for Freedom', he writes in *A New-Yeers Gift sent to the Parliament and Armie*, 'it is acting of the Curse and lifting him up higher; and do thou uphold it by the Sword, we will not; we will conquer by Love and Patience, or else we count it no Freedom: Freedom gotten by the sword is an established Bondage to some part or other of the Creation . . . Victory that is gotten by the Sword, is a Victory that slaves gets one over another . . . ' (W 378–9). Moreover, the work of building community was a divine work, and for Winstanley violence could have no part in God's plan: working for liberty, he maintains in *The True Levellers Standard Advanced*, 'we shall not do . . . by force of Arms, we abhorre it'; rather it would be done 'by obeying the Lord of Hosts who hath Revealed himself in us, and to us, by labouring the Earth in righteousness together . . . ' (W 256).

Further, given the eschatological dimension of the work of remaking the earth a common treasury, the question of using violent means to achieve it would have seemed to Winstanley an irrelevant one. The prelapsarian spirit of community and sharing was, after all, to be restored by Christ rising in his people (which for Winstanley meant potentially everybody), reawakening them to the rationality of that way of living by establishing the law of Reason within them. Transformation of this sort could hardly be achieved at the point of a sword; the means, rather, would be reasoned argument, practical example and the work of the Spirit. 'For this Conquest over [the landlords] shall be got, *not by Sword or Weapon, but by my Spirit saith the Lord of Hosts*', Winstanley writes at the end of *The True Levellers Standard Advanced* (W 266). As Sabine writes, 'Winstanley distrusted the efficacy of force to accomplish any permanent moral results, and this was altogether in accord with the belief that morality begins with a change of heart' (W 49).

It is important to keep clear a distinction between 'violent' action and 'direct' action, for as his projects on St George's Hill and at Cobham testify, Winstanley clearly believed in the latter. Undoubtedly the digging venture must be understood on several levels: as a symbol or sign of Christ inaugurating his return; as a common-sense response to the Diggers' own plight ('wee digg upon the Common to make the earth a common treasury, because our necessity for food and rayment require it', Winstanley told Lord Fairfax in December 1649 (W 344; cf. 272)); and as an attempt to bring back into use land that had been left idle in order to alleviate poverty and unemployment on a larger scale. Above all, though, it must be seen, as it was by many at the time, as a decisive and threatening political act. For while at no point did Winstanley go beyond advocating the digging of common or unenclosed land – the Diggers have no intent, he told Parliament, 'to meddle with any mans inclosures, or propriety . . . but only to improve the Commons and waste Lands to our best advantage . . . Let the Gentry and Freeholders have their inclosures . . . and let the common people have their Commons and waste lands' (W 301, 305) – a threat to the system which ensured the profitability of those enclosures was very clearly on Winstanley's agenda. As he writes in *The New Law of Righteousnes*, the whole purpose of the digging is to enable him to eat bread by the sweat of his brow, *'without either giving or taking hire*, looking upon the Land as freely mine as anothers' (W 194, emphasis added). In other words, since the rich landowners can only maintain their vast holdings by hiring the labour of others, Winstanley's call to labourers to leave their employment – repeated even more explicitly in later passages – and join him in digging the commons is effectively a call for a general strike, with the declared aim of bringing about a situation where no one would own more land than he or she could cultivate on their own. The labourers and poor people thus declare, Winstanley writes in *The True Levellers Standard Advanced*, ' . . . that they shall not dare to work, for Hire, for any Landlord, or for any that is lifted up above others; for by their labours, they have lifted up Tyrants and Tyranny; and by denying to labor for Hire, they shall pull them down again' (W 262). 'It was not expropriation', writes Hill, 'but it would have amounted to a piecemeal deprivation of the profits of ownership'; though as he goes on to observe, when the Diggers later extended the term 'common lands' to encompass forests, and Church, crown and monastic property, their claim then, if actualized, precisely *would* have amounted to expropriation, and on a large scale.[50]

Winstanley, then, offers a radical critique of the prevailing social order, a vision of a new and more equitable one to be built on its ashes, and a clear idea of how the transition from the one to the other might be effected; and is thus more consistently and profoundly revolutionary than many of his interpreters have acknowledged. Whereas they have found difficulty reconciling Winstanley's twin concerns of individual and structural transformation, and have tried to emphasize one (the 'religious') over and against the other (the 'political'), for Winstanley the two are essentially interconnected. True revolution, for him, consisted in overcoming the effects of sin and the fall at the individual and the social level simultaneously (for they are causally linked), in overthrowing *both* the divisive and unjust system of land-ownership and buying and selling, *and* the sense of guilt, depression and fear which such a system evoked and sustained in the majority of the poor, oppressed people. Where this programme does invite further analysis, of course, is at its point of contact with Winstanley's eschatological hopes which underpin it. This question, and the full implications his theological beliefs had for his revolutionary praxis, will be explored next.

6

'CHRIST RISING IN SONS AND DAUGHTERS': WINSTANLEY AS CHRISTIAN REVOLUTIONARY

Through his writing and digging Winstanley sought the complete overthrow of a socio-economic order rooted in the inherently inequitable principle of private land-ownership, and the construction on its ashes of a propertyless, moneyless – in short, communist – society; and he did so within a framework of thought which, though unorthodox, was recognizably Christian. He was both revolutionary and Christian, but what was the relationship between these two dimensions of his thinking? Can we find in Winstanley any pointers toward what might constitute a distinctive Christian contribution to revolutionary praxis? Does he provide any materials suitable for the shaping of a *Christian* political praxis?

There is, of course, no reason why this question should have made any more sense to Winstanley than it would have done to Müntzer. Whatever cultural differences there may have been between the milieux of the two men – and perhaps these were fewer than we might at first imagine – in terms of the framework within which they and their contemporaries interpreted the world there were broad similarities. In neither culture would a distinction between a 'religious' and a 'political' understanding of the world have been readily recognized, though this is not to say, as we argued in the case of Müntzer, that the guiding question of this book has no validity for us who more easily make just such a distinction. Nor, indeed, is it to impose modern interpretative categories upon Winstanley, and thereby lapse into the error identified in the previous chapter of attempting to drag him from his milieu into our own by 'going behind' his religious language to discover what he is 'really saying'. Rather it is to explore the beliefs which Winstanley uses his language to express, and ascertain the extent of their impact on his political analysis and programme.

It is possible to identify at least three aspects of Winstanley's revolutionary programme which owe their form and substance very largely to his Christian philosophy. First, the *historical* dimension of his programme, which is to say not only its interpretation of the process of history, but the nature of its relationship to the historical possibilities of the moment in which it was conceived. This is founded entirely upon a certain hope in the imminent arrival of the Christian millennium. Second, a *utopian* dimension, borne of a conviction in Winstanley's mind that, with the realization of his programme, a past Golden Age of innocence when all lived in true community would somehow be regained. And third, the concern apparent in his programme that there should be a consistency between means and ends, which is rooted strongly in Winstanley's assumptions about the origins and potentiality of human nature. To construct this typology is not to suggest that these strands are totally distinct and separate, for they are in fact very closely interdependent; nevertheless, in the interests of injecting some order into this discussion it would be helpful to deal with each separately.

Millenarianism

Belief in a thousand-year period of rule by Christ over a perfect kingdom on earth has long held a central place in the Judaeo-Christian tradition. Originally, as Norman Cohn points out in the introduction to his seminal work on the subject, the term 'millennium' was understood, on the basis of Revelation 20.4–6, quite literally as a kingdom of a thousand years, lasting from the second coming until the final judgement, and ruled by Christ and the martyrs for the faith who had been raised back to life in advance of the general resurrection. Since they expected the second coming in their own lifetime the early Christians soon began to broaden their interpretation of the martyred to include themselves, the 'suffering faithful', and further refinements were subsequently made in view of the millennium's delayed arrival. Some believers, however, continued to hold to an 'imminentist' position, while others increasingly came to regard it as a more remote event. Today, as Cohn points out, millenarianism is used in a more liberal sense still, the word having become no more than 'simply a convenient label for a particular type of salvationism'.[1] Peter Worsley, in his study of the Melanesian 'Cargo' cults, also adopts a loose definition, suggesting the term may be descriptive of any movement centred around 'an expectation of, and preparation for, the coming of a period of supernatural bliss' which may or may not be narrowly confined to a period of one thousand years. For Worsley the term can further be broadened to embrace both those movements which envisage the millennium occurring solely through divine intervention, and those which anticipate that some human agency will be necessary.[2] In his *Millennialism, Utopianism and Progress*, Theodore Olson suggests that, despite its religious associations, the millennium need not be exclusively linked to notions of 'the transcendent' or 'heaven', but can more broadly be understood as having to do with the present world, with the 'choices for action made by living communities' on the basis of an interpretation of history which sees it as a single drama in several acts, 'propelled by conflict among contending forces in a dialectical fashion'.[3] Karl Mannheim, too, suggests that 'absolute presentness' is 'the only true . . . identifying characteristic' of chiliastic (or millenarian) experience; 'promises of a better world removed in time and space are like uncashable cheques': it is the present 'propitious moment' which provides the opportunity — and which must therefore be seized — for the transformation of the world.[4] Rowland and Corner stress that millenarians have always rejected any temptation 'to polarize history and eschatology', recognizing instead, as did Jesus himself, 'that the eschatological reign is already at the doors and is evident in the ruins of the old age'.[5] To summarize, we may borrow Cohn's concise fivefold definition and characterize millenarians as those who expect salvation to be an event 'accomplished by, or with the help of, supernatural agencies', involving the transformation and perfection of life here on earth (rather than in heaven), and instituted suddenly, and probably imminently, for the benefit of all the faithful 'as a collectivity'. In the sense that the kingdom will be set up here on earth it is, as Olson says, a historical event, the 'climactic end state' of the drama of history.[6]

Winstanley shared with most of his contemporaries in the radical Protestant tradition strong millennial expectations. References to the final scenario described in the book of Revelation, to the fulfilment 'here' of biblical prophecies concerning the last days, and to St Paul's picture of nature groaning and travailing until it is delivered (Rom. 8.22), abound in his writings, no less in those produced *after* the digging began than in those written earlier. But how exactly did Winstanley perceive the millennium, and how significantly did it figure in his overall perspective?

Originally Winstanley's conception of the millennium appears to have been linked to a 'dispensationalist' view of history, as the title of his first tract (published in 1648) — *The Mysterie of God, Concerning the whole Creation, Mankinde, To be Made known to every man and woman, after seven Dispensations and Seasons of Time are passed over . . .* — makes clear.[7] According to this schema, as Winstanley explains in some detail in this work, biblical prophecies concerning the establishment of the kingdom of God on earth will one day be fulfilled, but 'in length of time, by degrees', God having been pleased to provide 'dispensations or discoveries of himselfe . . . which he will have the creature to passe through before he finish his work, to cast the Serpent, death and hell into the lake, and before he himself appeare . . .'[8]

These dispensations are divisions of history, each marked at their beginning and end by an event of great religious significance, and each symbolic of the progressing or deepening relationship between God and God's creation. The first, Winstanley tells us, is marked by the introduction of the law given by God to Adam forbidding him to eat of the tree of the knowledge of good and evil; the second spans the troubled years from Adam to Abraham; and the third covers the period from Abraham to Moses, having as its central theme Yahweh's promise that in the seed of the former 'all nations of the earth shall be blessed' (Gen. 18.18). The fourth dispensation stretches from Moses to Christ, and is one in which, more than those which went before, God 'did more manifestly set forth his love to his creature, and his wrath to the Serpent' by the institution of animal sacrifices which were 'types' and 'figures' foreshadowing Christ, 'the substance of all those sacrifices'. The fifth takes in the historically much shorter period from the birth of Christ to his appearance to the apostles following his resurrection, and the sixth the time from that appearance to 'the Resurrection day, or the great day of Judgement', which is the herald of the seventh and final dispensation. Winstanley, like all millenarians, is of course living in the sixth dispensation, during which the elect 'are to be gathered into one City, and perfected'.[9] But he is also assured that the seventh is not far off, when the whole creation will be set free, and the previously unrepentant and wicked will enter the city of Zion whither the elect have already gone. All humankind, as Winstanley constantly maintained, will ultimately be

111

saved, with only the Serpent – the prophecy of whose defeat was originally made during the first dispensation but is only now coming to pass – in line for eternal punishment. Winstanley's knowledge of the ultimate fate of the Serpent is clearly derived from Genesis 3.15 (the most frequently cited text in his works, according to Hayes), [10] in which God, addressing the beast, promises to 'put enmitie between thee and the woman, and between thy seed, and her seed, he shall breake thy head, and thou shalt bruise his heele'. [11] Indeed, it is this metaphor of the Serpent continually at war with the seed of Eve, though awaiting ultimately its final destruction, which gives Winstanley his clue to the proximity of the seventh dispensation, the millennium, though he is wise enough not to suggest an exact date for its arrival: that remains the mystery of God. He is clear that during the latter days of the penultimate dispensation, when the Serpent knows that its days are numbered, its rage increases, and thus its ever-increasing aggression, manifest in the 'reproaches, slanders, oppressions . . . and the multitude of temptations' which it now casts upon the saints, is a sure sign that it knows it is not much longer for this world. [12] The consolation which Winstanley offers the saints at this difficult stage is the knowledge that victory over the Serpent is ultimately certain: Revelation 12.7–10 and other biblical passages give grounds for assurance that 'though for the present many poor creatures lies under . . . bondage . . . the time is drawing neere that they shall be delivered, and the wicked one himself, the Serpent, shall be cast into the Lake, and perish for ever'. [13] The battle, however, is not to be joined by the saints themselves: they are to be patient and wait upon God, for it is God who will accomplish the release they so fervently await.

After *The Mystery of God* Winstanley's interest in dispensationalism appears to wane, though not his dependence upon the apocalyptic literature of the Bible to provide a key to understanding the signs of the times. The imagery of the Beast or Serpent, for example, representing those who oppose the work of the people of God, remains central to his thinking, and the biblical prophecies concerning its ultimate defeat continue to confirm to Winstanley that his hope is not in vain. He leans ever more heavily on the promise of Genesis 3.15: the verse itself occurs repeatedly in *The Breaking of the Day of God*, and its theme in many of his subsequent tracts. [14] In *A Declaration from the Poor Oppressed People of England* the Beast appears together with its enigmatic number '666', which Winstanley uses to argue, rather unconvincingly, that the reign of Charles I is 'to be the last Tyrannical power that shall raign' before 'people shall live freely in the enjoyment of the Earth, without bringing the mark of the Beast in their hands, or in their promise' (W 270).[15] This motif appears again in *A Humble Request*, written in the wake of the destruction of the digging community, where Winstanley castigates Parson Platt and the others who had violently attacked the Diggers as men who 'do so powerfully act the Image of the Beast' and bring by their actions the fulfilment of the prophecy of Revelation 13.17. Their days, however, are numbered too, for the work of digging, 'or the appearance of Christ in the earth . . . hath ripped up the bottom of their Religion', and 'when the Lamb turnes into the Lion, they will remember what they have done, and mourne' (W 436–7).

In *Fire in the Bush* another variation of the theme of the Beast appears, this time drawn from the Old Testament: 'the foure Beasts, which *Daniel* saw rise up out of the Sea' (W 464). These, it turns out, are Winstanley's old adversaries 'Kingly power', 'selfish Lawes', 'the thieving Art of buying and selling the Earth with her fruits to one another', and 'the Imaginary Clergy-Power', which, although they seem to flourish for a time, oppressing and burdening the creation, will 'run into the Sea againe, and be swallowed up in those waters; that is, into Mankinde, who shall be abundantly inlightened' at the glorious appearance of Christ (W 464–6).

Whatever imagery Winstanley draws on, his concern is always to show how the events foretold typologically by the biblical writers are materially to be fulfilled in his own day. He is considerably more subtle than some of his peers who, in a simplistic, and sometimes (to our mind) plainly absurd way,[16] attempted to make one-for-one correspondences between contemporary events and characters and images in biblical prophecies; yet neither is he content to leave these prophecies at the level of the abstract, wanting always to make the correspondence between the signifier and the thing signified particular and explicit. Behind each apocalyptic reference lies the assumption, sometimes implied and sometimes stated, that the final consummation of all things — of which the events in Revelation are a precursor — is even now at hand. The significance of his constant invocation of Genesis 3.15 is that the Serpent is *at this time* being overcome by the seed of the woman — Christ, or the power of universal love indwelling the saints. 'And now the Seed begins to worke, to bruise the Serpents head, and man begins to looke upward, towards the life of the Spirit within . . . ' (W 460).

Further pointers for Winstanley to the imminence of the new age are the prophetic biblical allusions to a figurative period of 42 months, or 'a time, times, and dividing of time', during which 'the Lord . . . gives this Beast a toleration to rule' (W 204). References to this period, which occur both in Daniel (7.25 and 12.7) and Revelation (11.2, 3 and 12.14), appear in a number of Winstanley's writings (as, of course, they did also in Müntzer's).[17] This scheme provided many (though not, as we shall see, Winstanley) with a seemingly very precise tool for understanding the times. The Puritan scholar Matthew Poole, a contemporary of Winstanley, noted that most interpreters agreed that the period 'a time, times and half a time' signified three and a half years, each of these years consisting of 360 'prophetical days' or ordinary years; and therefore the combined period of three and a half prophetical years is equal to a total of 1260 days or years, the period, according to Revelation 13.5, allowed to the Beast to exercise his power. It is therefore the case, Poole says, that 'if we could find out where any one of these [periods] began, we should find out the time of all the rest. Those who fix the rise of the beast in or about the year 400, must add to this 1260. Then in 1660 antichrist's reign should have determined . . . but if the rise of the beast were in the year 500, the expiration must be in 1760 . . .'[18] Christopher Hill has remarked on the importance of the 1260-year period in seventeenth-century thinking, noting that Protestants generally 'took Antichrist to be the Pope, whose rise was estimated to have occurred in 390–6 AD . . . [which] . . . pointed to the years 1650–56 for the destruction of Antichrist'. Hill also observes that some interpreters considered the Bishop of Rome to have emerged as pope a little later, around the years AD 400–6, which would give the year 1666 especial importance in the prophetic timetable.[19]

This method of historical interpretation bears a remarkable similarity to the myth, influential among radicals in Winstanley's day, of the Everlasting Gospel, formulated originally in the twelfth century by Joachim of Fiore. Winstanley incorporates this theory into his argument in *Truth Lifting up its Head* (W 122; cf. 100, 169).[20] As we have noted in our consideration of Müntzer, Joachim, breaking with the normal twofold division of history into 'before Christ' and 'anno Domini', advocated a trinitarian schema: the Old Testament dispensation, the age of the Father or 'time of the Law, when the people of the Lord served like a little child for a time under the elements of the world'; the New Testament or 'Gospel' dispensation, the age of the Son; and the third dispensation which 'will come towards the end of the world, no longer under the veil of the letter, but in the full freedom of the Spirit . . . '[21] Despite the active approval this doctrine was given by the papacy during Joachim's lifetime, it was, in fact, heretical in so far as it subverted the authority of the Church and placed greater significance upon the Spirit indwelling people than on the letter of Scripture. Thomas Edwards, a great scourge of the seventeenth-century radicals, identified the doctrine with universalism.[22]

Despite an adherence to a dispensationalist view of history, and a predisposition to interpret the present against the background of the apocalyptic drama set forth in Daniel and Revelation, Winstanley differed in two important respects from many who adopted a millenarian position. Firstly, although he never doubted he was living in the penultimate age or dispensation, that the world had come to the 'half day' or 'dividing of time' of Revelation and Daniel, he is never to be found offering a precise date or time by when he imagines the millennium will be installed. In this he differed from Joachim himself, who appeared to invest considerable significance in the year 1260, and, as we have noted, from a number of contemporaries – and not just unlettered sectaries. Detailed calculations about the end of the world occupied some of the best mathematicians and scholars of the seventeenth century (including Isaac Newton and Joseph Mede), among whom the year 1666 was (unsurprisingly) a favourite, as well as 1656, which corresponded to the number of years which were understood to have elapsed between the creation and the flood.[23]

That Winstanley avoids this sort of speculation in part arises from a second distinguishing feature of his millenarianism, namely his understanding of it in gradualist and immanentist, rather than metaphysical and triumphalist, terms. In the face of a widespread belief that Christ would suddenly and literally appear on Earth to reign in person – or, as the Fifth Monarchists hoped, through his elect, the saints – Winstanley saw the second coming in terms of Christ 'rising up' as it were within men and women, in order gradually to restore 'right Reason' within their hearts and forge them together once more into a true egalitarian community. 'Christ in his first and second coming in flesh . . . is Justice and Judgement ruling in man', Winstanley wrote in *The New Law of Righteousnes* (W 204–5).

It was not a widely held position, and Winstanley shared it with only a few of the more extreme radicals of his time. Winstanley is in fact quite explicit in his rejection of a literal, physical appearance of Christ, and from his earliest writings argued against portrayals of Christ as a man separate from the rest of humanity. Christ, he asserted in *The Saints Paradice*, 'is not a single man at a distance from you; but . . . is the wisdom and power of the father, who spirits the whole creation, dwelling and ruling King of righteousnesse in your very flesh'.[24] Or, as he had earlier put it in *The Breaking of the Day of God*, Christ should not be understood as separate from the saints, 'his body and spirituall house'.[25] Thus his equation of the second coming of Christ with the gradual transformation of humanity is consistent with his overall theological position. And it *is* an equation: for Winstanley the work of digging was evidence that the 'return' of Christ had begun, and it is therefore misleading to suggest, as Hayes for example does, that he held to a dichotomy between the two, that he 'wanted to set about building Christ's kingdom on earth without waiting for a Second Coming'.[26]

Winstanley also takes the wholly unorthodox step of equating Christ's second coming with his resurrection, ruling out the possibility, as Hill observes, of there being any sharp contrast in his thinking between 'Christ rising in sons and daughters' and his 'descending from heaven at a much later date'.[27] To expect Christ to 'come in one single person', as Winstanley says in *The Saints Paradice*, is to 'mistake the resurrection of Christ'; 'you must see, feel and know from himself his own resurrection within you, if you expect life and peace by him . . .' And Christ is 'now rising and spreading himselfe in these his sons and daughters, and so rising from one to many persons, till he enlighten the whole creation (mankinde) in every branch of it . . .'[28] 'Upon the rising up of Christ in sons and daughters', Winstanley wrote later in *The New Law of Righteousnes*, 'which is his second comming, the ministration of Christ in one single person is to be silent and draw back . . .' (W 162). Winstanley's conviction was therefore that society would be changed gradually; the third age would arrive, not on the heels of a literal return of Christ in person, but as the result of a spiritual transformation of individual women and men. 'Christ's resurrection and second coming collapse into each person's sanctification', as David Dawson has put it.[29] And the effect of this, Winstanley claims on the basis of another original insight, will be true community or communism:

when he hath spread himself abroad amongst his Sons and daughters, the members of his mystical body, then this community of love and righteousnesse, making all to use the blessings of the earth as a common Treasurie amongst them, shal break forth again in his glory, and fil the earth, and shal be no more supprest: And none shal say, this is mine, but every one shal preserve each other in love. (W 205)

Communal ownership and the resurrection of Christ were interchangeable concepts.

Despite Winstanley's immanentist understanding of the millennium, and apparent lack of concern about the exact date of its arrival, it can hardly be doubted that, for at least the early part of his literary career, a belief in its more or less impending arrival shaped his political programme; and the implications of this will be considered shortly. First, however, it would be useful to explore a little more closely a question touched on in the preceding chapter, namely whether he *consistently* held to a millenarian position *throughout* his digging career and up to the publication of *The Law of Freedom*, or whether his experiences on St George's Hill, and Cromwell's suppression of the Levellers at Burford in May 1649, prompted him, as we earlier noted Juretic arguing, to forgo his millenarian outlook and make a more realistic assessment of the prevailing political situation. The question is an important one since, if Juretic is right, Winstanley's millenarianism can be dismissed as having no significant part to play in his practical programme of political and economic reform.

The nub of Juretic's case, we observed in the previous chapter, is that although Winstanley's communist programme was originally inspired by his millenarian outlook, Winstanley *the Digger* was no millenarian. Assuming (it would seem) socialism and millenarianism to be by definition mutually exclusive, Juretic argues that once his commune began to get established Winstanley exchanged his millenarian dream of 'a return to the "primeval perfection of the first Adam"' for a 'political and social critique of England founded upon the real world'. This did not happen overnight, of course, as Juretic readily admits, but Winstanley's millenarian hopes disintegrated fast once the commune took off, and it was only a matter of time before his mysticism was discarded completely. *The True Levellers Standard Advanced* was 'pivotal in his development toward a secular radicalism', though the changes he underwent were often subtle: 'what

Winstanley failed to say', argues Juretic, 'was as crucial as what he included in this manifesto'.[30]

Juretic's case falls on at least three important points. First, the argument that one can draw significant inferences from what Winstanley *fails* to say – from what Mulligan *et al.* call his 'meaningful silences' – seems less than watertight. Surfacing again here, as these writers point out, is the tendency among some Winstanley scholars to want to excavate his writings in the hope that beneath his language some 'subterranean idea' will be unearthed.[31]

Second, it is not clear in any case that the 'silences' Juretic needs are in fact there. Even taking Winstanley's first Digger tract, *The True Levellers Standard Advanced*, which Juretic argues marks the watershed in his political career, the number of millenarian references is hardly significantly smaller than in the immediately preceding work, *The New Law of Righteousnes*. On only the third page we find Winstanley drawing on that perennial theme, the promise of Genesis 3.15 (W 253), and on the following page looking forward to the time when 'the Earth becomes a Common Treasury again, as it must, for all the Prophecies of Scriptures and Reason are Circled here in this community . . . ' In fact, in this short work of seventeen pages (actually numbered '6' to '22') may be found at least six direct attempts to link the work on which the Diggers were embarking on St George's Hill with the promises of Scripture concerning the last time; and three of these, with their talk of the world having 'come to the half day' and to the present being the 'Age' of the Spirit, and so on, suggest very strongly that Joachim's Everlasting Gospel still had an influential place in Winstanley's thinking (W 260–5).

Although, with the exception of *Fire in the Bush*,[32] references to the millennium do not feature so prominently in writings of the Digger period as in his earlier works, they *are* there, and do not appear to have taken anything like the subordinate role in Winstanley's programme that Juretic perceives. Thus in *A Declaration from the Poor Oppressed People*, written in the wake of the first outbreak of hostility toward the Diggers in June 1649, may be found a discussion of the significance of the number 666 in Revelation 13, and an assertion that 'the age of the Creation is now come to the Image of the Beast, or Half day . . .', and 'Covetousness . . . hath been permitted to raign for a time, times, and dividing of time, and his government draws to the period of the last term of his allotted time . . .'(W 270–2). A letter to Lord Fairfax, written that same month, refers to

Christ 'that is now rising up to restore all things from bondage' (W 290), and *A New-Yeers Gift* (written for publication at the beginning of 1650) contains further references to Christ who, 'now in these latter dayes', is casting 'the other Serpent and fiery scorpion out' (W 365), and to the fulfilment of prophetic scriptures concerning the last times, including that in Genesis 3.15 (W 380). In *Fire in the Bush* itself there is, in addition to several references to Christ rising, an extended discussion of some of the apocalyptic imagery of the book of Revelation – particularly that concerning the four beasts which, as we have noted, Winstanley uses as a framework for an analysis of contemporary English society – and the observation that the world has reached 'the dividing of time' (W 464f., 487). *A Humble Request*, the last Digger writing (April 1650), has references to the fulfilment of prophecy concerning the Beast in Revelation 13.17 and to the work of digging being synonymous with the appearance of Christ in the Earth (W 436–7); and even *The Law of Freedom* refers to the need for the work of building the Commonwealth to go on lest we 'shew our Government to be gone no further but to the half day of the Beast, or to the dividing of Time . . . ' (W 535).

We need to reiterate, of course, that the mere inclusion of a number of references in his work to the end time is by no means conclusive proof that Winstanley actually *believed* in its proximate arrival, nor that hopes that the millennium might be inaugurated in England in the 1650s actually motivated or sustained his programme of digging. Yet the frequency with which they appear throughout his writings, the seriousness with which he appears to treat them, and the uncontrived manner in which he incorporates them into an argument or theme he is developing, supports at least a *prima facie* case that he shared the general millenarian expectations of the time. The burden of proof lies with those who want to claim that such expectations did not sustain him throughout the digging venture and beyond.

A third problem with the position Juretic represents is that it is too much of a piece with the 'Engelsian' tendency identified in the previous chapter which rejects *on principle* the possibility of any synthesis between genuine and informed revolutionary commitment and a theological *Weltanschauung*. For Juretic, the process of transition which led Winstanley, once the digging began, to become 'more politically orientated' and focus his analysis 'more and more upon the actual social structure of English society', is only complete if, concomitantly, 'the millenarian underpinning of his pre-Digger tracts' begins also to disappear;[33] and this is argued in the face of evidence to the contrary contained in Winstanley's writings.

What is required is a more nuanced understanding of Winstanley's position, one such as that offered by Hill in his stimulating monograph *The Religion of Gerrard Winstanley*. In this work Hill suggests that Winstanley 'initially expected a sudden conversion to Reason . . . as Christ rose everywhere in sons and daughters', and would certainly have been encouraged in this conviction by the abolition of the monarchy – just a fortnight before the digging began – and the subsequent declaration that England was to be made a free Commonwealth. The hostility which the Diggers then had to endure, however, forced him to accept that he had underestimated both the 'institutional power of the Beast', and 'the hold of the serpent over the minds of [people]', and so 'clearly a period of education was needed before Christ arose in a sufficient number of sons and daughters to overthrow kingly power'.[34] Hill's argument is borne out by the tone of some of Winstanley's later writings, including *The Law of Freedom*, where the writer's early belief that the state could be uprooted by working people withdrawing their labour and cultivating the commons, gives way to an acknowledgement that the new society would have to be won with the assistance of those with real power, namely Cromwell and his supporters. Perhaps Winstanley looked forward, as Hill suggests, to a 'transitional period' of Commonwealth's government, during which Parliament would 'break the Tyrants bands', 'abolish all their oppressing Laws', and 'give Orders, Encouragements and Directions unto the poor oppressed people of the Land, that they forthwith plant and manure this their own Land, for the free and comfortable livelyhood of themselves and posterities' (W 558).[35] In any case, the appeals to the poor which had so characterized his early writings are replaced in his final work by a plea, indeed the dedication of the whole work, to the future Lord Protector. As Petegorsky notes, the whole temper of this work 'is the sober realization that the propertyless themselves do not have the power to force through those changes without the support of those in power'.[36] 'And now', Winstanley writes to Oliver, 'I have set the candle at your door, for you have power in your hand . . . to Act for Common Freedome if you will; I have no power' (W 510).

If Winstanley slowly lost the expectations he originally harboured of an imminent millennium by the time he came to pen *The Law of*

Freedom, his deep underlying hope that Christ would *ultimately* be seen rising in his sons and daughters and restoring again a true spirit of community remained. He can still express a hope that he is seeing the days of the resurrection to power of 'the spirit of universal Righteousness dwelling in Mankinde', and that in England,

> where this Commonwealths Government shall be first established, there shall be abundance of peace and plenty . . . and the Law shall go forth from that *Sion*, and that Word of the Lord from that *Jerusalem*, which shall govern the whole Earth. There shall be no Tyrant Kings, Lords of Manors, Tything Priests, oppressing Lawyers, exacting Landlords, nor any such like pricking bryar in all this holy Mountain of the Lord God our Righteousness and Peace; for the righteous Law shall be the Rule for every one, and the Judg of all mens actions. (W 534–5)

The closing lines of this work –

> O death where art thou? wilt thou not tidings send?
> I fear thee not, thou art my loving friend.
> Come take this body, and scatter it in the Four,
> That I may dwell in One, and rest in peace once more

– may sound like Winstanley's swan-song (W 600), a recognition that his hopes had been in vain, but it should also not be forgotten that he had begun this treatise with the claim that 'the Spirit of the whole Creation . . . is about the Reformation of the World, and he will go forward in his work' (W 502).

It is reasonable to conclude, then, both that a belief that the digging signified, and would serve to advance, the long-awaited reign of Christ on earth inspired and sustained Winstanley throughout and beyond the life of his community; and that although Winstanley's optimism during the heady days of 1649 that 'the time of Deliverance is come' was perforce tempered by his experience of the violent determination of the Beast, kingly power, to preserve its privileges and power, an underlying assurance that England was even now 'under the dividing of time' sustained him right through, even until the publication of *The Law of Freedom* some eighteen months after the final collapse of the digging. These convictions clearly contributed in a significant way to his overall political philosophy, but in what way? What *singular* contribution did they make to his theoretical analysis and revolutionary programme?

A response to this question was offered briefly in the previous chapter when, in citing Winstanley's millenarianism to rebut accusations that he merely used biblical themes to disguise an essentially secular philosophy, it was suggested that the effect of his millenarian position was to dehistoricize the struggle in which he was engaged. His programme was undoubtedly revolutionary in theory, it was argued, but deficient of any account of how it could be realized with reference to the historical conditions of the time; and this lack was rooted in his millenarianism – or more precisely, the demands which he placed upon it.

In fact, Winstanley's position is considerably more nuanced than a cursory reading – and some of his critics – may suggest. First, he did not embark on his programme without *any* reference to the prevailing circumstances, or with no grounds at all for supposing that Christ was beginning to rise in his people. Hayes, for example, has implied that the Digger leader was guilty of portraying 'contemporary sociological conditions in a timeless religious context at a time and in a place of acute political and theological conflict'.[37] This, however, is to suggest that the digging venture had more of a *utopian* than a *millenarian* underpinning, a distinction which will be discussed more fully below. The call of God which he felt within him to the work of digging; the speed with which he was joined by others (in Surrey and further afield) in whom Christ was also manifestly working; and the execution of Charles, which portended so clearly the imminent demise of the Beast in its many forms; these together provided him with enough 'empirical' evidence to sustain his belief that the time for his programme was now. Much the same can therefore be said of Winstanley's millenarianism as was argued with respect to Müntzer's apocalypticism, namely that in so far as it enabled him to recognize the present as a *kairos*, a 'breach through which what was previously inward' could burst out suddenly and transform the world, as Mannheim has put it, it could not of itself be said to have prompted a misreading of the times.[38] Further, Winstanley never saw Christ's coming as an isolated or disengaged event, an irruption into history without reference to social, political and economic conditions, since for him it was intrinsically linked to the restoration of a communitarian form of social organization. Yet ultimately the *demands* which he placed upon his eschatology, that Christ be brought back into history *now*, led him to believe that the reign of God, in the form of a truly communist society, could be achieved now without reference to material agencies and conditions.

It is also necessary to nail the myth that Winstanley held a *regressive* view of history. Sabine has suggested, *a propos* the attention Winstanley pays to history as a struggle between good and evil, that his reading of history is essentially spiritual and 'in no way implies progress or a gradual development but the contrary' (W 42). To a point Sabine is correct: Winstanley's interpretation of history *is* spiritual, as many of his commentators have acknowledged.[39] Since the fall, humankind has been prey to the power of the Serpent, and the subsequent history of the race can essentially be seen as a struggle within each heart between God, or 'right Reason', and the Serpent, manifest in the form of a spirit of selfishness. And Winstanley saw this struggle also taking place on a grander scale in the world at large: 'if you desire to know the Beast', he wrote in *The Breaking of the Day of God*, 'look first into your owne hearts: for there she sits; And after that ye have beheld her confused workings there against Christ, then looke into the world, and you shall see the same confusion of ignorance, pride, self love, oppression and vain conversation acted, against Christ . . .'[40] Yet he also sees history, albeit in a crude and simplistic way, moving towards a climax. Whether he adopts a sevenfold dispensationalism, or Joachim's trinitarian model, Winstanley sees the struggle between light and darkness moving inexorably toward an 'omega' point, towards a moment when the Serpent will be cast out, all will be saved, and society will be reordered on communitarian lines according to the dictates of 'right Reason'. This may not constitute a 'progressive' interpretation of history in the modern sense – a concept which was, in any case, unfamiliar before the eighteenth century – and has virtually nothing in common with a materialist conception of history as found in Marx. Nevertheless, to argue that the idea behind Winstanley's reading of history implies the *reverse* of progress and gradual development is totally unrealistic, and suggestive again of a completely 'timeless' quality to his programme. Which is not to deny that there is *one* sense in which Winstanley's programme is backward-looking, and this will be considered shortly; but it is not the overall direction of his thinking.

Winstanley's millenarianism also contributed to his revolutionary programme a sense of *hope* – in the New Testament sense of 'certain expectation' – in the establishment of a new social order, this hope being grounded upon the central place of the new order in the revealed promise of God. For Winstanley, as for many other people of faith, hope of this sort can play an immensely positive role in stimulating and sustaining revolutionary activity, though to do this, as we shall discuss more fully in the concluding chapter, it must always remain *future-orientated*, recognizing the penultimate and partial character of all achievements in the direction of the kingdom (until the final inauguration, by God, of the kingdom itself). Where Winstanley's programme fails is in its collapsing of the future into the present, in its dependence for its ultimate realization upon the divine initiative at some historical point, precisely the present. What Winstanley demands, in other words, as Denys Turner has put it, is something which 'clearly no adequate eschatology can deliver', namely, 'the full significance of Christ's coming, fully available within history and now'.[41]

Thus if Winstanley's eschatological hope provides, in the form of a dynamic, a positive contribution to his thinking and action, his conviction that this hope could and would be realized 'here and now' does weaken its usefulness; his conviction that the communist society he was working to achieve would materialize in a short time removed an imperative to take cognizance of the economic and political transformation occurring around him, to relate his programme to the prevailing historical conditions (which, as may be seen with hindsight, were ripe for the emergence of a *bourgeois* revolution).[42] Yet is his 'mistake' rooted in his millenarianism *per se*, as Engels would want to argue? Is a propensity to misread history an *inevitable* consequence of a Christian revolutionary position? Or does our difficulty with Winstanley lie more with the particular demands he makes upon his eschatology, specifically that it be *realized*; and might not a more 'nuanced' eschatology offer a less ambiguous contribution to revolutionary praxis? These are issues to which we shall turn in the concluding chapter.

There is one final point worth making *a propos* Winstanley's 'collapsed' eschatology. We noted in an earlier chapter how, following the bloody termination of the digging project, Winstanley returned to hiring out his labour, to involvement in the world of property ownership and buying and selling, and to the more established practice of religion; and it is more than idle speculation to suggest a link between these developments, and an ever-increasing loss of faith, as the months and years passed, in the realization of the millennium.

One result of reducing eschatological expectations to a given time and place is that, with their non-fulfilment, these expectations lose their efficacy; and Winstanley has a lesson here for contemporary Christians tempted to identify the kingdom of God with any particular temporal society which, since it *will* be temporal, will always be vulnerable to the suppression or loss of those values upon which its similarity to the kingdom is predicated. One vital consequence of the kingdom always remaining in essence a *promise*, a *future* reality, is its power to sustain hope, even through defeat. As Terry Eagleton once put it, the fact that Christians do not limit their sights to the historical success of any one specific revolutionary venture but to the 'fruitfulness of that venture (even if it historically fails) in building up the future kingdom, should have one obvious effect: it should make [them] . . . struggle harder'. Revolutionary Christian faith, with its sense of certainty that the struggle will ultimately bear fruit, 'should therefore make its difference felt most in situations where the fight seems historically fairly hopeless'.[43] And by the same token, the loss of that vital distinction between 'history' and the kingdom, the collapsing of the one into the other, serves only to deepen the experience of defeat.

Utopianism

The distinction between millenarianism and utopianism has not always been recognized in scholarly literature. Theodore Olson, in his classic study of these phenomena and their relationship to the idea of 'progress', bemoans an all-too-frequent imprecise usage of the terms: utopianism, he notes, is employed as a term for *all* visions of a better world or better age, and millenarianism 'arbitrarily separated from its setting in main-line Hebrew and Christian thought, the better to distance these religions today from a tradition seen as belonging to wild-eyed visionaries and fanatics'.[44] J. C. Davis has taken Karl Mannheim to task for making the same conceptual error in the latter's influential study *Ideology and Utopia*: 'For Mannheim', Davis writes, 'Chiliastic Anabaptism was part of the modern utopian tradition'. Davis' problem with Mannheim is that his definition of utopia – essentially any set of ideas which threatens the *status quo* – is far too broad, embracing 'all that it would be possible, and that one might (with some impatience) wish, to call simply "radical"'. For Davis 'millennium' and 'utopia' are more accurately to be understood,

with 'Cockaygne', 'Arcadia' and the 'Perfect Moral Commonwealth' as distinct types of 'ideal society'.[45] Yet one of the most
recent scholarly studies of this topic, Krishan Kumar's *Utopia and
Anti-Utopia in Modern Times*, appears also not to recognize any firm
distinction between the two. 'Of all the heterodox currents in Christianity', Kumar writes, the one 'most replete with utopianism' was 'the
idea of the millennium . . . millenarianism was the form in which
Judaism made its major contribution to Christian utopianism'. In
complete contrast to Davis, Kumar eschews any precise definition
of terms: 'it seems best not to insist on some "essentialist" definition
of utopia', he writes, 'but to let a definition emerge: by use and
context shall we know our utopias'. The nearest he gets to any
definition is a loose 'Mannheimian' one: 'Utopia', he writes in an
earlier essay, 'is a secular, rational form of inquiry concerned with
the transformation or reconstruction of human life on earth'.[46]

It is hardly necessary here to explore fully the distinction between
'millennium' and 'utopia', or the debate it has generated, so the
briefest summary will suffice. Broadly speaking it is possible to identify
four distinctions between the two concepts: (i) millenarianism is of
very early origin, having emerged during the exile of the Hebrews
in Babylon in the sixth century BC, whereas utopianism – as a literary genre – only emerged in the sixteenth century AD with Thomas More (albeit there are themes in Plato which later utopian writers
developed); (ii) millenarianism is concerned primarily with divine
intervention in human affairs and the transformation of humanity
and nature, while utopias are secular and generally accommodating
of human fallibility; (iii) millenarianism is historically rooted, anticipat-
ing divine intervention at a given moment in history (namely the
present), whereas utopias are essentially 'timeless' and concerned
with transcendent truths; and (iv) millenarians are hardly concerned
at all with the form that the new order will take, only with the fact
that it *will* come, while utopians generally set out in great detail the
way in which their new society is to be ordered.

Many of Winstanley's interpreters would accept that there is a
utopian dimension to his thought, though not that it is in any
meaningful way rooted in a Christian world-view. Generally the
claim for Winstanley as a utopian thinker is made on the basis of
the blueprint for a new society he outlines in *The Law of Freedom*,
though by the time this work was penned he had largely abandoned
the millenarianism which informed his 'earlier' ideas.[47] Davis, for

example, having studied in considerable detail the utopian aspect of Winstanley's thought, stresses that there is an important distinction to be made between the Digger with his 'millenarian expectancy', and the writer of *The Law of Freedom* with his 'utopian reliance on a dynamic secular state and its agencies . . .' For Davis, perhaps the most significant development in Winstanley's thought is the shift from 'an anarchist position', characterized by a waiting upon God to establish a new order, to a dependence upon the *state* to usher in a better society – a shift which occurs with the writing of his final work which is essentially secular.[48] An argument could be sustained that underpinning Winstanley's whole platform is a conception of human nature which may owe something to his Christianity, and in fact this will be explored shortly; but the shape of Winstanley's utopian society as outlined in *The Law of Freedom*, despite the scattering of biblical references in its support, and the evidence (adduced in an earlier chapter) that it does not necessarily point to a complete rejection of the millenarianism its author espoused as a Digger, has little which could be identified as 'specifically Christian'.

There is, however, one strand of Winstanley's programme which *is* both utopian (if not according to Davis' narrow definition) and Christian, namely that which identifies the establishment of communist society, not only with the fulfilment of the millennial prophecies in the Bible, but in some sense with the *restoration* or recovery of a past age of perfection. In terms of its utopian dimension this aspect of Winstanley's thinking has received surprisingly little attention, though it appears consistently in his writings. 'In the beginning of Time, the great Creator Reason, made the Earth to be a Common Treasury', Winstanley writes at the beginning of *The True Levellers Standard Advanced* and elsewhere, and to make the earth a common treasury *again* is the basis of the Diggers' programme: 'they that are resolved to work and eat together, making the Earth a Common Treasury, doth joyn hands with Christ, to lift up the Creation from Bondage, and restores all things from the Curse' (W 262). Indeed, it is clear to Winstanley that the system of common ownership he envisaged would be established in his day would be a restoration of the perfect order instituted at the creation which had been shattered by the introduction of private property. 'I see that the whole earth stinks', he writes in *The New Law of Righteousnes*, 'by the first *Adams* corrupt Government; therefore it is the fulness of time, for *Jacob* to arise, extream necessity cals for the great work of restoration, and when the restorer of the earth hath a little more manifested himself, he wil make the earth a common treasury, and sweep away all the refuge of lies, and all oppressions . . .' (W 188). 'Upon *Israels* returne from captivity', he says a few pages later, 'the Lord himself wil burn up the curse, and restore the Creation, fire, water, earth and air from that slavery, and make the earth to be a common treasury to them all' (W 191). 'You swore in your National Covenant to endeavour a Reformation according to the Word of God', he reminds the House of Commons in July 1649, 'which Reformation is to restore us to that Primitive freedom in the earth, in which the earth was first made and given to the sons of men, and that is to be a common treasury of livelihood to all, without working for hire, or paying rent to any, for this is the Reformation according to the Word of God before the fall of man, in which there is no respect of persons' (W 305).

It is important to establish what status the idea of a 'Golden Age' had in Winstanley's scheme of things. Christopher Hill has argued in *The World Turned Upside Down* that, like the other biblical stories he draws upon, Winstanley treated the narrative of the garden of Eden 'as an idle tale unless taken allegorically', and that his 'poetic concern with spiritual meaning rather than with historical truth enabled Winstanley to blend the myth of the Fall with the myth of the Norman Conquest'.[49] On both counts, however, Hill could be mistaken. First, although Winstanley clearly *does* use the Genesis stories as allegories, as the quotations Hill offers bear out – 'The Apple that the first man eats . . . is the objects of creation', 'We may see *Adam* every day before our eyes walking up and downe the street' – this is not the extent of Winstanley's interest in them; indeed, in another quotation Hill provides, Winstanley actually makes plain that he finds both spiritual *and* historical significance in the Genesis narrative, though Hill's rendering of the text makes this less obvious at first reading. In *Fire in the Bush* Winstanley writes that ' . . . this Innocencie, or plaine heartednesse in man, was not an estate 6000. yeare agoe onely; But every branch of mankinde passes through it, . . . ' (W 480–1). Hill, however, in line with his already noted tendency to 'modernize' Winstanley, decapitalizes the first letter of 'But' and omits the preceding semi-colon altogether, a practice which may possibly be designed to minimize the import of the word 'only'.[50] But Hill also appears to mislead in suggesting that Winstanley's lack of concern about 'historical truth' led him to fuse the fall and the Norman Conquest: in *A Letter to Lord Fairfax* (omitted from Hill's collection) Winstanley is quite clear that the two are separate events, and that England is about to experience a restoration of the spirit of community unknown since prelapsarian times:

> The Reformation that England is now to endeavour, is not to remove the Norman *Yoke* only, and to bring us back to be governed by those Laws that were before *William the Conqueror* came in, as if that were the rule or mark we aime at: No, that is not it; but the Reformation is according to the Word of God, and that is the pure Law of righteousnesse before the fall, which made all things, unto which all things are to be restored: and he that endeavours not that, is a Covenant-breaker. (W 292)

To make these points is not merely to extend the discussion of the previous chapter about the centrality or otherwise of Winstanley's theological convictions to his political programme; rather it is to show specifically that the utopian ideal of a past Golden Age played a greater role in providing for Winstanley a vision of a new society, towards the creation of which revolutionary action could be directed, than may sometimes be suggested.

Winstanley's utopianism may be seen as a second aspect of his revolutionary design deriving its form and content from the theological framework within which he operated: and in so far as it showed up in sharp relief all the imperfections and injustices of the present, and offered a vision of a perfect alternative, it was, like Müntzer's, a valuable and constructive one. Its power lay also in its potential to mobilize the Digger communities actually to bring it to pass in their day, to work to undo the curse and make the earth once more a 'Common Treasury'. Yet must it not also be recognized that its mobilizing potential only 'worked' for Winstanley and his followers because of the historical framework within which they operated, and that to the modern mind the idea of the recapturing of a past age seems little more than romantic and nostalgic, 'utopian day-dreaming' according to the most pejorative use of the term? Unlike other (literary) utopias, as Christopher Kendrick says, Winstanley's 'does not exist in *parallel*, either to the (English) nation or to the city'.[51] In an attempt, perhaps, to make contemporary sense of Winstanley's utopia,

William D. Lindsey has suggested that Winstanley's 'mythic retelling . . . of the creation myth . . . is intended to provoke the transformation of society here and now';[52] and in a similar vein T. Wilson Hayes argues that 'Winstanley's postulation of the previous existence of a lost Golden Age lends historical validity to his desire to restore it. What happened once can happen again.'[53] But an argument from 'historical validity' will surely only 'provoke' those for whom it appears to be a realistic historical possibility − those, in other words, like Winstanley and his contemporaries to whom, if Olson is right that 'progress ha[d] few if any advocates prior to the eighteenth century', calls for a restoration or recapturing of the past would not have appeared misplaced.[54] If, however, Christians are to argue today that modern revolutionary theory can be enhanced and deepened by the addition of a utopian element, to which they themselves can contribute, such assertions will achieve credibility only in so far as they display a consistency with the forward-looking perspective of revolutionary activity. This is another area to which we shall return in the concluding chapter.

Human Nature

A third important aspect of Winstanley's programme is what might be called the humanistic or moral element, a concern to achieve consistency between the *end* to which his revolutionary activity is directed, and the *means* by which that activity is effected. Two aspects of this concern may be identified: a rejection of violence, and an interest in individual transformation.

The issue of violence was touched on briefly in the previous chapter, and little need be added here by way of additional comment. Winstanley, it was noted, held the use of violence to be inconsistent with his programme to liberate his fellow country-people from 'Kingly Power' and bring about a restoration of true community: 'weapons and swords shall destroy . . . but they shall never build up' (W 182). 'Freedom gotten by the Sword is an established Bondage to some part or other of the Creation . . . Victory that is gotten by the Sword, is a Victory that slaves gets one over another . . . ' (W 378–9). True freedom from oppression could not, for Winstanley, be achieved by oppressive means. And, consistently, Winstanley not only outlawed the use of violence by the Diggers, he could not countenance any group using it to seize power on behalf of the people. In what is perhaps a veiled reference to the New Model Army, he cautions that the ending of oppression and the rising up of the universal power which will destroy selfishness 'is not done by the hands of a few, or by unrighteous men, that would pul the tyrannical government out of other mens hands . . .'; rather it is achieved by 'the universall spreading of the divine power, which is Christ in mankind making them all to act in one spirit, and in and after one law of reason and equity' (W 181).

The emphasis on Christ appearing in men and women to make them *all* to act in one spirit exposes the human aspect of Winstanley's programme: the conviction underlying it is that, since the new community is to exist for the benefit of all, the work of making it a reality must be undertaken by all — or, at least, all must be given the opportunity to participate in it. And the inclination of men and women so to participate would increase, Winstanley held, as each experienced inward transformation, the rising of Christ within the heart to restore there the rule of 'right Reason'. Petegorsky, adopting the either/or approach we have observed before in some of Winstanley's interpreters, suggests that the essence of Winstanley's doctrine 'was his realization that social change had to be initiated neither by the spirit of love nor by the force of reason, but only through the direct action of politically-conscious individuals'.[55] In fact it was by a combination of all three: Winstanley perceptively realized that a society built upon the basis of mutual co-operation can only be brought into being by those in whom this spirit of co-operation has already taken root; it cannot be achieved, let alone maintained, at the point of a sword.

Winstanley's conception of human nature is at the very nub of his revolutionary programme. It is also the key to a proper understanding of his utopian vision of recapturing the Golden Age, and his millenarianism, since for him the rekindling of the prelapsarian universal spirit within each heart is nothing other than the second coming of Christ. As Christ begins once again to rule in each person, so he replaces selfish desires with a spirit of fellowship and effects his work of making the earth once more a common treasury.

Winstanley's position, at least until the writing of *The Law of Freedom*, amounts to a belief in the ultimate perfectibility of humanity, and in this, again, he was going against the tide; Hobbes was not to publish his *Leviathan* until 1651, but his ideas were in the air. Further, as we noted in the previous chapter, while many in his time may have believed in the existence *once* of a Golden Age, most would have felt, with Calvin, that the fall no longer made humanity's return to such a state of innocency a possibility. Yet for Winstanley any doctrine of original sin was to be rejected: 'Looke upon a childe that is new borne', he writes in *Fire in the Bush,*

> or till he growes up to some few yeares, he is innocent, harme-lesse, humble, patient, gentle, easie to be entreated, not envious; And this is *Adam*, or mankinde in his Innocency; and this continues till outward objects intice him to pleasure, or seeke content without him; And when he consents, or suffers the imaginary Coveteous-nesse within to close with the objects, Then he falls, and is taken captive, and falls lower and lower. (W 493-4)

Indeed, so far from the present corrupt society being a product or consequence of human sinfulness, it was society itself that was largely responsible for shaping the human condition: we have already noted Winstanley's assertion that 'the inward bondages of the minde . . . are all occasioned by the outward bondage, that one sort of people lay upon another', and it seems clear that, quite early on, he sensed that there was nothing immovable or eternal about human nature, but rather that social conditions played an influential role in shap-ing and fashioning it. As R. Eccleshall has suggested, Winstanley 'rejected, more fully and explicitly than any previous writer, the assumption that human nature was a fixed datum of which the established political system was the natural and invariable counterpart'.[56]

It is important to realize that Winstanley is not suggesting that men and women must be changed or 'saved' *before* a system of com-mon ownership can be reintroduced; rather he sees the internal and external transformation proceeding together. As we observed earlier, both are different manifestations of the struggle between good and evil, between Reason and Imagination, which every person experi-ences in their own being, and which occurs continually in the world at large. Each heart is the locus of a perpetual conflict between the forces of good and evil, but this conflict also finds expression in the institutions through which people's relationships are mediated; and the restoration of society to the rule of Reason can be envisaged taking place on both levels simultaneously. Thus Winstanley's belief in the potential of every person to know the spirit of Reason led him to the conviction that as the spirit spread, breaking the root of selfishness in each heart, so the external manifestations of that selfishness, the system of buying and selling and private property would disintegrate also; and the overthrow of these practices, since it was they themselves that corrupted men and women in the first place, would in turn hasten their transformation.

It would be difficult to argue that Winstanley's belief in the 'perfectibility' of humankind constitutes another distinctively *Christian* contribution to his programme, save in as much as it augments his utopian and millenarian convictions upon which we have already commented; indeed, in so far as he believed in the power of social forces to influence human nature, he is decidedly secular. But where Winstanley does have something to offer is in his concern that a political revolution should effect a transformation, not simply of institutions and structures, but of individuals themselves. This is not to place Winstanley alongside those conservative theorists who argue that by a piecemeal process of individual conversion society may somehow be improved; Winstanley's concern is rather that only through a truly communitarian system, created by people in whom the spirit of community had already taken root, can real freedom be guaranteed – and not only economic and political freedom, but freedom from 'Imagination' in the heart which 'feares where no feare is' and which 'stirs up warres and divisions [and] makes you lust after every thing you see, or heare of' (W 456, 452). As Sabine has argued, Winstanley 'could not content himself with a religious experience that ended with a change of personal morality, nor imagine a moral reform that did not include the elimination of poverty and the removal of political oppression'. Since all the corruption and deceit of the clergy, lawyers, landlords and the king were rooted in self-love and covetousness, he 'could not envisage a political reform which was not at the same time economic, [n]or a form of civil liberty that could coexist with poverty and economic dependence'. Hence he looked to the revolution of his time to bring forth a real reformation, 'to make the earth a common treasury and England a community in which the king of righteousness should rule in every heart' (W 51).

One final consequence of Winstanley's humanism was his concern that even those who oppress under the present system should not be excluded from participating in the new society, or the work of bringing it into being. His universalism led him to believe that the seed of Reason could take root even in the most barren soil, in those who upheld the kingly power, and that as Christ rose, they, too, would be swept into the reformation and join those working towards the communization of the land. They might for a time resist, of course, but even then the logic of Winstanley's position was that eventually they would not be able to maintain their economic superiority, nor the system which supported it, due to the gradual withdrawal on a massive scale of their hired labourers. It is not difficult to see, in the light of this, how Winstanley could consistently eschew the use of violence: the oppressors were to be 'coerced', either by the power of Reason rising within them, or by the momentum of the revolution, or perhaps both. There was no need for them to be eliminated. This is not to suggest that non-violence is a distinctively or even necessarily Christian position, nor to play down the obvious naivete of Winstanley's approach, with its expectation that the spirit of Reason or love would ultimately triumph in everybody by virtue of its inherent power and strength. Winstanley, in any case, was well aware that rulers will seldom voluntarily relinquish the power and privileges they enjoy, but he did not draw what to some would be the logical, practical conclusion of that observation and advocate the overthrow of the oppressor by force. For some political theorists this has left Winstanley facing something of a dilemma,[57] though the dilemma only exists for those for whom the 'means' may, if necessary, be subordinated to 'ends'. For Winstanley and (as we shall argue next) for other Christian revolutionaries, this cannot be an option, and in so far as Winstanley maintains a consistency between the method by which the new order is to be achieved, and the nature of that order itself, he has, *qua* Christian, an important lesson for all who actively promote political change.

'True Religion, and undefiled', Winstanley wrote in the last month of the digging,

is this, To make restitution of the Earth, which hath been taken and held from the Common people, by the power of Conquests formerly, and so *set the oppressed free*. Do not All strive to enjoy the Land? The Gentry strive for Land, the Clergie strive for Land, the Common people strive for Land; and Buying and Selling is an Art, whereby people endeavour to cheat one another of the Land. Now if any can prove, from the Law of Righteousness, that the Land was made peculiar to him and his successively, shutting others out, he shall enjoy it freely, for my part: But I affirm, It was made for all; and true Religion is, To let every one enjoy it.

Therefore, you Rulers of *England*, make restitution of the Lands which the Kingly power holds from us: *Set the oppressed free*; and come in, and honour Christ, who is the Restoring Power, and you shall finde rest. (W 373–4)

PART THREE

—

CONCLUSION

7

BUILDING THE KINGDOM: TOWARDS A CHRISTIAN CONTRIBUTION TO REVOLUTIONARY PRAXIS

T he guiding thread of our discussion has been the question of a Christian contribution to revolutionary theory and praxis, the identification of a *distinctive* contribution which Christians, *qua* Christians, might offer to a revolutionary programme. A suspicion that clues to formulating a response to this question might be discerned in an analysis of some figures within the Christian revolutionary tradition led us to an examination of the experience and writings of Thomas Müntzer and Gerrard Winstanley, and to the identification of strands within their revolutionary programmes which owed their origin and substance, in good measure, to the Christian world-view within which both operated. It is now time to draw together these strands and, in so doing, go on to develop a more general response to our preoccupying question. To make a more 'general' response need not entail introducing themes other than those which have already emerged (though the probability that new themes could be discovered will be readily admitted); rather it will involve draw-ing on a range of sources somewhat wider than that used hitherto, in order to argue that what have so far been identified as 'specifi-cally Christian' aspects of the thinking of Winstanley and Müntzer might also have wider applicability within revolutionary politics gener-ally.

First, to put the discussion into some sort of perspective, it is necessary to recognize in what sense it is being argued that Christian theology *can* make its presence felt within revolutionary discourse; will its 'contribution' be found at or near to the core of such discourse, or operate at a more peripheral and insignificant level? For some writers, if the 'core' of revolutionary theory is understood to embrace a 'scientific' critique of the prevailing political and economic order and a programme for its overthrow, then Christianity's inability to provide – or even contribute to – that core would seem axiomatic: 'at that level', as Alfredo Fierro has rather baldly put it, Christians 'have nothing to do or to contribute as Christians. There is no Christian social theory, no Christian praxis, no Christian politics.' Christians who want to know how to make their political commitment effective must always draw on 'the concepts furnished by social theory'.[1]

Fierro writes from a European perspective, but his position has been echoed in both South and North America. The Brazilian sociologist and theologian Hugo Assmann, for example, while recognizing the validity of the question of a 'specifically Christian' contribution, and offering some positive responses to it, has argued that, whether in Latin America or elsewhere, 'neither the structures of the Church nor the theology in vogue offer any natural resources for a specifically Christian contribution to liberation'. Thus instead of worrying about their 'specific contribution' to revolution, 'what Christians in growing numbers ought to do is to make a real contribution to the process as they find it'.[2] The Uruguayan theologian Juan Luis Segundo, too, while acknowledging that 'the social doctrine of the Church' represents 'an attempt to determine and spell out the "specifically Christian contribution" to the process of bettering and improving the existing real-life situation', suggests that it could not pass for a political programme, any more than could 'a sermon on socioeconomic morality . . . take the place of a consistent and effective political policy'.[3] Pietro Brugnoli, also writing from within a Latin American context, argues that any 'specific contribution' that Christianity can make to political discourse will not be in terms of content but rather the motivation which faith and hope can provide.[4] And in his influential and pioneering work *The Secular City*, the North American theologian Harvey Cox considers that as Christians enter the discussion about social ethics and social philosophy 'it must be made clear . . . that there are no specifically Christian answers to the inclusive problems of social planning any more than there are to the piecemeal problems with which we have usually been concerned. The kingdom of God does not come in the same way everywhere . . . Christians possess no blueprint for the heavenly city.'[5]

Underlying some of these comments is the principle of the 'priority of praxis', a central theme in liberation theology which affirms that it is only in the course of active commitment to political struggle that the task of theorizing or theologizing about what is being done can begin. Theology is always the 'second step', as Gustavo Gutiérrez has put it, reflection upon, rather than the source of, pastoral activity.[6] According to a liberation perspective, therefore, political engagement is not undertaken in accordance with laid-down principles, rather the truth relevant in a given situation is discerned by and through praxis to transform that situation. Truths applicable to one situation cannot necessarily be applied outside their original context as general principles; there can be no 'timelessly appropriate abstract answers', as Nicholas Lash has put it, to questions concerning the social and political implications of Christian hope.[7] This position, it is argued, reflects a conviction that, for the biblical writers, 'truth . . . is a relation not between things and concepts but between promise and fulfillment', not the 'theoretical contemplation of abstract truths' but 'an active relationship with reality';[8] yet the whole thrust of this argument, in so far as it explicitly rejects the possibility that objective 'truths' can be incorporated into a political or revolutionary programme, would appear to limit further the openings for a specifically Christian contribution to such programmes. Indeed, this was explicitly acknowledged by the authors of the Final Document of the 'Christians for Socialism' convention held in Santiago in 1972 when they wrote that 'the specific nature of the Christian contribution should not be viewed as something prior to revolutionary praxis, as something ready-made that Christians bring with them to the revolutionary struggle. Rather, in the course of their real-life experience in that struggle, faith reveals its capacity to provide creative contributions . . .'[9] And the consequences of taking any other line – of, for example, attempting actually to impose 'evangelical conditions' on a revolutionary process *a priori* – are spelled out by Segundo: the conditions 'eventually turn into third-way stands' and 'into counter-revolutionary forces when and if the revolution becomes feasible'. There is, Segundo concludes, 'no such thing as Christian theology or a Christian interpretation of the gospel message in the absence of a prior political commitment. Only the latter makes the former possible at all.'[10]

The conclusion to which this premise leads, that Christianity needs the mediation of secular ideologies in order to become historically relevant, is also a commonplace among political, and particularly, liberation theologians. According to José Míguez Bonino, for example, Christian obedience requires a concrete and specific form of analysis of reality, and Marxism, understood as 'an analysis of the way in which socio-economic-political reality functioned at a certain point in history' and 'an hypothesis [which] has been tested against our knowledge of the past' can provide this.[11] For Fierro the gospel offers 'regulatory ideas', but no guidelines for concrete action in response to any given situation. The gospel command to love may act as a general horizon for all human actions, but, lacking any 'scientific and theoretical analysis', it cannot help us to determine what means will be necessary to translate it into concrete action; this can be provided by Marxism, an example *par excellence* of that 'scientific' knowledge of society which Christianity needs in order to become historically relevant.[12] A priest who has experienced the reality of political revolution, Fernando Cardenal of Nicaragua, has also spoken of the need for Christianity to have recourse to the social sciences – and among these Marxism – 'to help . . . in the practical building up of this new society, which the kingdom of God obliges us to build'.[13] The central point here, as the British philosopher and theologian Denys Turner has spelled out, is that Christianity, unlike Marxism, 'is not *itself* a political doctrine' with 'the appropriate revolutionary strategy, correct for any, let alone every, age', and therefore the Christian Church has 'had constantly to redefine its historical mission . . . for every age and in terms of the revolutionary issues of that age'. Thus where capitalism is the prevailing ideology, Christianity *needs* Marxism 'because Marxism is the knowledge of what those conditions are, under capitalism, which, in preventing [people] from being human, require that humanity to be expressed in the form of the sacred'.[14]

There are a number of questions which could be raised about the whole drift of this argument, the tendency of some of these writers to speak in Althusserian terms of Marxism as a science, and the apparent ease with which Marxism escapes the limitations earlier imposed on Christianity regarding the question of supplying 'truths' with application to a wide number of situations. But more disturbing, perhaps, is the way in which Christian theology explicitly here buys into the notion that revolutionary discourse is essentially if not entirely 'secular', leaving no space for theology to make any concrete or otherwise material contribution; and in this respect the work of Stanley Hauerwas,[15] John Milbank[16] and Oliver O'Donovan[17] offers a radically different approach.

A central concern of Milbank's *Theology and Social Theory* is that theologians have rather too readily assumed that, 'because theology has rightly become aware of the (absolute) degree to which it is a contingent historical construct emerging from, and reacting back upon, particular social practices . . . most of what is to be known about social processes in general and the socio-historical "aspects" (an unwarranted qualification) of Christianity in particular, must be learned from social scientists'.[18] For Milbank it is all too clear that, once theology concedes that it *requires* the mediation of social science – once 'social science presents theology with the social object perfectly described and perfectly explained' – its task will amount to little more than a restatement of revolutionary objectives in its own terms and the provision of divine endorsement of them;[19] or there will be, as O'Donovan bluntly concludes, 'no political theology'.[20] For Milbank there *is* a distinguishable social theory – and, indeed, a sense in which theology is itself a social science – and this is so because there is also 'a distinguishable Christian mode of action', namely the enactment of the Christian metanarrative (a term unashamedly reclaimed from the wastebasket of postmodernism!) predicated on the ontological priority of non-violence, harmony and peace over against those (dialectical) conceptions of the world which accept violence, conflict and anarchy as foundational.[21] Of a piece with its preparedness to allow 'secular reason' to 'police the sublime' is liberation theology's attachment to the priority of praxis. For Milbank this further 'render[s] insignificant any specifically Christian practice', making the content of Christianity essentially theoretical and preventing a unity of theory and practice.[22] Similarly, for O'Donovan the notion that our total knowledge and understanding of the world may be gained from practical engagement leaves no space for any specific divine irruption into the process: 'our action becomes the predetermining matrix for whatever God may say to us, ensuring that we hear nothing from him but the echo of our own practical energies'. There is, says O'Donovan, 'in the space between reflection and deliberation . . . a moment of transcendent criticism, a moment of obedience to God's word; and that is squeezed out by collapsing the two, the backward and the forward glance, into one moment'.[23]

In so far as it wants to assert that there is within the Christian tradition a (virtually forgotten) narrative of revolutionary politics, and within political discourse a (no less neglected) tradition of Christian revolution, this present book is (in albeit a more modest and unsophisticated way) about the same business as O'Donovan and Milbank. Mine is an attempt, not only to retell a neglected chapter of the Christian metanarrative, but to relate elements of the Christian revolutionary tradition meaningfully to the contemporary form of that discourse, to refuse to yield up 'secular space'. It is time to see how this might be done.

Eschatology, Utopia and the Kingdom of God

A central concern in the writings of Christian revolutionaries has been the eschatological, the final consummation of all things in the long-anticipated millennium or reign of God. Both Müntzer and Winstanley had deeply-held convictions that the reign of Christ foretold in Scripture would shortly be inaugurated in their own day; indeed, the realization of their respective revolutionary projects depended upon just that eventuality. These convictions thus informed two characteristics of their revolutionary programmes: first, a sense of 'sure and certain hope' about the realization of those programmes, based on their 'convergence' with the millennium which, of course, has a central place in the promises of God; and second, as a consequence of their unrealistic hopes about the fulfilment of their programmes, a tendency to pay scant regard to the actual economic and political circumstances of the time. Both characteristics might be considered 'distinctively Christian', though not in a wholly positive sense.

This tendency within the Christian revolutionary tradition – and it was not entirely absent from more recent figures like Camilo Torres[24] and some Christian Sandinistas in Nicaragua – to collapse the future into the present, has the potential to undermine the effectiveness of any revolutionary programme. Such a one-sided eschatology can give rise to false expectations about the historical potential of any revolutionary programme, these expectations being grounded less on any realistic analysis of the prevailing socio-economic conditions than on a belief that the divine 'promise' is to be realized at a certain historical moment, namely the present. Although one can discern in a Müntzer or a Winstanley a clear conviction about the need for the revolutionary transformation of a given situation, and an active and committed response in the light of that conviction, the sense of certainty which their eschatological perspective tended to provide about the outcome of the programme to which they were committed had the potential to override any serious attempt to engage that programme with the historical possibilities of the moment in question. Indeed, an assurance of 'success' (in the historical sense) renders unnecessary any such analysis. So, while we can find in Winstanley's tracts a profound and clear-sighted understanding of the roots of power in Stuart England, and of the way in which the poor and oppressed people owed their status as such to the class-divided society under which they existed, he appears to take little cognizance of the new socio-economic – and subsequently political – order emerging around him shaped by the new, assertive and upwardly-mobile bourgeois merchant class. Similarly Thomas Müntzer's decision, in the wake of the princes' refusal to act against the wicked, to take matters into his own (and a handful of peasants') hands, signals a comparable naivete about the actual possibilities for the social and economic transformation to which he was committed. All of which is not to detract from the revolutionary nature in principle of the political programme of these figures: indeed, in so far as they focus upon the need for transformation at the level of the individual and, in Winstanley's case, envisage a truly propertyless and moneyless society, it could be argued that their programmes are more consistently revolutionary than those of many of their contemporaries. But to be revolutionary *in principle* is not, in the end, to be revolutionary; to adopt an important distinction made by Turner, as *ideas* the programmes of a Müntzer or a Winstanley may be revolutionary, but when conceived, as it were, 'out of time' – in disjunction from the real possibilities of the moment – they may *as events* be positively reactionary.[25]

Does Christianity, in the light of this, need to abandon its eschatological dimension if it is to avoid placing a block on revolutionary advance, or does the problem lie more specifically with the demands which revolutionaries like Müntzer and Winstanley may place upon their eschatologies? We shall return to this question shortly, but it is necessary, first, to examine the argument that to adopt a Christian perspective on the world is *inevitably* to see it in distorted, unrealistic and ahistorical terms. This view has been a commonplace in the Marxist tradition, though it is distinct from another feature of Marx's critique of religion, that which sees religion as an imaginary substitute for real liberation. '*Religious* distress', as Marx wrote in a celebrated passage in 1844, 'is at the same time the *expression* of real distress and also the *protest* against real distress', but it is capable of providing only '*illusory*' rather than '*real*' happiness because it desensitizes the suffering masses (as opium does the body) to the actual cause of their distress, namely the 'existing state of affairs'.[26] The argument I am addressing here does not doubt that Christian commitment can be channelled in the direction of seeking, through political revolution, the alleviation of the root – namely *economic* – causes of human suffering, but contends that a preoccupation with eschatology will always in the end render historically impotent any Christian revolutionary programme. Ernst Bloch has put it like this: 'When the hereafter seeks to leap down to earth, or when the inner life seeks to leap out into the world outside, then there appears in the subjective factor a fresh turn – not an opiate but an explosive without rival, a desire to fashion heaven here on earth'; but what have been the historical consequences of this desire? 'The revolutionary passion fed by those means was abstract and mythological. It did not and could not have any sense of reality. It simply gave wings to the subjective desire to change the world without proposing any concrete method of effecting such change'.[27]

This view receives perhaps its most vigorous application in Friedrich Engels' treatise on the peasant struggles (and Müntzer's part in them) in Reformation Germany.[28] In this work Engels argued that, because of the conditions of the time, that is, the existence of a strong religious culture, what was straightforwardly a class struggle between plebeians and bourgeoisie was conducted behind a screen of religious language: 'all the revolutionary social and political doctrines . . . had, mostly and simultaneously, to be theological heresies'. Yet he recognized that this 'religious reading' of the situation was not without serious consequences for the way in which the revolutionary elements in the struggle, in particular Müntzer, shaped their response to it. Müntzer's programme was undoubtedly revolutionary and communistic in that he looked for 'a society in which there would be no class differences or private property and no state authority independent of or foreign to the members of society'; but, as Engels in the same breath points out, this new society was conceived by Müntzer as the materialization of the kingdom of God, the prophesied millennium, and this millennium 'and the Day of Judgement over the degenerated Church and corrupted world . . . seemed to Müntzer imminently close, what with the Reformation and the general unrest of his time'.[29]

Thus for Engels, Müntzer's programme, based on 'the chiliastic dream visions of early Christianity' amounted to no more than a 'sally beyond both the present and even the future . . .' Müntzer's preoccupation with the fulfilment of prophecy obscured the necessity for him to relate his programme to the process of history, specifically – for the Marxist – to recognize that the communitarian order he sought could only be established on the ruins of the bourgeois capitalist system to which the present revolution was giving birth, and to which, of course, he was opposed. Thus Müntzer's sally beyond the present had, of necessity, to fall back into the narrow limits set by the actual contemporary situation: 'The anticipation of communism nurtured by fantasy becomes in reality an anticipation of modern bourgeois conditions.'[30]

The conclusion which Engels appears to draw from his analysis of Müntzer is that there is an inevitable connection between a religious way of looking at the world and a failure to see that world realistically. Christianity is either something disengaged from the real world and therefore politically vacuous, 'a set of abstract platitudes' as John Maguire has put it,[31] or else, when it does appear to inspire commitment to real-life struggles, it inevitably gives rise to a distorted understanding of the context of those struggles and an inability to read their real possibilities. Or to put the argument another way, Christianity serves either to provide language for the restatement of propositions which have already been reached by other (secular) routes, in which event it serves to cloud a 'true' or 'scientific' analysis of reality; or, if it does appear to stimulate a serious and informed revolutionary commitment, it has simply ceased to be recognizable as Christianity. Engels thus sees in Müntzer's political development (as other writers, we observed, have discerned in Winstanley's) two stages – first, theologian or millenarian, and second 'outright political agitator' and communist – with the transition being effected as the religious language characteristic of the earlier stage falls away to reveal the straightforwardly political agenda which was there all the time – and, moreover, the atheism upon which it was 'really' based. So according to Engels, Müntzer could be found, shortly before his death, addressing on the one hand 'the people . . . in the only language they could then comprehend, that of religious prophecy; and, on the other . . . the initiated, to whom he could disclose his ultimate aims'.[32] In a similar vein we noted Christopher Hill writing of Winstanley that, had he lived fifty years later than he did (that is, into the early

Enlightenment period), he would have been able to have expressed his philosophy free from the requirement, imposed on him by the milieu in which he actually did live, to adopt biblical metaphor and imagery.[33]

Another commentator on Winstanley, Perez Zagorin, perhaps reveals most clearly the train of thought underlying these arguments when he writes that we can see in Winstanley's last tract, *The Law of Freedom in a Platform*, his philosophy completing the circuit 'along which its inner logic has impelled it'.[34] But what is this *'inner logic'* which supposedly leads inexorably from millenarianism to materialism, and according to which Winstanley and others are essentially reductionists who, in their earlier 'incarnations' employ religious language decoratively but who find it, as they come politically of age, an encumbrance which can be swept away? Simply, it must be argued, the logic of the position of these writers and interpreters themselves, who can make sense of the presence of religious language in revolutionary discourse only as a screen to conceal an essentially atheistic and materialistic philosophy. Yet such an extreme position cannot do justice to the close relationship which can be identified between the theological and political convictions of revolutionary activists like Müntzer and Winstanley. As Michael Löwy rightly points out, if we consider the faith and religious identity of people motivated, as Christians, to participate in revolutionary struggle as a cloak, 'we fall into a sort of reductionist approach which prevents us from understanding the richness and authenticity of the real movement'.[35] Or as Maguire puts it with some force, this whole thesis that if religious language generates knowledge it has no religious content, and if it has any religious content it is not knowledge-generating but metaphor, must be dismissed as 'Kafkaesque'; it is a theory based not on empirical evidence but on an *a priori* definition of Christianity, and is the basis upon which, in the end, Engels and others cannot in principle believe in the Christianity of any genuine revolutionary.[36]

If, however, as has been the implicit assumption throughout this book, one *does* want to take seriously the Christianity of genuine revolutionaries, can anything be rescued from the discussion so far to advance the enquiry into the possibility of a distinctive Christian contribution to revolutionary politics? And can this contribution amount to anything more than the provision of a new vocabulary in which to express revolutionary demands or the generation of unrealistic expectations about the outcome of revolutionary praxis?

Can it be argued that to operate within the perspective of the kingdom of God is not *of necessity* to adopt an ahistorical reading of a given revolutionary situation?

On the basis of the empirical evidence we have considered so far the prospects would not appear to be hopeful. Whether, as for Müntzer, it was to be fought for with weapons or, as for Winstanley, worked for through more peaceful means, the point of the kingdom was that it would be realized within the struggle in which each was involved. Yet, and this is the important point, it is not imperative to infer from this a *necessary* connection between a political perspective grounded in a belief in the coming of the kingdom, and a conviction that the kingdom must be realized imminently. Or to put it another way, to see the world religiously, and even to hold that its ultimate destiny is the kingdom of God, is not, *pace* Engels, inevitably to see it unrealistically. The root of the mistake in Winstanley and Müntzer is not to be found in their Christian perspective on the world, nor indeed in Christian eschatology *per se*, but rather in the particular demands they placed upon that eschatology, specifically that the kingdom be realized 'for them'. Thus the route to a more consistently revolutionary position need not lie, as Engels or Hill might imagine, in the direction of the abandonment of a Christian *Weltanschauung* or an eschatological perspective, but rather in the construction of a more balanced or measured eschatology. Once *this* point is accepted one can begin to move forward, not only towards a *distinctive* but also a *constructive* Christian contribution to the praxis of political revolution.

The most suggestive thinking in this area is currently being done in the two-thirds world, particularly Latin America, by Christians working out the theological implications of a commitment to economic, social and personal liberation in situations characterized by injustice, oppression and corruption.[37] For these 'theologians of liberation' the concept of the kingdom of God, as both a sign and goal of God's activity in human history, retains an absolutely central place, but importantly they reject the unreconstructed millenarianism characteristic of earlier radicals like Müntzer and Winstanley.[38] Within the mainstream writings of liberation theology the chief significance of the kingdom lies both in its relationship to the concrete process of history *and* its dynamic nature as a perpetually *future* phenomenon, one of the central models being employed being that of utopia.

Two Latin American theologians who, in their early writings, explored in some detail the relationship between eschatology, utopia and political struggle were José Míguez Bonino, a Protestant academic from Argentina, and Gustavo Gutiérrez, a Peruvian priest whose book *Teología de la liberación*, published in 1971, is usually considered to be the seminal work of liberation theology. For both writers utopia is defined fairly broadly: Míguez Bonino, for example, points to the 'inspiring and critical power of the Christian faith' and refers approvingly to Jürgen Moltmann's thesis in *Theology of Hope* that 'Christian hope . . . is a constant disturbance of reality as it is and a call to move ahead to the future';[39] and for Gutiérrez the term 'utopia' can be said to refer to 'a historical plan for a qualitatively different society and to express the aspiration to establish new social relations among [people]'.[40] Both writers understand the term utopia differently from the way it is popularly defined: as Gutiérrez puts it, the main characteristic of utopia is 'its *relationship to present historical reality*,' as demonstrated by the fact that it is both (to borrow some terms from Freire) a 'denunciation' of the *status quo* and an 'annunciation' of what is to come, 'the forecast of a different order of things, a new society'.[41] Rubem Alves, another liberation theologian, has also stressed that the essential feature of Christian utopianism is a 'belief in the non necessity of *this* imperfect order . . . it affirms that there is no reason for us to accept the rule of the sinful structures that now control our society'.[42] Because of this link between utopia and history, the utopian vision is not to be held solely as an ideal to which all praxis should be directed: rather it must be found operating within that praxis at an inspirational and critical level. The plan for the new person in a new and more free society is not for later, when political liberation has been realized, but ought rather to inform the struggle for a more just society at all times.[43]

Míguez Bonino and Gutiérrez assert that utopian thinking plays an important if not vital role in saving revolutionary activity from what might be called 'one-dimensionalism'; while 'utopia without political science is romantic, ineffective day-dreaming', Míguez Bonino writes, 'science without a mobilising dream is inhuman or merely functional'.[44] The relationship between scientific analysis and utopian visions is broadly dialectical: the former, by exposing the reality of the situation and the real possibilities for change, opens up new horizons for revolutionary activity, while utopian thinking, with its overarching vision of new people in new relationships, serves to stimulate science to explore new fields of possibility. Without the element of what Gutiérrez calls 'creative imagination' provided by utopian thinking, science and political activity could fall all-too-readily into dogmatism and bureaucratism, or even generate new structures of oppression.[45]

The main focus of utopian thinking for liberation theologians is the creation of new men and women in new non-oppressive relationships, and it is here that the possibility of a creative and positive relationship between utopia and the Christian category of the kingdom becomes clearer. Christian faith, in other words, has a role to play in stirring and stimulating utopian imagination, in providing it with a dynamic which is specific in so far as it points ahead to a concrete vision of full personhood in perfect solidarity – in short, to the kingdom of God. And this vision, because it is of God, is for the Christian 'certain': faith, writes Gutiérrez, proclaims that the community which Christians seek through the abolition of human exploitation 'is something possible, that efforts to bring it about are not in vain, that God calls us to it and assures us of its complete fulfilment . . . '[46] Thus Christian faith challenges and stimulates revolutionary action precisely by drawing on its eschatological content, by prompting it in the direction of historical realizations of the kingdom in the form of the establishment of justice, peace and new non-oppressive relationships between people. The liberation which Christ offers is both *gift* and *task*, as Gutiérrez says; it is received freely in faith, but is also to be made efficacious in the world.[47]

For most theologians a distinction needs to be maintained between the kingdom of God and utopia. Jürgen Moltmann, for example, contends that Christian eschatology 'supersedes' utopian visions of the end-state and exposes their relativity and provisionality, and Karl Rahner has argued in a similar vein that Christian eschatology operates on a different plane from this-worldly utopias – indeed, Christian hope 'fills the vacuum left by Marxist expectations for the future'.[48] Gutiérrez and Míguez Bonino also decline to conflate the kingdom and utopia. Yet even if the kingdom does not serve *itself* as a utopian vision but operates in a more general way to stir or kindle the 'utopian imagination' with its vision of full solidarity, in terms of opening up the possibility of a Christian contribution to revolutionary activity the identification of a relationship between these concepts seems both valid and fruitful.

It may be argued that in stimulating the revolutionary imagination Christianity performs no unique task, since few political activists, when confronted by what they perceive to be situations of injustice, oppression and exploitation, will operate without any vision of some alternative world which will right these wrongs. Nor is it obvious that the kingdom offers to the revolution a more concrete project for liberation than that provided by, for example, Marxism, since in reality both Marxism and Christianity will want to argue that the future is actually being shaped in the course of concrete historical engagement in the present. Which is not to say that both do not contain the idea, as David McLellan has put it, 'that history has a purpose that is being relentlessly worked out and a powerful vision of future harmony to contrast with present discord':[49] but both will want to avoid the charge of 'idealism' and, in the pejoratively Marxian sense, 'utopianism', often laid at the door of any form of socialism lacking some scientific analysis of the existing conditions or the possibilities for change. Notwithstanding this, Assmann has suggested that where (as in Latin America) 'the political situation and the urgency of the struggle . . . tended to lead left-wing groups to reduce to a minimum their statement of a clear historical project', Christians had a real contribution to make in the area of offering 'plans for the objectives of liberation in the form of a historical project . . .'[50]

The way in which we can begin to support such an assertion, and move towards identifying something more distinctive in the concept of the kingdom, is by examining two of its central features, both of which are intimately connected; the *depth* of the revolution for which it calls at the level of the individual and the social, and its inherently *eschatological* nature. Nicholas Lash has suggested that the 'transformation of [people], and hence of patterns of social relationship, envisaged in the Christian proclamation of the reign of God, is far more radical than that envisaged by any political movement, including Marxism', and this is so because Christian hope is always yet to be fully realized; it envisages a depth of liberation which no actual political or social movement can realize or satisfy.[51] Both these features have critical and practical repercussions in the political realm.

Again, claims for 'distinctiveness' in this area may need some qualification. On the first point, for example, the question may be raised as to how far Christian hopes for the transformation of the individual can be distinguished from the Marxist-Leninist concept of the social-ist so-called 'new person' (or, to be historically authentic, 'new man'!). Clearly, in so far as Christianity announces the possibility of a 'new creation' it suggests a transformation qualitatively different from that of Marx, for whom the advent of communist society, while it would allow the full realization of human potential hitherto suppressed by an alienated existence under capitalism, would not involve a *total* transformation of human nature.[52] José Miranda may well be right when he argues that 'not even in Marx do we find such a strong expression of . . . total transformation as that coined by Paul in the term "new creation"', though claims by Gutiérrez that 'the life and preaching of Jesus postulate the unceasing search for a new kind of [person] in a qualitatively different society', must be set alongside comments such as Che Guevara's that 'in [the] period of the construc-tion of Socialism, we can see the new man being born. His image is as yet unfinished; in fact, it will never be finished, for the process advances parallel to the development of new economic forms . . .'[53] One important function of any transformation of men and women, though, must be the overcoming of what Rosemary Radford Ruether calls a 'lust for domination', and here the example of Jesus can be of value in so far as he offers a new concept of leadership based on service to others – even unto death – rather than power. As Ruether writes, unless the hunger for power is overcome, any successful revolu-tion will simply replace one domination with another; yet 'in the new community based on the life of service to others, the lust for domination will be overcome at its source'.[54]

We can make three points here, the latter two perhaps more concrete than the first. Firstly, even if their claims in the area of individual transformation might not be wholly distinctive, Christians may still contribute alongside others in the revolutionary process, using their own categories of sin, redemption and conversion; secondly, the central-ity of the 'qualitatively new human' to the kingdom does, in contrast to some revolutionary projections, have important consequences now in terms of the ethics of revolutionary struggle; and thirdly, the eschatological nature of the kingdom encourages a permanently critical stance towards all historical events, however liberative, since it recognizes that the full and total transformation of individuals, and their social relationships, will only be fully realized with the advent of the kingdom, in the direction of which it therefore seeks to stimulate all revolutionary activity. We shall consider the last of these points now, and the second in a moment.

It has been suggested that it is in so far as it maintains its *eschatological* dimension that the kingdom can perform a critical or judgemental role *vis-à-vis* revolutionary activity, and in view of the earlier critique of Winstanley and Müntzer, it is necessary to make clear precisely what is meant by this term. We have already argued that there were weaknesses in the eschatological perspectives of both men, not in the sense that they discerned a *kairos* or directed their praxis towards the establishment of the reign of God, but in so far as they anticipated that reign being inaugurated immediately. With similar force, though, another common position within the Christian tradition should be disclaimed, that which, while it avoids the reductionism of a Winstanley or a Müntzer with its propensity to read historical events in terms of the fulfilment of the promise of the kingdom, does so at the price of acknowledging there to be *any* relationship between the kingdom and the process of history. According to this scheme the kingdom is an essentially *spiritual* entity, God's activity in the world being confined to redemption from the power of sin in the individual sphere of life and the rescuing of souls for the next; and while such a conception of the kingdom can clearly complement and deepen a broader 'political' one, it implies, when taken alone, a form of historical dualism according to which the kingdom comes into being apart from, and indeed incidental to, the linear path of history. Since it is predicated upon an individual's 'vertical' relationship with God rather than upon social relations *between* individuals, it is being established whatever historical circumstances obtain; it assumes, in fact, as Denys Turner puts it, that 'the history which Christians are struggling to write is governed by some higher text *which has already been written* and to which they have privileged access'.[55] An eschatological perspective of this sort would tend more towards an accommodation to present conditions than to historical action, and be possessed of no greater applicability in the realm of political struggle than that embraced by those with a 'reductionist millenarianism'; and so clearly what is needed, if Christianity is to make any meaningful contribution to the revolutionary cause, is an eschatology which is neither fideistic nor reductionist but which somehow operates between the two – which is, in other words, both historically-referenced and future-orientated. As already indicated, the suggestion in liberation theology that the kingdom may operate at the level of utopia is of help here, to the extent that it emphasizes its function (using Freire's terminology) of 'denouncing' the old order and 'announcing' the new, though there is a more profound relationship between the kingdom, history and the future which it would be useful to explore.

If we look again at some of the thinking done by political theologians in the southern hemisphere, one of their most helpful insights, not least for our purposes, is that which identifies the kingdom as both a present *and* a future reality – or, to put it more precisely, the kingdom as present *partially* within history but, in terms of its full realization, always a future event. (It is perhaps hardly necessary to point out that in this scheme the 'two histories' model is explicitly rejected in favour of an integral one which sees Christ's redemptive work as embracing all dimensions of life to bring them to completeness.) The growth of the kingdom, then, is to be discerned within 'liberative' events in history – where liberation means greater human fulfilment – but these events or signs, either individually or collectively, are not *the* kingdom in its fullness. As Leonardo and Clodovis Boff have put it, 'the kingdom of God is something more than historical liberations, which are always limited and open to further perfectioning, but it is anticipated and incarnated in them in time, in preparation for its full realization with the coming of the new heaven and the new earth'.[56] The mission of Jesus himself demonstrates this: although he was actively opposed to the authorities of his day, the main point, as McLellan has summarized it, 'is that, for Jesus, the liberation of the Jewish people was only part of a universal revolution with more profound and permanent consequences than could be encompassed by the political liberation of a single people'.[57]

The kingdom, then, has a place both in history and in God's eschatological time; or, to adopt somewhat more dynamic terminology, it is both 'already' and 'not yet'. Indeed, 'dynamic' describes well the relationship between the kingdom and history: Harvey Cox articulates the possibility of speaking of 'an eschatology which is *in process of realizing itself*', and as Míguez Bonino writes, 'The Kingdom is not . . . the natural dénouement of history. Quite the contrary, history arrives at the Kingdom through suffering, conflict, and judgement . . . History, in relation to the Kingdom, is not a riddle to be solved but a mission to be fulfilled.'[58] Nicholas Lash and Christopher Rowland have drawn suggestive analogies with the Eucharist in the Christian tradition, which not only exhibits criteria by which all that is imperfect in our social relationships may be judged, but also, as a 'parable' or 'pledge' of our 'future glory', anticipates with each celebration 'the glory it proclaims'. Not that this anticipation takes the form of a 'precise preview' of our future, which remains hidden in God; but the Eucharist does link, in however tenuous a way, the present and the future in so far as it 'declares, announces, celebrates the fact that, in God's time and way, "all shall be well . . ."'.[59]

To place the kingdom within this eschatological tension has, it would seem, at least three important consequences. Firstly, as mentioned before, it has ethical implications for the conduct of revolutionary struggle, in the sense that if the kingdom is both future *and* partially anticipated in the present, then the future makes ethical demands on present praxis to realize it; and this will be explored shortly. Secondly, it suggests the possibility of discovering a deeper level of meaning to the process of history, and to this we shall also return later. And thirdly it enables Christians to exercise what Rowland has called a 'continuous critique of every project and institution, whether temporal or spiritual, in the light of the reign of peace and justice to come'.[60] Christians, in other words, will recognize the penultimate and partial character of all achievements in the direction of the kingdom, and, following Augustine, never sanctify any one particular system but rather affirm that all – even the best imaginable – are flawed and under the judgement of God.[61] But retaining a permanently critical perspective towards individual revolutionary 'successes' is only possible if this temptation to 'absolutize' the kingdom, to identify it wholly with any one political event, is overcome. What must be maintained, in other words, is the *transcendence* of the kingdom over against all historical projects, since it is only on this basis that the kingdom can exercise its vital critical role. For as we observed with Winstanley, when this transcendence is lost, when Christians invest all their hope in the realization of one particular project on the basis of an identification of that project with the reign of God, the consequence of the failure or 'turning in on itself' of that project will be, not only an individual or collective crisis of faith, but the devaluation of the kingdom as a model or vision for revolutionary enterprise.

For some, this line of argument can form part of a response to the central question of this book. Terry Eagleton, for example, taking up this theme in the 1970s, suggested that Christians can promote (in a term he acknowledged as Trotsky's) a form of 'permanent revolution' or 'revolution within the revolution', and concluded that 'on this theory, the distinctive practice of revolutionary Christianity lies in its permanently critical, negative, transcending role within a revolutionary society . . .'[62] Writing from a similar theological and political perspective (and chronological distance!), Herbert McCabe also speaks of Christians embracing the concept of the permanent revolution, and of their being those 'for whom the coming of the kingdom demands a continual remaking of institutions and of the structures of life and thought'.[63] And Arthur Rich has also argued for a specifically Christian contribution to revolution in the form of 'the theological task of proclaiming that no revolution can bring about the kingdom of God – which is to say, the total solution of our afflictions in this world'.[64]

These comments can take us some way towards finding a positive response to the question of a distinctive Christian contribution to revolutionary politics, in so far as they suggest that an eschatological perspective which recognizes *partial* or 'germinal'[65] evidences of the kingdom in history, but the full realization of it to be always 'up ahead', can offer a perpetual critique of historical struggles and an incitement towards new and deeper possibilities of liberation. As John Marsden has well put it, ' . . . if the Christian hope of the coming Kingdom of God implies a power which is also manifest *within* human history, then far from hindering the revolutionary process, this hope provides the power and impetus for the transformation of historical conditions'.[66]

Again, though, this is not to suggest that Christianity has a *unique* role to play in this respect: Marxism, except perhaps in its extreme Stalinist form, is hardly inclined towards a fetishizing of the socialist order, and indeed sees revolution as the inauguration rather than the culmination of human history. As James Klugmann has argued, the Marxist vision of the future is open, stretching 'ever-changing into infinity', aware that people 'will always be engaged in struggle against nature, will always find new aims, new needs, and in changing nature, will always change themselves' – which should not, however, blind us to the fact, as Alistair Kee has pointed out, that Marx's 'whole life and vocation were based on the assumption that it is possible to achieve at last something like a secular version of the Kingdom of God on earth'.[67] Whatever the case, even if 'a monopoly of continuous criticism' is not to be cornered by the Church so that it becomes, in Eagleton's words, 'simply one element within a series of "Left Oppositions"', it does nevertheless, on that level, offer a singular contribution.[68]

There are at least two difficulties to be faced with this line of argument, however. The first is the possibility that the concept of the kingdom may ultimately prove too abstract to be of use in concrete political struggle, that its transcendence may be emphasized to the extent that it ceases to be recognizable by other revolutionaries as related in any way to the struggle in which they are engaged. The praxis of Christians, in other words, orientated towards the kingdom, could become increasingly tangential to the historical process to which they suppose themselves to be committed, such that they are, in fact, fighting a different revolution. Richard Shaull, for example, warns of the danger of Christians perceiving only 'a relative coincidence of direction' in certain situations between the revolution and 'God's humanising action in the world',[69] and in Eagleton's reflections cited above this danger is not far below the surface: for him, the price of drawing a distinction between Christianity and Marxism on the grounds that, according to the former, 'the kingdom is of God and not just of man', is the postulation of a future state which appears to bear little or no resemblance to the sort of socio-economic order towards which Marxist praxis is directed. Marxists, Eagleton says, must face the reality that their project could be 'scuppered' for good by 'a few well-placed nuclear missiles'; the revolution, in other words, can be irrevocably lost. For the Christian, however, this cannot be so, even if history does end in a nuclear holocaust, 'for the kingdom does not come as top Doh in the lyrically ascending tune of history' but is in revolutionary continuity 'not with the final state to which human history arrives, but with the underlying significant trajectory of history itself: the project of building human community, of which the Church is sacrament'. Revolutionary Christian faith, then, is characterized by a 'certainty that the struggle will finally bear fruit, if not on this side of history, then on the far side of the *parousia*'.[70] Notwithstanding that he entitles his book *First the Political Kingdom*, Brian Wicker displays a similar tendency in this work when he describes the whole purpose of the revolution, both within the Church and within society, in terms of 'leav[ing] the field clear for the coming of Christ'.[71]

Perhaps Karl Barth's comments on Romans 13 demonstrate most clearly the distinction that Christians will want to draw between 'revolution' attempted at a human level and 'the Revolution' which is God's prerogative. Barth perceives in Paul a profoundly revolutionary attitude towards human rulers, but not a mandate for human projects to bring them low through revolutionary struggle. For Barth, it is *God* who stands ultimately in judgement over all existing orders, *God* who is the 'minus sign' suspended against all existing orders, and *God* who alone can effect the true Revolution and create the wholly new. Thus even the most radical humanly-engineered revolutions essentially change nothing: they do no more than set what *exists* against what *exists*, and lead to the restoration of the old in a new and more powerful form.[72] For Barth, then, 'no revolution, however radical, which takes place within the realm of history, can ever be identical with the divine minus sign outside the bracket, by which the totality of human ordinances is dissolved'.[73] This sounds disturbingly close to a call for passivity – a stance which of course Barth famously did not adopt in his own life – until it is realized that what is in fact advocated is the ultimate act of nonconformity and challenge to the present powers, the practice of love, one of another. Love for Barth is the 'GREAT Positive Possibility . . . because it is veritably concerned with the denial and breaking up of the existing order . . . by love we do the "new" by which the "old" is overthrown'.[74]

As these comments make clear, in so far as Christians understand the kingdom to be *ultimately* God's prerogative, and forbear ever to identify it fully with any concrete historical project, tension between the two will be inevitable. Yet it must also be said – and this is the second issue we must confront – that the kingdom, if it is to have any real significance, must be held to be ultimately a future *event*. Christians, in other words, may want to stress with Moltmann the God 'ahead' of us, with Gutiérrez the God who is 'a force in our future', or with Miranda (in *Marx and the Bible*) the God whose very name Yahweh expresses his 'essential futureness';[75] but there must be underlying any conception of the kingdom, if it is to be more than an idle dream (or a 'utopia' in the common, more pejorative, sense of the term), a belief that at some point it is to be realized.[76] Fierro captures the essence of this argument when he coalesces into a single dichotomy the aspirations of Christian revolutionary politics. 'On the one hand', he says

> we might maintain that the Christian hopes for the same thing that other human beings hope for: i.e., a more humane society; the only distinctive element in the Christian hope is that it regards

a more humane society as a promise and gift from God. Or, on the other hand, we might claim that the Christian hopes for something in addition to that hoped for by other human beings: i.e., for a kingdom of God that is to be realized in a future that will transcend history and this world.[77]

The first alternative, which amounts to the view that divine salvation and resurrection are simply the transcendent side of historical liberation, we have explicitly rejected on the grounds that the Christian contribution to revolution cannot be reduced to the mere restatement in theological language of the political aspirations of secular philosophies. To accept the second, however, leads to the dilemma raised above. Before going further, however, we should note that to hold to the ultimate realization of the kingdom is to accept that, in an ultimate sense, Christian eschatology is not as open to the future as are 'secular ideologies', and our comments earlier about the perpetually critical capacity of the kingdom *vis-à-vis* historical praxis may need to be qualified to that extent. Indeed, Klugmann has contrasted Marxism and Christianity precisely on the point that the former's vision of the future is the more open-ended of the two: Marxism differs from aspects of Christian eschatology because 'there is no communist *last* day of judgement, no *final* reckoning, no end'.[78] Fierro is also right to argue that, despite claims by theologians that Christian eschatology serves to prevent the absolutizing of revolution, it is only Christianity that makes any claims for the possibility of an 'absolutely perfect society'.[79] And what is more, of course, the kingdom is to be realized as the result of a divine act, which must be the whole point of claims by, for example, Gutiérrez, that 'the coming of the Kingdom . . . is . . . a gift', and of references in Moltmann to 'the Promise' which speaks of 'the reality which is coming'.[80] For Fierro, using Althusserian categories of knowledge, the proposition that the kingdom will ever 'be' is of course problematic: one can talk meaningfully about 'the future of history' but not 'representations of Christian hope'.[81] Though as Löwy puts it, both Christianity and Marxism 'come down to a question of faith and are not demonstrable on the exclusive level of factual judgements'.[82]

At the heart of Christian revolutionary politics, then, is a tension between, on the one hand, the postulation of an eschatology orientated wholly towards the future – but a future ultimately to be consummated in a kingdom *of God* – and, on the other, a concern for Christian praxis within historical situations to be authentic and meaningful. And while we should not presume that this tension can be resolved at the theoretical level, the key does seem to lie in the central plank of our critique of Winstanley and Müntzer, namely that because all that is known about the *coming* of the kingdom is that it is a promise, in practical terms the Christian will continue to work for what will be recognized as only partial realizations of it, and these within, of course, concrete political projects. I think what Rowland says of Müntzer – that he 'may have been able to recognize when the *Kairos* had come but he did not have the gift of recognizing when the *Kairos* was no longer propitious'[83] – is very apposite here, for where the problem lies is not in holding to a belief that history will at some point be consummated in the kingdom, nor that there can be those liberative events in history which foreshadow the kingdom's final appearance, but in recognizing the difference between the two.

What has been argued, then, is that, *pace* Engels and others, to view the world as a Christian is not *necessarily* to adopt a distorted perspective with regard to the process of history and the possibility for revolutionary change in the political realm. Nor is theological talk always a mere linguistic embellishment, imposed by the conditions of the time and both dispensable and incidental to the true nature of a revolutionary programme. And this claim is made, moreover, not at the price of evacuating Christianity of its eschatological dimension, but, on the contrary, by upholding its absolute centrality to the faith – in short, with Moltmann, recognizing that 'from first to last, and not merely in the epilogue, Christianity is eschatology, is hope, forward looking and forward moving, and therefore also revolutionizing and transforming the present'.[84]

Means and Ends

In our earlier discussion of Winstanley a consistency was perceived between the goal of his revolutionary programme and the means employed to bring it into being, and this is suggestive of a further contribution Christianity may offer to revolutionary politics. Christians, of course, claim no monopoly in the realm of what might be called 'ethical insight', and it would hardly be difficult to cite examples of revolutionaries from within other traditions who have been sensitive to moral considerations. But Christian theology does have a powerful and salutary word to utter within the discourse of revolutionary ethics.

Winstanley, we noted, was concerned that concomitant with structural and institutional transformation should also be individual transformation, affecting both oppressed and oppressors. Only a truly communitarian – that is, moneyless and propertyless – system could guarantee real freedom for all, but only if those who were to enjoy its benefits had themselves already experienced liberation from all the fears and desires generated by the old 'kingly' system; if, in other words, the spirit of co-operation, of 'right reason', had already taken root within them individually. And since by the logic of Winstanley's programme – and the eschatological assumptions underpinning it – the oppressing minority under the kingly system would themselves also be drawn into the momentum of the revolution, they were not to be overthrown by violent means. It is in so far as Winstanley maintains this consistency between the values of the social order he aspired to help create, and the means to be employed in its creation, that he has an important lesson for revolutionary theory, not least since a similar harmony between means and ends is prescribed by the concept of the kingdom, towards the building of which Christian praxis is orientated.

It is worth considering first, however, especially in view of its centrality to Winstanley's programme, the question of non-violence and its alternatives. It was suggested when discussing Winstanley earlier that a non-violent position was not a distinctively or even a necessarily Christian one, and a brief consideration of the stance adopted by more recent Christian revolutionary figures like Camilo Torres and some of the Catholic Sandinistas in Nicaragua might help to suggest why. Torres' perception of the situation in Colombia was that the oppression generated by the system was of such an intensity that it precluded the possibility of Christian love being practised effectively, and a similar conclusion was reached by many Nicaraguans who suffered under the severe Somoza regime. Only by structural change could the gospel command to love – to feed the hungry, clothe the naked, house the homeless and heal the sick – be carried out effectively; and, in the absence of an abdication of power by the ruling oligarchies in the face of majority pressure, the only way to achieve this change, in view of the violence by which those structures were maintained, was to resort to counter-violent measures (which, of course, Torres and many Nicaraguans did). Torres was quite explicit on this point: 'the seizure of power by the majorities must be preached', he wrote; 'The majority must take over the government to change the structures through economic, social, and political reforms that favour the majority. This is called revolution.'[85]

A good deal could and indeed has been written on the ethics of violence in political change,[86] but the central point to be made is that, if violence is inherent in the system to which one is subject, then some engagement with violence cannot be avoided, whatever response is made to that system. As Rosemary Radford Ruether has put it, where there exists a situation of total violence 'there is no way to protest or struggle without evoking violence. Violence is already the dominant reality.' The Christian, she argues, 'should be primarily with those who suffer rather than those who inflict suffering, even on the oppressors. But in real struggle, there is no way to keep one's hands clean.'[87] Any programme to overthrow the system, in other words, will have to recognize that violent measures will be necessary if it is to succeed, while to opt not to join such a revolutionary programme is, in effect, to side with those enforcing the system. Either way violence is endorsed, though it is of course imperative to address the question of the circumstances in which its use could be said to be legitimate and illegitimate. J. G. Davies argues in favour of distinguishing between the terms 'violence' and 'force', and maintains that a valid distinction can be made between an 'illegitimate' use of force, such as that used by an oppressive regime to uphold its authority, and a 'legitimate' use of force which may be necessary, in response, to achieve justice.[88] Archbishop Oscar Romero, in his third pastoral letter (issued in August 1978), also identified various kinds of violence – including 'institutionalized violence', 'repressive state violence', 'terrorist violence', the spontaneous violence of people attacked for defending their rights, the violence of legitimate self-defence, and the violence of non-violence – noting that the judgement of the Church is different upon each type.[89] It is noteworthy, also, that a resort to violence in the face of 'manifest, long-standing tyranny' was even tacitly accepted by Pope Paul VI in his 1967 encyclical letter *Populorum Progressio*.[90] It is perhaps possible to assert that, while in a strictly moral sense violence can never be 'good', that is not to say that it is never 'right'.

In situations of structural or institutional violence, therefore, the point would seem to be that it is not only the violent response that has to be justified but also the *non*-violent. The latter may appear superficially to be the more distinctively 'Christian' option, but its effect may ultimately be merely to allow the perpetuation of a *status quo* founded on violence and injustice. Míguez Bonino summarizes the issue helpfully when he contrasts the often rehearsed argument about the 'social cost of structural changes' with the little-recognized 'human cost of postponing such change'. Revolutionary change may sacrifice human lives, but how many more lives are sacrificed 'by prolonging for a century or two a form of production or distribution of goods that has ceased adequately to serve the needs of the people?'[91]

In summary, then, there would appear to be a sense in which it can be argued that the violent course is not *per se* incompatible with the work of building the kingdom; and this is perhaps to make clearer the distinction between the kingdom itself and its 'partial realizations' within history. When the kingdom comes and relationships are perfected, then violence will have no place, but this point has not yet been reached and Christians cannot live as if it had. In seeking to build the kingdom, therefore, they will need to recognize the imperfection of the present situation. The kingdom is about full reconciliation between people, but in the present, where, as Albert Nolan says, it may be necessary to face 'cases of conflict due to injustice and oppression', reconciliation cannot be made 'an *absolute principle* that must be applied in *all* cases of conflict'. '"Bringing the two sides together" in such cases', as Nolan writes, 'is actually extremely beneficial to the oppressor, because it enables the status quo to be maintained; it hides the true nature of the conflict, keeps the oppressed quiet and passive and it brings about a kind of pseudo-reconciliation without justice.'[92] Or as the *Kairos Document*, also written from within the old South Africa, bluntly put it, to have made a plea for reconciliation and peace under the apartheid system *before* the injustices of that system were removed would have been 'totally unChristian' and 'sin'.[93]

There are, of course, major problems with this argument, not the least of which is how, once the use of violence in some form is permitted, a compatibility between individual and structural transformation is maintained. This has been a central concern of Christian advocates of non-violent change like the Brazilian archbishop Hélder Câmara, one of the best-known defenders of this position in Latin America. Like Winstanley he offers a diagnosis of the situation in his part of the world that is as thorough and uncompromising as any revolutionary's, and in fact he does not condemn those who feel called to revolutionary involvement, holding Torres and Che as much in respect as Martin Luther King. But he will not condone their violence, because his priority is individual transformation before political revolution. For him, a revolution which changes structures is not thorough enough and, because it presupposes that a new society can be built without first creating new people to live in it, unworkable. What is needed is individual conversion among people, not as an alternative to structural change but as a prerequisite to it.[94]

Although this position clearly deserves a more thorough consideration than it has received here, to dwell further on it may blur the distinction suggested earlier between commitment to non-violence, which, it was argued, was not a specifically Christian dimension of Winstanley's programme, and concern to achieve consistency between the means and ends of a programme, which arguably was. Thus, on the assumption that the question of a violent response will have to be faced at some point by any serious revolutionary project, and that such a response is not *per se* incompatible with a Christian one, our concern should be to examine the possibility of Christianity having something 'distinctive' to say on that question.

If, as has been argued, the kingdom is both an intrahistorical reality and a future event, then the process by which it is to be built will be governed by the values and qualities of that final state itself. The relationship that exists between the kingdom's (partial) appearance within history and its final manifestation in the future makes it imperative, in other words, for a consistency to be achieved between that full realization and the form and nature of the struggle to achieve it; and thus, in addition to being the future horizon of revolutionary activity, the kingdom will make 'moral demands' on that activity in order that, as Turner has put it, 'a reference to that future is already inscribed in the historical vicissitudes of the present'.[95] In specific terms, if the revolution is about creating the possibility of a fully *human* existence, practices such as indiscriminate or mass killing, terror, torture, wanton destruction and action harmful to those who are neutral will be outlawed. There can be no 'teleological suspension of ethics' as Míguez Bonino writes: 'no human class, group or generation can be considered as merely instrumental', nor human values subordinated to tactical considerations. 'No really human achievement can be obtained through the denial of the humanity of some [people] or of a generation.'[96] Thus the doctrine attributed to Lenin that 'good is what advances the cause of the revolution' will be rejected *on principle* by the Christian, who will argue that not *all* means can be appropriate, that the success of the revolution is not to be achieved at *any* cost. Indeed, 'success' in the sense of the historical realization of a project is not the be-all and end-all of Christian revolutionary praxis, which, as a consequence of its concern for ethical consistency and fidelity to gospel values, may well issue ultimately in projects which, from a utilitarian perspective, might appear to be 'unsuccessful' – like, in fact, digging the commons. But then, as Rowland has put it, from such a perspective the gospel is itself 'a story of "ineffectiveness" and of apparently "futile gestures"'.[97]

One powerful effect of this orientation will be the stance it suggests toward the oppressor. We noted earlier that one of Winstanley's particular concerns was that even those who oppressed the Diggers and upheld the kingly power should, so far from being 'eliminated', not be excluded from sharing in the new society or from the work of creating it. Winstanley was never so naive as to imagine that the oppressing class would voluntarily relinquish its privileges and power in the face of a revolutionary challenge; yet the logic of his position was that, as the revolution gathered momentum, those opposed to it would be swept along by it, either because Christ or Reason had begun to rise up in them (as in all people), or as a consequence of the gradual erosion of their power base.

To draw out a theological point here, the Christian seeks through revolution the emancipation not only of the oppressed but also of the oppressor. In an 'evangelical' spirit, the believer offers to those who oppress an opportunity to rediscover their full humanity by opening themselves up to others (and therefore to God). Because their confinement within the structures of society is somewhat more comfortable in nature than that of the oppressed, they are likely to reject this offer of 'liberation', yet in forcing through the revolution against their wishes the Christian revolutionary acts consistently with the praxis of Jesus who, as Jon Sobrino has put it, 'out of love for the poor . . . took his stand *with* them; out of love for the rich . . . took his stand *against* them'.[98]

Underpinning this thesis is an important distinction, which a 'kingdom' perspective suggests, between opposition to one's enemies and hatred of them. As McCabe has argued,

It is not a question of vindictive violence against individuals seen as personally wicked; the revolutionary, who will reject all conspiracy theories of society, is the last person to blame the corrupt social order on the misdeeds of individuals; there is no place for such infantile hatred in the revolution. However difficult it may be to see this, the revolution is for the sake of the exploiter as well as the exploited.[99]

'There are contexts in which there just is and will be violence, and the problem is how to make it redemptive.'[100] McCabe also suggests that an eschatology which understands the present and the future to be in direct continuity, which recognizes Christ as 'not only the Omega point' but one who 'lives in us even now', makes possible a 'genuine *forgiveness*' and an ability to love 'both the just and the unjust'. This does not make the unjust any less unjust, he writes, or diminish the requirement that they be overthrown, 'but it does, in the end, make hatred impossible'.[101] Violence is thus not to be confused with hate: as Severino Croatto has put it, love and hate are opposite poles, not love and violence.[102]

It would be wrong to suppose that adequate answers to these questions can or should be worked out at the level of theory, nor can we avoid the fact that the Bible itself does not unambiguously denounce 'enmity and hatred'; such concepts, far from being absent, are unashamedly attributed to the pioneers of the faith, and even to Godself. But these are questions which Christians are surely right to raise if the ultimate object of political praxis is the reality of a 'new person' in a new community of sister- and brotherhood. They present paradoxes, but not, perhaps, ultimately contradictions.

The Revolutionary Gospel

One characteristic we observed as common to the writings of both Müntzer and Winstanley was a rejection of the traditional formulations of the Christian faith promulgated by the forces of reaction of their day, and the radical re-presentation of core doctrines the better to release the revolutionary potential of the Christian gospel; and such activity may point the way towards a further distinctive contribution to the praxis of revolution which Christians have to offer.[103] Hugo Assmann, for example, has recognized the value to revolutionary struggle of a process of what he calls 'breaching the superstructure',

superstructure here being used in the precise Marxian sense to refer to the political, legal and religious forms in society which arise from, and to an extent reflect, the 'base' of that society, namely 'the economic structure' or relations of production. 'If one analyzes the impact made to date by the presence of Christians in liberation movements', Assmann writes, 'the area in which they have been most effective is that of the superstructure represented by traditional bourgeois values, in which they have opened a major breach'.[104] Míguez Bonino has observed, too, that in so far as Christianity has been 'co-opted into the present oppressive structures and is constantly manipulated for their preservation, a Christian faith which has rediscovered its revolutionary vocation can explode this reactionary instrumentalising of Christianity from within and thus unblock the conscience of Christians for an effective revolutionary participation'.[105] For revolution to succeed in a religious context, therefore, it is essential for religion to be given a 'revolutionary' political interpretation: 'there will be no "theology of revolution"', as Moltmann has said, 'until there is a revolution in theology'.[106] And this re-theologizing, it is argued, can be most effectively undertaken from within the Church itself.

The substance of this argument is that one priority for revolutionary Christians, at least in regions where very deep religious cultures subsist, must be to work to end the Church's traditionally close ties with the ruling elites, and rescue from the ideological use to which they have been put, for a more 'revolutionary' interpretation, the message, symbols and practices of the Christian faith. Theology has to keep alive what Johann Baptist Metz (after Walter Benjamin) has called the 'dangerous memory' of the people,[107] their own fragile accounts of their identity and history which are in radical and subversive contradistinction to 'official' and potentially overpowering interpretations of 'the way things really are'. Exploding the 'reactionary instrumentalising of Christianity from within', therefore, implies both the release of the faithful from slavish adherence to expressions of Christianity promulgated by the forces of reaction and conservatism, and the recovery and retelling of their own story of oppression and marginalization, thereby to provide a dynamic for revolutionary change. Indeed, as Karen Lebacqz argues, such storytelling is a vital imperative, since the people's knowledge of 'justice' is grounded in their memory of God's dealings with them: 'if the story is not told, justice will die'.[108]

Central to this argument is a recognition that, in societies where the majority follow the Church's teaching in all areas of life, whatever *political* expression – consciously or unconsciously – is given to religion will be very influential; indeed, the right to determine what constitutes 'knowledge' is an object of all political struggle, no less within the Church than without. The development of a political consciousness must therefore involve engagement with what Mary Grey has called 'a structured amnesia, a structural blotting out of the voices of resistance, the voices of all who are "Other" to the dominant story', together with a hearing of those voices in order to give *their* story 'a privileged place in the discourse and to construct from it an alternative politics of truth'.[109]

There is a strong general case to be made on empirical grounds for the value of a Christian contribution of this sort to the revolutionary project. The process of 'going to the poor' which preoccupied some sections of the Catholic Church in Latin America in the 1950s and 1960s (and led to the Church's articulation of 'a preferential option for the poor') is a case in point. Here, among a people where for centuries a highly spiritualized and fatalistic form of Christianity had been a virtual fact of life, a process of demythologizing (after, for example, the teaching of Freire) the social order, and demonstrating that poverty and suffering were not divinely ordained but rooted in humanly constructed and therefore transformable economic and political arrangements, had profound consequences in raising the political consciousness of many communicants. And the more so, when, as political aspirations were aroused, they were given solid expression within a new theological framework which stressed that God, far from ordaining or even condoning conditions of inequality, slavery and injustice, actually takes the side of the poor – and, as the narrative of the Exodus, for example, testifies, has for an ultimate purpose their liberation from captivity. The roots of the revolutionary process in Nicaragua have also been traced back to the Church's *concientización* work in the preceding decades, and Ivan Vallier has recorded how in Colombia in the late 1960s a group of priests influenced by the example of Camilo Torres attempted with some success to build an oppositional movement to the ruling elite.[110]

On a more theoretical level there are perhaps two questions to ask about this general thesis that Christianity has a role to play in the revolutionary process at the level of the superstructure. The first recognizes that, according to a materialist conception of history, the initial priority for a revolutionary movement should be the reconstruction of the economic base of society rather than the superstructure which arises from it. Assmann recognizes the force of this point, but argues that Christian activity directed at the superstructure can be of value in Latin America – the context out of which he is writing – when one takes into account the peculiar features of that continent, in particular the 'relative autonomy' of the elements which make up the superstructure. This is the level, he argues, where many obstacles to the revolutionary process are to be found, notably the prevalence of *petit bourgeois* values and the tendency towards passivity and acquiescence among the people; and these are obstacles, moreover, which owe much to 'pseudo-Christian traditions and values both in origin and maintenance'. Assmann also argues that to hold to a materialist understanding of history is not to be committed to the view that the focus of political activity must *exclusively* be economic relations, and cites evidence of a non-dogmatic stance on this point by Marx and Engels: in a letter to Joseph Bloch in September 1890 Engels wrote that although 'the *ultimately* determining element in history is the production and reproduction of real life . . . the various elements of the superstructure . . . also exercise their influence upon the course of the historical struggles and in many cases preponderate in determining their *form*'.[111]

A second objection to the usefulness of this contribution could be raised on the grounds that it can only possibly have any relevance in societies and cultures where religion has traditionally played a significant if not central role. Che Guevara's famous prognostication about the invincibility of the revolution once Christians 'dare to give a revolutionary testimony',[112] or the Sandinista Luis Carrión's statement that 'Religion is a strong ideological force that can hinder or accelerate the coming to consciousness of the people', would hardly make any sense if uttered, for example, in a pluralist culture like that of modern Britain.[113] Nevertheless, as Kee has shown, the work of trying to liberate Christianity from identification with authoritarianism and oppression, the more easily to incorporate it into the consciousness-raising process, has also been undertaken with effect among deeply religious groups within a largely alien culture, for example, blacks in the United States. Kee notes attempts by James Cone, Albert Cleage and others to 'break the identification of Christianity with the white community'; to show that the racism practised by many mainstream churches in the States was not the only expression, if indeed it was an expression at all, of Christianity; and to show, moreover, that Christianity, 'if properly understood, was concerned with precisely the issues of freedom and humanity which were central to Black Power'.[114] The name of Cleage's church in Detroit, the Shrine of the Black Madonna, and the title of his major work, *The Black Messiah*, offer clues as to how this work of rescuing Christianity from white hands is to be approached. The project of mainstream feminist theologians in differing cultures to release God-talk and all the language and symbolism of Christianity from centuries of service to patriarchy and male domination and hegemony, and to recover and retell the stories of women of faith hitherto hidden in histories of the Church written by, for and about males, is another example of the potency and effectiveness of this 'contribution'.

One further thing this argument suggests is that the negativity of those writers who deny the possibility of any sort of distinctive Christian contribution to revolutionary politics lacks a degree of subtlety and refinement. Even if it was true, as Kee notes, that for US black theology Black Power set the agenda,[115] Christian attempts to create a breach for that movement within the churches were clearly going to be a *sine qua non* for socio-economic change, given the deep religious commitment of the people and the historical influence of the 'White Man's religion'. And much the same can be said with respect to Latin America, where even if questions of political analysis and strategy were settled by reference to Marxism, revolutionaries had also to reckon with a strong traditional religiosity – the legacy of their oppressors and their political descendants – and its profound effect on the consciousness of the people.

A Deeper Meaning to the Struggle?

Our project has so far led us to explore, among others, the eschatological, the utopian, and the ethical dimensions of the faith, yet if there is one Christian doctrine which more than any other would seem suggestive in terms of distinctive Christian practice it would be the resurrection of the body; and so, in conclusion, let us consider briefly the question of a place for this teaching in revolutionary theory and praxis.

In the course of our earlier consideration of Müntzer we hinted at the possibility that belief in an after-life may in some sense increase the Christian's 'availability' for revolutionary participation, and allow theology to help uncover a 'deeper meaning' to political struggle. Following a similar train of thought, Míguez Bonino has suggested that only on the basis of a conviction that death is not the end can one make sense of the human *cost* of the struggle, the self-sacrifice of those revolutionaries who are 'ready to go beyond what is demanded, to pay in their own person . . . the cost of transformation'; 'only a faith that transcends death', he writes, 'can responsibly undertake the awful decision of indispensable but costly transformations'. In a passage which echoes our earlier discussion of the kingdom, Míguez Bonino argues that, for Christians, because tragedy, suffering and death do not have the last word, and because beyond all our own efforts lies the certainty of God's own promise 'there is nothing contradictory, but quite to the contrary, the deepest secret and ethos of Christian spirituality, in Paul's paradoxical exhortation: "Rejoice in suffering!"'[116] Indeed, Moltmann argues that Christians ought to be the 'joyous revolutionaries' because they recognize that, 'even in martyrdom, a revolution can look like a procession of the liberated'. With their belief that God is present in the revolution Christians ought to 'laugh and sing and dance as the first to be liberated in creation'![117]

While recognizing that Marx himself was a man of deep compassion and sensitivity, Míguez Bonino's view is that Marxism suffers from a profound inability to make sense of the deep experiences – 'joy, personal fulfilment, hope and love' – which many revolutionaries, through their commitment, beautifully illustrate.[118] Taking the question further, Lash alludes to the 'abstract character' of Marx's account of human essence, 'an account unduly neglectful of the mortality both of the individual *and* of the species'.[119] Klugmann offers a partial corrective to this argument from a Marxist perspective: 'Death is never easy', he writes, ' . . . [b]ut a Communist who helps to bring about the advance of humanity sees himself living in those that he leaves behind. Armed with the feeling that his contribution has been worthwhile he can look death in the eyes.'[120] This was a judgement echoed by the French Marxist Roger Garaudy (who later converted to Catholicism) when he spoke of Marxists conceiving life as having an 'eternal dimension' in the sense that the individual is defined in terms of her or his relationship with others and with all human beings 'in the totality of their history'.[121]

To the Christian, the concepts of *resurrection* and *immortality* suggest a deeper understanding of humanity itself, of the intrinsic worth of the individual, and therefore of the meaning and praxis of liberation, which must ultimately include liberation from death. Assmann recognizes something of this when he suggests that the direction in which we should look for a 'specifically Christian contribution' is in 'what is specifically and fully human, in the line of fidelity to all that is involved materially in loving one's neighbour'. This is not a theoretical point, he argues, since Christians have an overall vision of humankind's ultimate purpose to urge us into action. Marxism's deficiencies in this area are also made plain: 'A truly historical reading of the Bible', Assmann writes, 'particularly of the message of Christ, leads to a whole series of radical questions to which Marxism has not paid sufficient attention, of which perhaps the most significant is the Christian affirmation of victory over death, that final alienation to which Marxism can find no satisfactory answer.' For Assmann the central point of the Christian's affirmation of victory over death is not the (potentially selfish) belief in 'something after death', but the importance, underlined by the resurrection of Jesus from the dead, of *life*, human life: 'Since life is God's "medium", he also wants it to be [our] sphere above all else', and when this is understood 'we come to the marrow of the loving mystery of what it means to risk one's life for one's fellow[s]. Marxism asks all revolutionaries to be prepared to do this, but I do not believe it can really answer the question of the human sense of laying down one's life for others – so deeply relevant to revolutionary practice – nor that it has really tried to see the importance of the problem.'[122]

Eagleton also makes the connection between an eschatological hope and a preparedness to lay down one's life, and argues that, as a consequence of their certainty with respect to both the coming of the kingdom *and* their place within it, there may be a specific space in the revolutionary struggle which Christians may be particularly suited to fill. What distinguishes Christians from certain other types of revolutionary is that they are neither utilitarian with regard to their own death, nor adventurist with regard to revolutionary engagement. Their perception of a 'deeper dimension' to revolutionary struggle rescues them from the former: their conviction that what might be lost to history might nevertheless be rescued for the kingdom means that their faith makes its difference felt most in situations where the fight seems historically fairly hopeless. And their certainty with regard both to the coming of the kingdom *and* of their place within it leads them, not to mere adventurism, but to a greater readiness to die than the revolutionary 'for whom the future society must, inevitably, be radically unsure, and for whom personal death is an absolute end'. All of which leads Eagleton to suggest that

> what would be extremely useful to any revolutionary movement would be the presence of a number of [people] who believed that what hinged on the degree of intensity with which they fought was not simply historical liberation for themselves and others, but eternal life. A number of non-Christian revolutionaries of my acquaintance would certainly be prepared to die, and gladly, if they thought that the action had a reasonable chance of furthering the revolutionary cause; not many, understandably, would be ready to face extinction if the chances of political victory were extremely slender. Yet there comes a point, in many revolutionary processes, where a precarious twilight area opens up between calculative probability on the one hand, and self-squandering adventurism on the other; and this may just be the area that Christians are called on to occupy.[123]

For Moltmann, the eschatological perspective of revolutionary Christians suggests for them a role as 'the fools of revolution', those who, while being deeply committed to it, can at the same time laugh about it '*because* they are the forerunners of a yet greater revolution, in which God will abolish even greater oppositions than any human revolution can envision'.[124]

The doctrine of the resurrection is bound up very closely with what has been the central theme of this whole essay, the kingdom of God; it has something to say about the kingdom both in the sense of its being a future reality, and in the emphasis it places on the importance of keeping human values to the forefront of the struggle. We are back, in other words, with the question of eschatology, and the contribution that the doctrine of resurrection may be thought to make to the revolution must be seen in the light of our earlier discussions. What, perhaps, could be underlined in conclusion is the claim that the Christian's confession of faith in the resurrection of the body and the life everlasting is not to be understood in terms of a selfish hanging on to life, nor compensation for one lived in misery and oppression, but rather a confident affirmation of the ultimate triumph of God's love, of God's identification with humankind, and of the coming reign of God's kingdom of justice and peace. It is this eschatological faith which makes it possible for Christians to invest their lives in the struggle for a temporary and imperfect human order, with the certainty that neither they nor their effort will ultimately be meaningless or lost.

NOTES

Notes to Introduction

1. I share the current general unease about the term 'kingdom' with its androcentric and monarchical overtones, but have retained it for the most part here because it has become such common currency and any change might seem distracting. The term 'kin-dom' used by, among others, my colleague Mary Grey (see for example 'Epilogue' in Mary John Mananzan *et al.*, eds, *Women Resisting Violence*, NY, Orbis, 1996, pp. 173f) has a certain appeal, as does (for more reasons than one) 'commonwealth', once suggested to me by another colleague, Andrée Heaton. (I notice that Bishop Peter Selby used this term in a recent lecture (see *Theology*, May/June 1995, p. 166), so perhaps it will catch on.) When used in this text, 'kingdom' can be taken to mean 'a domination-free order', an expression coined by Walter Wink, in *Engaging the Powers*, NY, Fortress, 1992, which seems to encapsulate the vision of it held by Jesus himself. This order, Wink writes, is characterized by 'partnership', 'interdependence' and 'mutual respect between men and women that cuts across all distinctions between people'; to which I would add that, when we reach it, our relations with one another will not be mediated in any way, whether through a 'market' or any other system or mechanism.

Notes to Chapter 1

1. Georg Theodor Strobel, *Leben, Schriften und Lehren Thomae Müntzers, des Urhebers des Bauernaufruhrs in Thüringen*, Nürnberg, 1795.
2. Tom Scott, *Thomas Müntzer: Theology and Revolution in the German Reformation*, London, Macmillan, 1989, p. xvii.
3. Hans-Jürgen Goertz, *Thomas Müntzer: Apocalyptic Mystic and Revolutionary*, tr. Jocelyn Jaquiery, ed. Peter Matheson, Edinburgh, T. & T. Clark, 1993, pp. 31ff.
4. CW 362.
5. CW 6, n. 1.

6. This was the view of, for example, Ernst Bloch; see Goertz, *Thomas Müntzer*, pp. 33–4.
7. See CW 36, n. 223.
8. The expression 'the fiery love of purity' possibly reflects the influence of mystical writers in Müntzer's circle of friends at this time.
9. See for example Scott, *Thomas Müntzer*, p. 9, and the letter from the rector of St Martin's School, Brunswick, to Müntzer in CW 9–12.
10. CW 447–50.
11. For a discussion of the possible order in which these were written see CW 353–4.
12. See CW 439, and Scott, *Thomas Müntzer*, pp. 167–8.

Notes to Chapter 2

1. Hans-Jürgen Goertz, *Innere und äussere Ordnung in der Theologie Thomas Müntzers*, Leyden, 1967; 'The Mystic with the Hammer: Thomas Müntzer's Theological Basis for Revolution', *The Mennonite Quarterly Review*, 50, 1976, p. 91.
2. See Peter Matheson, 'Christianity as Insurrection', *Scottish Journal of Theology*, 44, 1991, pp. 321–2.
3. Georg Theodor Strobel, *Leben, Schriften und Lehren Thomae Müntzers, des Urhebers des Bauernaufruhrs in Thüringen*, Nürnberg, 1795.
4. Gordon Rupp, *Patterns of Reformation*, London, Epworth Press, 1969, p. 255, and *Thomas Müntzer, Hans Huth and the 'Gospel of All Creatures'*, Manchester, The John Rylands Library, 1961, p. 494.
5. CW 17; cf. Reinhard Schwarz, 'Thomas Müntzer und die Mystik', in Siegfried Bräuer and Helmar Junghans, eds, *Der Theologe Thomas Müntzer: Untersuchungen zu seiner Entwicklung und Lehre*, Göttingen, Vandenhoeck & Ruprecht, 1989, pp. 284–5; Rupp, *Patterns*, pp. 277–8, n. 2.
6. James M. Stayer, 'Thomas Müntzer's Theology and Revolution in Recent Non-Marxist Interpretation', *Mennonite Quarterly Review*, 43, 1969, pp. 146, 147, 150; cf. Rupp, *Patterns*, pp. 282–3, and Thomas Nipperdey, 'Theology and Revolution in Thomas Müntzer', in James M. Stayer and Werner O. Packull, tr. & eds, *The Anabaptists and Thomas Müntzer*, Dubuque, Iowa, & Toronto, Kendall/Hunt, 1980, p. 108.
7. Peter Matheson, 'Thomas Müntzer's *Vindication and Refutation*: A Language for the Common People?', *Sixteenth Century Journal*, 20, 1989, p. 605.

8. cf. CW 214, n. 1.

9. Schwarz, 'Thomas Müntzer und die Mystik', pp. 285–6.

10. See Schwarz, 'Thomas Müntzer und die Mystik', pp. 286–7.

11. Christopher Rowland, *Radical Christianity: A Reading of Recovery*, Cambridge, Polity Press, 1988, p. 97.

12. Rupp, *Patterns*, p. 283.

13. Goertz, 'The Mystic with the Hammer', pp. 102–3; see also Nipperdey, 'Theology and Revolution in Thomas Müntzer', p. 115, and James M. Stayer, *The German Peasants' War and Anabaptist Community of Goods*, Montreal & Kingston, McGill-Queen's University Press, 1991, p. 109. A recent book with themes which echo Müntzer's dialectic between inner and outer transformation is Charles Elliott, *Memory and Salvation*, London, Darton, Longman & Todd, 1995.

14. Eike Wolgast, 'Die Obrigkeits- und Widerstandslehre Thomas Müntzers', in Bräuer and Junghans, *Der Theologe Thomas Müntzer, passim*; cf. Ulrich Bubenheimer, *Thomas Müntzer: Herkunft und Bildung*, Leyden, 1989, p. 230.

15. Wolgast, 'Die Obrigkeits- und Widerstandslehre Thomas Müntzers', p. 197.

16. ibid., p. 201.

17. Siegfried Bräuer, 'Konturen des Theologen Thomas Müntzer', in *Ich Thomas Müntzer, eyn knecht gottes*, Berlin, Henschelverlag, 1989, p. 82; Peter Matheson, 'Thomas Müntzer and the Sword of Gideon', *Theology*, 84, 1981, p. 113.

18. Rupp, *Patterns*, pp. 301–2; see also Ernst Bloch, *The Principle of Hope*, tr. N. Plaice, S. Plaice and P. Knight, Oxford, Blackwell, 1986, p. 488, and Stayer, *The German Peasants' War and Anabaptist Community of Goods*, pp. 107ff.

19. Günter Vogler, 'Gemeinnutz und Eigennutz bei Thomas Müntzer', in Bräuer and Junghans, *Der Theologe Thomas Müntzer*, pp. 174–94.

20. Elliger and Scott think he did; Goertz, Wolgast and Stayer do not.

21. Tom Scott, *Thomas Müntzer: Theology and Revolution in the German Reformation*, London, Macmillan, 1989, pp. 171–2; cf. Matheson, 'Christianity as Insurrection', p. 320.

22. Hans-Jürgen Goertz, 'Thomas Müntzer: Revolutionary between the Middle Ages and Modernity', *Mennonite Quarterly Review*, 64, 1990, p. 30.

23. Hans-Jürgen Goertz, *Thomas Müntzer: Apocalyptic Mystic and Revolutionary*, tr. Jocelyn Jaquiery, ed. Peter Matheson, Edinburgh, T. & T. Clark, 1993, p. 206.

Notes to Chapter 3

1. R. J. Bauckham, 'Apocalyptic', in Sinclair B. Ferguson, David F. Wright, and J. I. Packer, eds, *New Dictionary of Theology*, Illinois & Leicester, Inter-Varsity Press, 1988, p. 34.

2. Christopher Rowland, *The Open Heaven*, London, SPCK, 1982, p. 2; *idem*, *Revelation*, London, Epworth Press, 1993, p. 20.

3. Rowland, *The Open Heaven*, p. 26; cf. *idem*, '"Upon Whom the Ends of the Ages have Come": Apocalyptic and the Interpretation of the New Testament', in Malcolm Bull, ed., *Apocalypse Theory and the Ends of the World*, Oxford, Blackwell, 1995, p. 47, where Rowland observes (though not in this case with specific reference to Müntzer) that 'access to privileged knowledge of the divine purposes' can sometimes be 'linked to decisive action'.

4. Marjorie Reeves, 'Joachim of Fiore', in Gordon S. Wakefield, ed., *A Dictionary of Christian Spirituality*, London, SCM, 1983, p. 228.

5. Richard Bailey, 'The Sixteenth Century's Apocalyptic Heritage and Thomas Müntzer', *Mennonite Quarterly Review*, 57, 1983, p. 33.

6. Abraham Friesen, 'Thomas Müntzer and the Old Testament', *Mennonite Quarterly Review*, 47, 1973, pp. 13–14.

7. Gordon Huntston Williams, *The Radical Reformation*, London, Weidenfeld & Nicolson, 1962, p. 858.

8. F 373, n. 14.

9. Marjorie Reeves, *The Influence of Prophecy in the Later Middle Ages: A Study in Joachimism*, Oxford, Clarendon Press, 1969, p. 48.

10. Bailey, 'The Sixteenth Century's Apocalyptic Heritage', pp. 35–6.

11. The book of Jeremiah proved a rich vein for Müntzer to tap – there are well over a hundred allusions to it in his writings – and he closely identified himself with the prophet's sufferings, particularly those occasioned by warning the people of the dangers to come (see, e.g., CW 236, 360–1). The 'sickle' metaphor was not unknown to Winstanley's contemporaries: see J. F. McGregor and B. Reay, *Radical Religion in the English Revolution*, Oxford, Oxford University Press, 1984, p. 170.

12. Müntzer's references to 'sharpness' have distinct echoes of the *via negativa* of mysticism, and he frequently alludes to the 'bitterness' of Christian experience (see, e.g., CW 62, 84, 135, 196, 220, 300, 389, 403). The 'bitter faith', of course, stands in contrast to the faith of those who think they can achieve conformity to Christ by 'honey-sweet thoughts' (CW 366, cf. 220).

13. Müntzer's comments to Luther were later thrown back at him from Wittenberg by Agricola (CW 29).
14. cf. Müntzer's use of musical imagery to goad Luther in the *Vindication and Refutation* (p. 345).
15. The Jude reference is suggested by James M. Stayer, *Anabaptists and the Sword*, Lawrence, Kansas, Coronado Press, 2nd edn, 1976, p. 81.
16. The 'game' metaphor had earlier been introduced in a letter of July 1524 (CW 84).
17. Müntzer had spoken of 'tear[ing] the godless from their judgment seats and rais[ing] up humble, coarse folk in their place' in *A Manifest Exposé* written the preceding year (CW 286/8).
18. Müntzer toned down his language considerably in the other two versions of this Manifesto!
19. Eric W. Gritsch, *Thomas Müntzer: A Tragedy of Errors*, Minneapolis, Fortress Press, 1989, pp. 56, 41; CW 296, 297, 308.
20. Gordon Rupp, *Patterns of Reformation*, London, Epworth Press, 1969, pp. 302, 268, 303; cf. Hans-Jürgen Goertz, 'Thomas Müntzer: Revolutionary between the Middle Ages and Modernity', *Mennonite Quarterly Review*, 64, 1990, p. 28, and *idem*, *Thomas Müntzer: Apocalyptic Mystic and Revolutionary*, tr. Jocelyn Jaquiery, ed. Peter Matheson, Edinburgh, T. & T. Clark, 1993, p. 60. For evidence of a possible similar tendency in Winstanley see John P. Burgess, 'Biblical Poet and Prophet: Gerrard Winstanley's Use of Scripture in "The Law of Freedom"', *Journal of Religious History*, 14, 1987, pp. 276–7.
21. A leitmotif of the *Manifest Exposé* is the call the author feels himself to have had to 'launch himself' into the godless (e.g. CW 262).
22. The other witness is usually understood to be Enoch, who, like Elijah, did not see death, 'because God took him' (Gen. 5.24; Heb. 11.5; cf. Jude 24). Cf. Reinhard Schwarz, *Die apokalyptische Theologie Thomas Müntzers und der Taboriten*, Tübingen, 1977, pp. 62ff.
23. cf. Steven E. Ozment, *Mysticism and Dissent: Religious Ideology and Social Protest in the Sixteenth Century*, New Haven & London, Yale University Press, 1973, p. 94. The reference to 'judgement' (*urteyl*) in this context is significant in the light of Gottfried Maron's study suggesting that Müntzer's usage of the term always has eschatological and in fact apocalyptic overtones (Gordon Rupp, '"True History": Martin Luther and Thomas Müntzer', in D. Beales and G. Best, eds, *History, Society and the Churches: Essays in Honour of Owen Chadwick*, Cambridge, Cambridge University Press, 1985, p. 82).

24. Tom Scott, *Thomas Müntzer: Theology and Revolution in the German Reformation*, London, Macmillan, 1989, p. 154.

25. That Müntzer subscribes to a doctrine of predestination is not to be doubted, though he rejects the 'double' kind which would attach responsibility to God for the presence of evil in the world. He makes this explicit in one of his tirades against Luther: you distort scripture 'and make God the cause of evil . . . You . . . try to blame God for your being a poor sinner . . . You have conjured up such fantasies from your Augustine . . .' (CW 345; cf. 375).

26. Surprisingly, in view of its clear apocalyptic tone, Müntzer never refers to the parable of the sheep and the goats in Matthew 25; cf. CW 105, n. 821.

27. See Tom Scott, 'From Polemic to Sobriety: Thomas Müntzer in Recent Research', *Journal of Ecclesiastical History*, 39, 1988, p. 561, and Werner Packull's review of Gabriel Müntzenberg's *Thomas Müntzer ou L'illuminisme Sanglant*, in *Archiv für Reformationsgeschichte*, Beiheft/ Supplement, Literaturbericht/Literature Review, 1990, p. 57, n. 204.

28. Stayer, *Anabaptists and the Sword*, p. 89; Bailey, 'The Sixteenth Century's Apocalyptic Heritage', p. 42.

29. For some reflections on the appropriateness of the concept of 'covenant' to contemporary revolutionary politics see Jürgen Moltmann, 'Revolution, Religion and the Future: German Reactions' in the Concilium volume *1789: The French Revolution and the Church*, ed. Claude Geffré and Jean-Pierre Jossua, Edinburgh, T. & T. Clark, 1989, pp. 48f.

30. Müntzer can use the self-same expression to speak of God wiping out evil-doers like Count Ernst – 'Das soltu . . . ausgereutet werden' – and rooting out weeds and thistles from the soil of the heart – ' . . . Got selbern dein unkraut, disteln und dorner aus seinem fruchtbaren lande, das ist aus deinem hertzen, reutet'; CW 155, 199 (F 468, 233).

31. Goertz, *Thomas Müntzer: Apocalyptic Mystic and Revolutionary*, pp. 21–2.

32. Cited in José Míguez Bonino, *Christians and Marxists: The Mutual Challenge to Revolution*, London, Hodder & Stoughton, 1976, pp. 135–6.

33. ibid., p. 138.

34. The idea that there might be a natural theology in Müntzer has recently been revived by Ulrich Bubenheimer ('Thomas Müntzer und der Humanismus', in Siegfried Bräuer and Helmar Junghans, eds, *Der Theologe Thomas Müntzer: Untersuchungen zu seiner Entwicklung und Lehre*, Göttingen, Vandenhoeck & Ruprecht, 1989, pp. 302–28), though it has been contested by some scholars, for example Ozment (*Mysticism*

and Dissent, p. 88). For a brief discussion of Müntzer's 'theology of the creatures' see CW 357, n. 6.

35. In the version of the Bible with which Müntzer was familiar this Psalm appeared as '18', and is so numbered whenever it is referred to in his writings.

36. Schwarz, *Die apokalyptische Theologie Thomas Müntzers*, pp. 110ff.

37. cf. Siegfried Bräuer, 'Konturen des Theologen Thomas Müntzer', in *Ich Thomas Müntzer, eyn knecht gottes*, Berlin, Henschelverlag, 1989, p. 81.

38. cf. CW 46, n. 293, and Matheson, 'Thomas Müntzer's Marginal Comments on Tertullian', *Journal of Theological Studies*, 41, Pt 1, April 1990, p. 85.

39. cf. CW 412 and Matheson, 'Thomas Müntzer's Marginal Comments', p. 87.

40. The differing eschatologies of Müntzer and Luther also helps to explain their political differences: Luther's expectation that the world would be wound up with the sudden, imminent appearance of Christ checked any inclination he might have had to change the world; for Müntzer, however, notwithstanding that he clearly saw salvation in supernatural terms, the 'Christianization' of the world was a possibility; see Eike Wolgast, 'Die Obrigkeits- und Widerstandslehre Thomas Müntzers', in Bräuer and Junghans, *Der Theologe Thomas Müntzer*, p. 206.

41. Rupp, *Patterns*, p. 294.

42. cf. Rupp's translation of this passage, 'All knowledge of the Creatures is to be related to the Whole', *Patterns*, p. 294 (cf. p. 329). The original Latin reads: *In toto exordienda est omnis scientia creaturarum* . . . (F 534).

43. Schwarz, 'Thomas Müntzer und die Mystik', in Bräuer and Junghans, *Der Theologe Thomas Müntzer*, p. 289; idem, *Die apokalyptische Theologie Thomas Müntzers*, p. 115. The terms were also familiar to Karlstadt, who published a tract in 1523 entitled *Von manigfeltigkeit des eynfeltigen eynigen willen gottes*.

44. Note that the sexual imagery continues further on in the same paragraph.

45. Schwarz, *Die apokalyptische Theologie Thomas Müntzers*, ch. 5, pp. 87ff.

46. Thomas Nipperdey, 'Theology and Revolution in Thomas Müntzer', in James M. Stayer and Werner O. Packull, eds, *The Anabaptists and Thomas Müntzer*, Dubuque, Iowa, & Toronto, Kendall/Hunt, 1980, p. 116.

47. Reeves, *The Influence of Prophecy*, p. 291.

48. Cited in Scott, 'From Polemic to Sobriety', p. 566.

49. Schwarz, *Die apokalyptische Theologie Thomas Müntzers*, pp. 46–7, 55–6.

50. Míguez Bonino, *Christians and Marxists*, p. 127.

Notes to Chapter 4

1. J. D. Alsop has recently pointed out that the evidence linking Edward the mercer and Edward the burgess is not conclusive but has come to appear so through constant repetition. Alsop also argues that a burgess was not necessarily a person of wealth or high status; J. D. Alsop, 'A High Road to Radicalism? Gerrard Winstanley's Youth', *The Seventeenth Century*, 9, 1994, pp. 12, 14.

2. For a discussion of this point see Alsop, 'A High Road to Radicalism?', pp. 13f. Some writers have inferred strong Puritan tendencies on the part of Winstanley's parents from evidence that an 'Edward' Winstanley and his (unnamed) wife were presented to the church courts in 1605 for holding conventicles; Alsop, however, points out that the Winstanley presented was in fact 'Edmund', and in any case (as R. C. Richardson had earlier observed) the charge was dismissed (Alsop, 'A High Road to Radicalism?', pp. 12–13).

3. Christopher Hill, *Winstanley: The Law of Freedom and other Writings*, Harmondsworth, Penguin, 1973, p. 11; Alsop, 'A High Road to Radicalism?', p. 14.

4. On Winstanley and the established church see Alsop, 'A High Road to Radicalism?', pp. 16ff.

5. Hill, *Winstanley: The Law of Freedom*, p. 11; he knew Coke (W 322) and may have read Foxe (T. W. Hayes, 'Gerrard Winstanley and Foxe's "Book of Martyrs"', *Notes and Queries*, 222, 1977, p. 210).

6. David W. Petegorsky, *Left-Wing Democracy in the English Civil War*, London, Gollancz, 1940, pp. 122–3. This book was reissued in 1995.

7. ibid., p. 123, where the case is discussed fully; cf. W 6 and Hill, *Winstanley: The Law of Freedom*, p. 12.

8. For a full discussion of this episode see R. J. Dalton, 'Gerrard Winstanley: The Experience of Fraud 1641', *The Historical Journal*, 34, 1991, pp. 973ff.

9. See James Alsop, 'Gerrard Winstanley's Later Life', *Past and Present*, 82, 1979, p. 75.

10. Cited in Hill, *Winstanley: The Law of Freedom*, p. 12.

11. Referred to by the Diggers as 'George Hill' in conformity with the radical protestant tradition of not recognizing the saints of the established church.

12. Petegorsky, *Left-Wing Democracy in the English Civil War*, p. 162.

13. This is the most recently discovered of Winstanley's writings, and was

first published for a modern readership, with an introduction by G. E. Aylmer, in *Past and Present*, 40, 1968. Aylmer's comment is on p. 5.

14. For a full discussion of the dating of this tract see Keith Thomas, 'The Date of Gerrard Winstanley's "Fire in the Bush"', *Past and Present*, 42, 1969, pp. 160–2; cf. G. E. Aylmer, 'The Religion of Gerrard Winstanley', in J. F. McGregor and B. Reay, eds, *Radical Religion in the English Revolution*, Oxford, Oxford University Press, 1984, pp. 105–6.

15. Also referred to in some texts as Lady Eleanor Davies; of aristocratic birth, she was married first to Sir John Davies and subsequently to Sir Archibald Douglas, an illegitimate brother of Charles I. For a useful brief introduction to her ideas see Paul H. Hardacre, 'Gerrard Winstanley in 1650', *Huntington Library Quarterly*, 22, 1958–59, pp. 345–6, and Phyllis Mack, *Visionary Women*, Berkeley, University of California Press, 1992, *passim*. The standard biography is Esther S. Cope, *Handmaid of the Holy Spirit: Dame Eleanor Davies, Never Soe Mad A Ladie*, Ann Arbor, University of Michigan Press, 1992. The recently completed doctoral research of Carola Scott Luckens at the University of Southampton has deepened further our understanding of Lady Eleanor.

16. Hardacre, 'Gerrard Winstanley in 1650', pp. 349; the full text of the letter is reproduced here by Hardacre. See also Richard T. Vann, 'The Later Life of Gerrard Winstanley', *Journal of the History of Ideas*, 26, 1965, p. 133.

17. J. D. Alsop, 'Gerrard Winstanley: Religion and Respectability', *The Historical Journal*, 28, 1985, p. 708; also cited in Hill, *Winstanley: The Law of Freedom*, p. 31, Nigel Smith, ed., *A Collection of Ranter Writings from the Seventeenth Century*, London, Junction Books, 1983, p. 182, and George M. Shulman, *Radicalism and Reverence: The Political Thought of Gerrard Winstanley*, Berkeley, University of California Press, 1989, p. 245.

18. The Dedicatory Epistle is dated 5 November 1651, and the work was published the following year, both in complete form and partially in the newspaper *The Faithful Scout* and other literature (see Christopher Hill, *The Experience of Defeat: Milton and Some Contemporaries*, London, Faber & Faber, 1984, p. 39).

19. For two contrasting opinions about the reasons underlying Winstanley's shift from radical politics see Alsop, 'Gerrard Winstanley: Religion and Respectability', p. 709, and Shulman, *Radicalism and Reverence*, pp. 244ff.

20. Alsop, 'Gerrard Winstanley's Later Life', p. 80. For an amusing yet pointed reflection on Alsop's whole approach to Winstanley see James

Holstun, 'Rational Hunger: Gerrard Winstanley's *Hortus Inconclusus*', *Prose Studies*, 14, 1991, p. 196.

21. Dalton, 'Gerrard Winstanley: The Experience of Fraud 1641', p. 980; the case is given full treatment in this essay (pp. 977ff.). For a less than complimentary reference to lawyers in *The Law of Freedom* see W 504–5.

22. Hill, *The Experience of Defeat*, p. 40.

23. T. Wilson Hayes, *Winstanley the Digger: A Literary Analysis of Radical Ideas in the English Revolution*, Cambridge, Mass., & London, Harvard University Press, 1979, p. 246, n. 42.

24. Cited in Alsop, 'Gerrard Winstanley's Later Life', p. 80, n. 22.

25. Christopher Hill, *The Religion of Gerrard Winstanley*, Oxford, The Past and Present Society, 1978, p. 51.

26. Alsop, 'Gerrard Winstanley's Later Life', p. 81.

Notes to Chapter 5

1. One of the clearest statements of this position is Lotte Mulligan, John K. Graham and Judith Richards, 'Winstanley: A Case for the Man as He Said He Was', *Journal of Ecclesiastical History*, 28, 1977, p. 63.

2. ibid., p. 65; a similar line is taken in Maurice Goldsmith, 'Levelling by Sword, Spade and Word: Radical Equalitarianism in the English Revolution', in C. Jones, M. Newitt and S. Roberts, eds, *Politics and People in Revolutionary England: Essays in Honour of Ivan Roots*, Oxford, Blackwell, 1986, p. 77; William D. Lindsey, 'Gerrard Winstanley's Theology of Creation: An Approval', *Toronto Journal of Theology*, 4, 1988, p. 180; and David Mulder, *The Alchemy of Revolution: Gerrard Winstanley's Occultism and Seventeenth-Century English Communism*, NY, Peter Lang, 1990, pp. 10–11.

3. 'Complete' is not a strictly accurate description of this collection since, disappointingly, Winstanley's first three tracts appear only in heavily abbreviated form. Editions of these works are housed in the British Library (though *The Saints Paradice* may be read only on microfilm).

4. Paul Elmen, 'The Theological Basis of Digger Communism', *Church History*, 23, 1954, pp. 216–17.

5. Timothy Kenyon, *Utopian Communism and Political Thought in Early Modern England*, London, Pinter, 1989, p. 133 (cf. p. 137). Among other writers who stress the central role theology played in Winstanley's thinking are A. S. P. Woodhouse, *Puritanism and Liberty*, London, Dent,

1938; Winthrop S. Hudson, 'Economic and Social Thought of Gerrard Winstanley: Was He a Seventeenth-Century Marxist?', *The Journal of Modern History*, 18, 1946; and W. Schenk, *The Concern for Social Justice in the Puritan Revolution*, London, Longmans, Green, 1948.

6. Perez Zagorin, *A History of Political Thought in the English Revolution*, London, Routledge & Kegan Paul, 1954, pp. 52–3.

7. J. C. Davis, 'Utopia and History', *Historical Studies*, 13, 1968, p. 172. Another scholar taking a similar position is John Strachey, *The Theory and Practice of Socialism*, London, Gollancz, 1936.

8. George Juretic, 'Digger No Millenarian: The Revolutionizing of Gerrard Winstanley', *Journal of the History of Ideas*, 36, 1975, pp. 269, 276, 279, 270. Completely the reverse position to this – that the Diggers became 'less militant' and more 'millennial' over time – is argued by Christopher Kendrick, 'Preaching Common Grounds: Winstanley and the Diggers as Concrete Utopians', in William Zunder and Suzanne Trill, eds, *Writing and the English Renaissance*, London & NY, Longman, 1996.

9. Eduard Bernstein, *Cromwell and Communism*, Nottingham, Spokesman, 1980, p. 107; Bernstein is usually credited with the rediscovery of Winstanley's tracts in the 1890s, though they did not entirely disappear in the mean time: see Christopher Hill, *The Experience of Defeat: Milton and Some Contemporaries*, London, Faber & Faber, 1984, p. 42. William Blake, among others, may have been influenced by his ideas.

10. David W. Petegorsky, *Left-Wing Democracy in the English Civil War*, London, Gollancz, 1940, p. 206.

11. Christopher Hill, *Winstanley: The Law of Freedom and Other Writings*, Harmondsworth, Penguin, 1973, p. 55; idem, *The World Turned Upside Down*, Harmondsworth, Penguin, 1975, p. 94, cf. pp. 144, 264, 388.

12. Maurice Ashley, *England in the Seventeenth Century*, Harmondsworth, Penguin, 1961, p. 115; cf. Juretic, 'Digger No Millenarian', pp. 278–9. For a slightly more nuanced variation of the 'comprehensibility' argument see Margaret James, *Social Problems and Policy During the Puritan Revolution 1640–1660*, London, Routledge, 1930, p. 103.

13. See Petegorsky, *Left-Wing Democracy in the English Civil War*, p. 149, and Hill, *The World Turned Upside Down*, p. 139. Winstanley's first five tracts were published together, with a preface by the author, under the title *Several Pieces Gathered into One Volume*, on 20 December 1649.

14. Zagorin, *A History of Political Thought in the English Revolution*, p. 57.

15. Christopher Hill, *The Religion of Gerrard Winstanley*, Oxford, The Past and Present Society, 1978, p. 57; cf. idem, *The Experience of Defeat*, p. 39.

16. For an examination of some of these 'faint voices of protest on the very margins of the tradition' – including Winstanley and Müntzer – see Christopher Rowland, *Radical Christianity: A Reading of Recovery*, Cambridge, Polity Press, 1988.

17. Zagorin, *A History of Political Thought in the English Revolution*, p. 57.

18. Hill, *The Religion of Gerrard Winstanley*, p. 57. Hill has more recently reiterated this position: ' . . . when scholars laboriously demonstrate that . . . Winstanley [was] "primarily motivated by religion", they have proved no more than that [he] lived in the seventeenth century' (*The English Bible and the Seventeenth-Century Revolution*, Harmondsworth, Penguin, 1993, p. 34). This is of course to rule out of court the debate being conducted here, though it is partly because of attempts by Hill and others to sift out the 'religious' dimension in Winstanley in order to reveal a supposed 'core' of (secular) ideas beneath that it does seem necessary to keep it alive.

19. For some recent discussions of the use of this term see Nicola Baxter, 'Gerrard Winstanley's Experimental Knowledge of God (The Perception of the Spirit and the Acting of Reason)', *Journal of Ecclesiastical History*, 39, 1988, pp. 191ff.; Lindsey, 'Gerrard Winstanley's Theology of Creation', pp. 186f.; and Nigel Smith, *Perfection Proclaimed: Language and Literature in English Radical Religion 1640–1660*, Oxford, Oxford University Press, 1989, pp. 258f.

20. cf. Christopher Hill, 'Debate: The Religion of Gerrard Winstanley. A Rejoinder', *Past and Present*, 89, 1980, p. 147, and *idem, The Religion of Gerrard Winstanley*, p. 47.

21. James Holstun, 'Rational Hunger: Gerrard Winstanley's *Hortus Inconclusus*', *Prose Studies* 14, 1991, pp. 179f.

22. This of course refers to the original (1649) edition.

23. In his unique and refreshing attempt to understand Winstanley as a person of his own time David Mulder argues that it is because we want to claim the Digger as a modern that we cannot conceive of him believing that his 'revolutionary movement . . . [could] . . . provide for the most basic needs of the very poorest sort of people through what we would call magic'. Yet, Mulder argues, ' . . . it was not ludicrous to the men and women who in 1649 endangered their lives to make it happen'; Mulder, *The Alchemy of Revolution*, p. 11, cf. p. 206.

24. cf. John P. Burgess, 'Biblical Poet and Prophet: Gerrard Winstanley's Use of Scripture in "The Law of Freedom"', *Journal of Religious History*, 14, 1987, p. 279, and Kenyon, *Utopian Communism and Political Thought*, p. 163.

25. Denys Turner, *Marxism and Christianity*, Oxford, Blackwell, 1983, p. 182.
26. John Maguire, 'Gospel or Religious Language?: Engels on the Peasant War', *New Blackfriars*, 54, 1973, p. 350.
27. Frederick Engels, *The Peasant War in Germany*, Moscow, Progress Publishers, 1956, p. 42.
28. Petegorsky, *Left-Wing Democracy in the English Civil War*, p. 206; C. H. George, 'Gerrard Winstanley: A Critical Retrospect', in Robert C. Cole and Michael E. Moody, eds, *The Dissenting Tradition: Essays for Leland H. Carlson*, Athens, Ohio, Ohio University Press, 1975, p. 214; G. E. Aylmer, 'The Religion of Gerrard Winstanley', in J. F. McGregor and B. Reay, eds, *Radical Religion in the English Revolution*, Oxford, Oxford University Press, 1984, p. 95.
29. Hill, *Winstanley: The Law of Freedom*, pp. 10, 19, 55; *idem*, *The Religion of Gerrard Winstanley*, p. 57. For an excellent critique of Hill's thesis about Winstanley's use of religious language see Burgess, 'Biblical Poet and Prophet' esp. pp. 271 and 275; and for a strong and sustained plea for Winstanley not to be read as a modern but as a person of his own time – one whose 'basic mode of thought was "occult"' in the precise sense of that term – see David Mulder, *The Alchemy of Revolution*, *passim*.
30. I am indebted to Denys Turner for offering this definition with respect to Winstanley.
31. Which is not to suggest that there are *no* writers who doubt Winstanley's real revolutionary intent, as will be discussed below.
32. W. H. G. Armytage, *Heavens Below: Utopian Experiments in England 1560–1960*, London, Routledge & Kegan Paul, 1961, p. 25; Petegorsky, *Left-Wing Democracy in the English Civil War*, p. 177.
33. Hill, *Winstanley: The Law of Freedom*, p. 38; cf. *idem*, *Liberty Against the Law*, London, Penguin, 1996, pp. 276–7.
34. I have reflected briefly on Winstanley's ideas about the land, and their possible contemporary relevance, in 'The Earth as a Common Treasury: The Diggers and the Land Question', *Ecotheology*, 1, 1996, pp. 35–41.
35. James R. Knott, *The Sword of the Spirit: Puritan Responses to the Bible*, Chicago & London, University of Chicago Press, 1980, p. 102.
36. For Mulder these references to 'mother-earth' are thoroughly pagan; *The Alchemy of Revolution*, p. 239.
37. For a more detailed discussion of the differences between Hobbes and Winstanley see Hill, *The World Turned Upside Down*, pp. 387ff., and George M. Shulman, *Radicalism and Reverence: The Political Thought of Gerrard Winstanley*, Berkeley, University of California Press, 1989.
38. Gerrard Winstanley, *England's Spirit Unfoulded, Or An Incouragement to*

take the 'Engagement', *Past and Present*, 40, 1968, p. 13; cf. Aylmer, 'The Religion of Gerrard Winstanley', p. 99.

39. Woodhouse, *Puritanism and Liberty*, p. 71.

40. A. L. Morton, ed., *Freedom in Arms*, London, Lawrence & Wishart, 1975, p. 276.

41. Woodhouse, *Puritanism and Liberty*, p. 53.

42. John Lilburne, *The Charters of London*, 1646, p. 4, cited in Hill, *Winstanley: The Law of Freedom*, p. 49; I have borrowed the idea of juxtaposing these two quotations from Hill.

43. See for example the discussion in C. B. MacPherson, *The Political Theory of Possessive Individualism*, Oxford, Oxford University Press, 1964, p. 136.

44. Among them Turner (*Marxism and Christianity*, p. 145; 'Gerrard Winstanley', *New Blackfriars*, 62, 1981, p. 503), Hill (*Winstanley: The Law of Freedom*, p. 35; *The English Bible and the Seventeenth-Century Revolution*, p. 208), Petegorsky (*Left-Wing Democracy in the English Civil War*, p. 186), Shulman (*Radicalism and Reverence*, p. 133), and Holstun ('Rational Hunger', pp. 172, 186).

45. Walter F. Murphy, 'The Political Philosophy of Gerrard Winstanley', *The Review of Politics*, 19, 1957, p. 224.

46. Hudson, 'Economic and Social Thought of Gerrard Winstanley', pp. 6, 11, 21.

47. Knott, *The Sword of the Spirit*, p. 86. Others who also doubt Winstanley had any real revolutionary intent include: Schenk (*Concern for Social Justice*, p. 102), J. Max Patrick ('The Literature of the Diggers', *University of Toronto Quarterly*, 12, 1942, p. 315), and Elmen ('The Theological Basis of Digger Communism', p. 213).

48. Aylmer, 'The Religion of Gerrard Winstanley', p. 99; any assertion that Winstanley renounced violence has to be qualified to the extent that he appears to have endorsed the execution of Charles Stuart (see Shulman, *Radicalism and Reverence*, p. 175).

49. Shulman, *Radicalism and Reverence*, p. 151.

50. Hill, *The Religion of Gerrard Winstanley*, pp. 26–7.

Notes to Chapter 6

1. Norman Cohn *The Pursuit of the Millennium*, London, Paladin, 1970, p. 13.

2. Peter Worsley, *The Trumpet Shall Sound*, London, Paladin, 1970, p. 22.

3. Theodore Olson, *Millennialism, Utopianism and Progress*, Toronto, University of Toronto Press, 1982, pp. 15–16.

4. Karl Mannheim, *Ideology and Utopia: An Introduction to the Sociology of Knowledge*, London, Kegan Paul, Trench, Trubner, 1946, pp. 193, 196.

5. Christopher Rowland and Mark Corner, *Liberating Exegesis: The Challenge of Liberation Theology to Biblical Studies*, London, SPCK, 1990, pp. 119–20.

6. Cohn, *The Pursuit of the Millennium*, p. 13; Olson, *Millennialism, Utopianism and Progress*, p. 15.

7. References here are to the 1648 edition housed in the British Library, London, at reference 4377.a.51(1).

8. Winstanley, *The Mysterie of God*, p. 32.

9. ibid., pp. 33–40.

10. T. Wilson Hayes, *Winstanley the Digger: A Literary Analysis of Radical Ideas in the English Revolution*, Cambridge, Mass., & London, Harvard University Press, 1979, p. 16.

11. Winstanley, *The Mysterie of God*, p. 31.

12. ibid, pp. 43–5. A curious feature of this discussion is that on page 43 Winstanley employs the feminine pronoun for the Serpent, but in subsequent pages the masculine.

13. ibid., p. 30.

14. See for example W 113, 117, 202, 253, 382, 453, 460, 486, 582.

15. See Sabine's footnote on this page for a discussion of the difficulties of Winstanley's argument here. (The 'mark of the Beast', according to Rev. 13.16–17, is a sign in the right hand or forehead without which, in the last times, no person 'might buy or sell'.)

16. Arise Evans, for example, thought that certain chapters in Amos and Revelation described events he had witnessed in the 1640s, and that the door lintel mentioned in Amos 9.1 was a reference to the Speaker of the Long Parliament, William Lenthall (Christopher Hill, *The World Turned Upside Down*, Harmondsworth, Penguin, 1975, p. 94).

17. W 163, 174 (on Rev. 13.1), 204–5, 261, 270, 272, 383, 485–6.

18. Matthew Poole, *Commentary on the Holy Bible: Volume III, Matthew to Revelation*, McLean, Va., MacDonald, n/d., pp. 982, 976. This commentary was originally published posthumously in two volumes, *Genesis to Isaiah* (1683) and *Jeremiah to Revelation* (1685). Poole died in 1679.

19. Christopher Hill, 'Till the Conversion of the Jews', in *idem, The Collected Essays of Christopher Hill, Volume 2: Religion and Politics in 17th Century England*, Brighton, Harvester, 1986, pp. 270–1.

20. For a discussion of possible Joachite influences on Winstanley see Hayes, *Winstanley the Digger*, pp. 2, 35, 97, 146, 199; Hill, *The World*

Turned Upside Down, pp. 147–8; Krishan Kumar, *Utopia and Anti-Utopia in Modern Times*, Oxford, Blackwell, 1987, p. 16; and Christopher Rowland, *Radical Christianity*, Cambridge, Polity Press, 1988, p. 88.

21. Joachim, *Exposition of the Book of Revelation*, Introduction, ch. 5, cited in Tony Lane, *The Lion Concise Book of Christian Thought*, Tring, Lion, 1984, p. 90.

22. Thomas Edwards, *Gangraena* (1646), vol. I, p. 22, cited in Hill, *The World Turned Upside Down*, p. 148, n. 187.

23. See Hill, 'Till the Conversion', pp. 270–2, Keith Thomas, *Religion and the Decline of Magic*, Harmondsworth, Penguin, 1973, p. 168, and Poole, *Commentary on the Holy Bible: Volume III, Matthew to Revelation*, p. 976.

24. Gerrard Winstanley, *The Saints Paradice* (1648?), p. 116. References here are to the edition housed (on microfilm) in the Thomason Collection in the British Library, London, at reference E.2137. This edition is dated 1658, but since the work is included in *Several Pieces Gathered into One Volume* (1649) the date is either wrong or the edition not an original; see Sabine's note at W 91.

25. Gerrard Winstanley, *The Breaking of the Day of God* (1648), p. 32. References here are to the 1648 edition housed in the British Library at reference 4377.a.51(2).

26. Hayes, *Winstanley the Digger*, p. 48.

27. Christopher Hill, 'Debate: The Religion of Gerrard Winstanley. A Rejoinder', *Past and Present*, 89, 1980, p. 148.

28. Winstanley, *The Saints Paradice*, pp. 82–4.

29. David Dawson, 'Allegorical Intratextuality in Bunyan and Winstanley', *Journal of Religion*, 70, 1990, p. 197. Arguably a collapsing of 'resurrection' and 'parousia' is already present in the gospel of John.

30. George Juretic, 'Digger No Millenarian: The Revolutionizing of Gerrard Winstanley', *Journal of the History of Ideas*, 36, 1975, pp. 268, 276.

31. Lotte Mulligan, John K. Graham and Judith Richards, 'Winstanley: A Case for the Man as He Said He Was', *Journal of Ecclesiastical History*, 28, 1977, p. 63.

32. Which Juretic (among others) argues is really a product of the pre-Digger era which was 'laid aside then taken up again' ('Digger No Millenarian', p. 279, n. 100).

33. Juretic, 'Digger No Millenarian', pp. 268–9.

34. Christopher Hill, *The Religion of Gerrard Winstanley*, Oxford, The Past and Present Society, 1978, pp. 39–40; cf. F. D. Dow, *Radicalism in the*

English Revolution 1640–1660, Oxford, Blackwell, 1985, p. 77, and W 59–60.

35. cf. W 432–3, 544; Christopher Hill, 'Winstanley and Freedom', in R. C. Richardson and G. M. Ridden, eds, *Freedom and the English Revolution*, Manchester University Press, 1986, p. 159 (and more recently Christopher Hill, *A Nation of Change and Novelty*, London, Routledge, 1990, p. 125).

36. David W. Petegorsky, *Left-Wing Democracy in the English Civil War*, London, Gollancz, 1940, p. 212.

37. Hayes, *Winstanley the Digger*, p. 113.

38. Mannheim, *Ideology and Utopia*, p. 193.

39. See for example Petegorsky, *Left-Wing Democracy in the English Civil War*, pp. 126–30; Walter F. Murphy, 'The Political Philosophy of Gerrard Winstanley', *The Review of Politics*, 19, 1957, p. 220; Douglas E. Sturm, 'Winstanley, Seventeenth Century Radical: From the Mystery of God to the Law of Freedom', in J. Witte and F. S. Alexander, eds, *The Weightier Matters of the Law: Essays on Law and Religion*, Atlanta, Georgia, Scholars Press, 1988, p. 105; Dow, *Radicalism in the English Revolution*, p. 76.

40. Winstanley, *The Breaking of the Day of God*, p. 57.

41. Denys Turner, 'Gerrard Winstanley', *New Blackfriars*, 62, 1981, p. 507.

42. For two interesting reflections on this see Denys Turner, 'Gerrard Winstanley', pp. 506–7, and Christopher Kendrick, 'Agons of the Manor: "Upon Appleton House" and Agrarian Capitalism', in David Lee Miller, Sharon O'Dair and Harold Wheeler, eds, *The Production of English Renaissance Culture*, Ithaca & London, Cornell University Press, 1994, pp. 48–9.

43. Terry Eagleton, 'Faith and Revolution', *New Blackfriars*, 52, 1971, p. 161.

44. Olson, *Millennialism, Utopianism and Progress*, pp. 5–6.

45. J. C. Davis, 'Utopia and History', *Historical Studies*, 13, 1968, pp. 172, 166; cf. *idem*, *Utopia and the Ideal Society: A Study of English Utopian Writing 1516–1700*, Cambridge, Cambridge University Press, 1981, and 'The History of Utopia: The Chronology of Nowhere', in P. Alexander and R. Gill, eds, *Utopias*, London, Duckworth, 1984, pp. 8f.

46. Kumar, *Utopia and Anti-Utopia in Modern Times*, pp. 13, 26; *idem*, 'Religion and Utopia', in Dan Cohn-Sherbok, ed., *The Canterbury Papers: Essays on Religion and Society*, London, Bellew, 1990, p. 74. Kumar has drawn a much sharper distinction between 'utopia' and 'millennium' in 'Apocalypse, Millennium and Utopia Today', Malcolm Bull, ed.,

Apocalypse Theory and the Ends of the World, Oxford, Blackwell, 1995, pp. 200–24.

47. James Holstun (claiming Christopher Hill in support) considers *The Law of Freedom* to be more 'postutopian' than utopian – 'an attempt to understand England's failure rather than an optimistic proposal of its way to a rational settlement'; James Holstun, *A Rational Millennium: Puritan Utopias of Seventeenth-Century England and America*, NY and Oxford, Oxford University Press, 1987, p. 277.

48. J. C. Davis, 'Gerrard Winstanley and the Restoration of True Magistracy', *Past and Present*, 70, 1976, p. 92; *idem*, 'Utopia and History', p. 172. Davis' is a somewhat idiosyncratic reading of Winstanley, discerning strongly authoritarian tendencies on the part of the author of *The Law of Freedom*, though a not dissimilar line was earlier taken by Murphy ('The Political Philosophy of Gerrard Winstanley', p. 257). For a solid critique of Davis' and Murphy's position see Michael Rogers, 'Gerrard Winstanley on Crime and Punishment', *Sixteenth Century Journal*, 27, 1996, pp. 735–47.

49. Hill, *The World Turned Upside Down*, p. 145.

50. ibid., p. 145. Interestingly, in the collection of Winstanley's writings he was preparing around the same time as this book, Hill retains the semi-colon: *Winstanley: The Law of Freedom and Other Writings*, Harmondsworth, Penguin, 1973, p. 254.

51. Christopher Kendrick, 'Preaching Common Grounds: Winstanley and the Diggers as Concrete Utopians', in William Zunder and Suzanne Trill, eds, *Writing and the English Renaissance*, London & NY, Longman, 1996, p. 227.

52. William D. Lindsey, 'Gerrard Winstanley's Theology of Creation: An Approval', *Toronto Journal of Theology*, 4, 1988, p. 188.

53. Hayes, *Winstanley the Digger*, p. 40.

54. Olson, *Millennialism, Utopianism and Progress*, p. 6; see Hill, *The World Turned Upside Down*, p. 188, n. 23, and Hayes, *Winstanley the Digger*, p. 99, for other examples of believers in a past Golden Age. Lindsey has tried to suggest – I think unconvincingly – that Winstanley rejects a 'backwards-pitched utopianism' and that 'the perfect world which [he] envisages is not a golden age in the past . . . [but] . . . this present world made complete in the future'; 'Gerrard Winstanley's Theology of Creation', p. 188.

55. Petegorsky, *Left-Wing Democracy in the English Civil War*, p. 199.

56. Cited in Hill, 'Winstanley and Freedom', p. 162, and *A Nation of Change and Novelty*, p. 128; cf. Petegorsky, *Left-Wing Democracy in the English*

Civil War, p. 151, and Hayes, 'Gerrard Winstanley and Foxe's "Book of Martyrs"', *Notes and Queries*, 222, 1977, p. 210, col. 2.

57. For example, Petegorsky (*Left-Wing Democracy in the English Civil War*, pp. 198–9).

Notes to Chapter 7

1. Alfredo Fierro, *The Militant Gospel*, London, SCM, 1977, p. 255.
2. Hugo Assmann, *Practical Theology of Liberation*, London, Search Press, 1975, p. 143. It should be noted that the explicitly 'revolutionary' language in this and other early texts by liberation theologians generally becomes more nuanced in their subsequent writings.
3. Juan Luis Segundo, *The Liberation of Theology*, NY, Orbis, 1976, pp. 91–3.
4. Peter Hebblethwaite, *The Christian-Marxist Dialogue and Beyond*, London, Darton, Longman & Todd, 1977, p. 69.
5. Harvey Cox, *The Secular City*, Harmondsworth, Penguin, 1968, p. 173.
6. Gustavo Gutiérrez, *A Theology of Liberation*, London, SCM, 1974, p. 11 (this work was revised and reissued in 1988 but all quotations here are from the 1974 translation); cf. *idem*, *The Power of the Poor in History*, London, SCM, 1983, p. 61.
7. Nicholas Lash, *A Matter of Hope*, London, Darton, Longman & Todd, 1981, p. 238.
8. José Míguez Bonino, *Christians and Marxists: The Mutual Challenge to Revolution*, London, Hodder & Stoughton, 1976, pp. 118–19; Gustavo Gutiérrez, *The Truth Shall Make You Free*, NY, Orbis, 1990, pp. 94–5.
9. Alfred T. Hennelly, ed., *Liberation Theology: A Documentary History*, NY, Orbis, 1990, p. 157.
10. Segundo, *The Liberation of Theology*, pp. 94–5.
11. José Míguez Bonino, *Doing Theology in a Revolutionary Situation*, Philadelphia, Fortress, 1975, p. 97; perhaps the most extensive treatment of the theme of political mediation is Clodovis Boff, *Theology and Praxis: Epistemological Foundations*, NY, Orbis, 1987.
12. Fierro, *The Militant Gospel*, p. 255; cf. p. 238.
13. Teófilo Cabestrero, *Ministers of God, Ministers of the People*, NY, Orbis, & London, Zed, 1983, p. 77.
14. Denys Turner, *Marxism and Christianity*, Oxford, Blackwell, 1983, p. 214; this position has recently been restated by Peter Scott, *Theology, Ideology and Liberation*, Cambridge, Cambridge University Press, 1994, p. 2.

15. See for example Stanley Hauerwas, *A Community of Character: Toward a Constructive Christian Social Ethic*, Notre Dame & London, University of Notre Dame Press, 1981.

16. See in particular John Milbank, *Theology and Social Theory: Beyond Secular Reason*, Oxford, Blackwell, 1990. For useful introductions to and critiques of Milbank's work see *New Blackfriars*, 73, June 1992; *Modern Theology*, 8, October 1992; Richard Roberts, 'Transcendental Sociology?: A Critique of John Milbank's *Theology and Social Theory Beyond Secular Reason*', *Scottish Journal of Theology*, 46, 1993, pp. 527–35; and Pat Logan, *Policing the Sublime*, London, Anglican Association for Social Responsibility, 1995.

17. Oliver O'Donovan, *The Desire of the Nations: Rediscovering the Roots of Political Theology*, Cambridge, Cambridge University Press, 1996.

18. Milbank, *Theology and Social Theory*, p. 2.

19. ibid., pp. 248–9.

20. O'Donovan, *The Desire of the Nations*, p. 15.

21. Milbank, *Theology and Social Theory*, pp. 380, 249, 251, 411.

22. ibid., p. 249.

23. O'Donovan, *The Desire of the Nations*, pp. 13–14.

24. I have discussed this in some detail in my PhD thesis 'A Christian Contribution to Revolutionary Praxis? An Examination of the Significance of Religious Belief for the Political Philosophies of Gerrard Winstanley and Camilo Torres', University of Kent at Canterbury, 1989, upon part of which this book is based.

25. Turner, *Marxism and Christianity*, p. 182; cf. Abraham Friesen, *Reformation and Utopia*, Wiesbaden, Franz Steiner Verlag GMBH, 1974, p. 238, and Scott, *Theology, Ideology and Liberation*, pp. 25f.

26. Karl Marx, 'Contribution to the Critique of Hegel's Philosophy of Right', in Marx and Engels, *On Religion*, Moscow, Progress Publishers, 1975, p. 39.

27. Cited in Fierro, *The Militant Gospel*, p. 286.

28. Friedrich Engels, *The Peasant War in Germany*, 1850. For a critique of Engels' whole approach to this subject see Friesen, *Reformation and Utopia*.

29. Marx and Engels, *On Religion*, p. 98, and Lewis S. Feuer, ed., *Marx and Engels: Basic Writings on Politics and Philosophy*, Glasgow, Collins, 1969, p. 462.

30. Feuer, *Marx and Engels: Basic Writings*, p. 457.

31. John Maguire, 'Gospel or Religious Language?: Engels on the Peasant War', *New Blackfriars*, 54, 1973, p. 350.

32. Feuer, *Marx and Engels: Basic Writings*, p. 469.
33. Christopher Hill, *The Religion of Gerrard Winstanley*, Oxford, The Past and Present Society, 1978, p. 57.
34. Perez Zagorin, *A History of Political Thought in the English Revolution*, London, Routledge & Kegan Paul, 1954, p. 52.
35. Michael Löwy, 'Marxism and Religion: The Challenge of Liberation Theology', *International Marxist Review*, 2, 1987, p. 97. For Löwy's most recent reflections on religion, politics and liberation theology see *The War of Gods: Religion and Politics in Latin America*, London & NY, Verso, 1996.
36. Maguire, 'Gospel or Religious Language?', p. 350; cf. Turner, *Marxism and Christianity*, p. 168.
37. It is worth noting that, since 1989, most of this thinking has been done in the light of the failure of revolution as a model for social change.
38. This is not to ignore, as Christopher Rowland has pointed out (in *Radical Christianity*, Cambridge, Polity Press, 1988, pp. 144–6), that in Nicaragua in the 1980s some were tempted to err dangerously near to identifying one historical situation with the establishment of the kingdom.
39. Míguez Bonino, *Christians and Marxists*, p. 127; *idem, Doing Theology*, p. 144.
40. Gutiérrez, *A Theology of Liberation*, p. 232.
41. ibid., p. 233.
42. Rubem A. Alves, 'Christian Realism: Ideology of the Establishment', *Christianity and Crisis*, 17 September 1973, p. 175. Alves has more recently reflected on 'utopia' in an imaginative way in *The Poet, The Warrior, The Prophet*, London, SCM, 1990.
43. Gutiérrez, *A Theology of Liberation*, p. 237.
44. Míguez Bonino, *Christians and Marxists*, p. 127.
45. Gutiérrez, *A Theology of Liberation*, p. 237.
46. ibid.; cf. Míguez Bonino, *Christians and Marxists*, pp. 127–8, and *Doing Theology*, pp. 151–2.
47. Gutiérrez, *The Power of the Poor in History*, pp. 61f.; cf. p. 12, and Thomas Cullinan, *The Passion of Political Love*, London, Sheed & Ward, 1987, p. 102.
48. Fierro, *The Militant Gospel*, pp. 278–9 (a passage which contains a useful survey of theologians' views on the relationship between the kingdom and utopia); Hebblethwaite, *The Christian-Marxist Dialogue and Beyond*, pp. 28–9.

49. David McLellan, *Marxism and Religion*, London, Macmillan, 1987, p. 161; cf. José Míguez Bonino, *Toward a Christian Political Ethics*, London, SCM, 1983, p. 80.
50. Assmann, *Practical Theology of Liberation*, p. 142.
51. Lash, *A Matter of Hope*, p. 238; cf. the analogy drawn by Frei Betto of faith as the 'map' to take us ever further down the 'road' of politics: *Os Dez Mandamentos De Fe y Politica*, Brazil, n/d.
52. See John Marsden, *Marxian and Christian Utopianism: Toward a Socialist Political Theology*, NY, Monthly Review Press, 1991, pp. 173f.
53. José P. Miranda, *Marx and the Bible*, London, SCM, 1977, p. 256; Gutiérrez, *A Theology of Liberation*, p. 231; Ernesto Guevara, 'Socialism and Man in Cuba', in David McLellan, ed., *Marxism: Essential Writings*, Oxford, Oxford University Press, 1988, p. 382.
54. Rosemary Radford Ruether, *To Change the World*, London, SCM, 1981, p. 15. It is interesting to recall that after the revolution there Cuban leaders were exceptionally ruthless with their own ranks who transgressed in order to demonstrate the superiority of the revolutionary ethic.
55. Turner, *Marxism and Christianity*, pp. 217–19.
56. Leonardo and Clodovis Boff, *Introducing Liberation Theology*, Tunbridge Wells, Burns & Oates, 1987, p. 53.
57. McLellan, *Marxism and Religion*, p. 154; cf. Gutiérrez, *A Theology of Liberation*, p. 231.
58. Cox, *The Secular City*, p. 125; Míguez Bonino, *Doing Theology*, pp. 142–3; cf. David Jenkins, *God, Politics and the Future*, London, SCM, 1988, pp. 109–10.
59. Nicholas Lash, 'Conversation in Gethsemane', in Werner G. Jeanrond and Jennifer L. Rike, eds, *Radical Pluralism and Truth: David Tracy and the Hermeneutics of Religion*, NY, Crossroads, 1991, pp. 51–61; Christopher Rowland, 'Eucharist as Liberation from the Present', in David Brown and Ann Loades, eds, *The Sense of the Sacramental: Movement and Measure in Art and Music, Place and Time*, London, SPCK, 1995, pp. 200–15; cf. Milbank, *Theology and Social Theory*, pp. 238ff.
60. Rowland, *Radical Christianity*, p. 3.
61. See Graham Maddox, *Religion and the Rise of Democracy*, London & NY, Routledge, 1996, pp. 89ff.; Christopher Rowland and Mark Corner, *Liberating Exegesis: The Challenge of Liberation Theology to Biblical Studies*, London, SPCK, 1990, pp. 114f., 137; Milbank, *Theology and Social Theory*, p. 389; Robert Markus, 'The Legacy of St Augustine: A Political Revolutionary', *The Tablet*, 17 May 1986, p. 506.
62. Terry Eagleton, 'Faith and Revolution', *New Blackfriars*, 52, 1971, p. 159.

63. Cited in Brian Wicker, *First the Political Kingdom*, Notre Dame, University of Notre Dame Press, 1968, p. 124.
64. Cited in Fierro, *The Militant Gospel*, p. 282.
65. I have borrowed this expression from Pedro Trigo, *Creation and History*, Tunbridge Wells, Burns & Oates, 1992, p. 201.
66. Marsden, *Marxian and Christian Utopianism*, p. 170.
67. James Klugmann, 'Communism – the Future', in James Klugmann and Paul Oestreicher, eds, *What Kind of Revolution?*, London, Panther, 1968, pp. 185–6; Alistair Kee, *Marx and the Failure of Liberation Theology*, London, SCM, 1990, p. 108.
68. Eagleton, 'Faith and Revolution', p. 160.
69. Cited in Míguez Bonino, *Toward a Christian Political Ethics*, p. 31.
70. Eagleton, 'Faith and Revolution', pp. 160–1; the reference to the Church as a sacrament of human community links with Lash's comments earlier on the Eucharist.
71. Wicker, *First the Political Kingdom*, p. 80.
72. Karl Barth, *The Epistle to the Romans*, tr. Edwyn C. Hoskyns, London, Oxford University Press, 1933, pp. 480ff. Barth's comments must be seen in the light of the context in which he prepared the various versions of *Der Römerbrief* – the Bolshevik revolution and Lenin's espousal of the dictatorship of the proletariat, and events in Germany in the 1920s.
73. ibid., pp. 482–3.
74. ibid., p. 493.
75. Fierro, *The Militant·Gospel*, pp. 263–4; Gutiérrez, *A Theology of Liberation*, p. 165; Miranda, *Marx and the Bible*, p. 295.
76. Miranda himself recognizes this in a later work, *Being and the Messiah*, NY, Orbis, 1977, where he writes: 'To postpone the kingdom, to postpone the Messiah, is to prevent them from ever being real'; cited in J. Andrew Kirk, *Liberation Theology: An Evangelical View from the Third World*, Basingstoke, Marshall, Morgan & Scott, p. 136.
77. Fierro, *The Militant Gospel*, p. 298.
78. Klugmann, 'Communism – the Future', p. 185.
79. Fierro, *The Militant Gospel*, p. 283; cf. Rosemary Radford Ruether, *Sexism and God-Talk: Towards a Feminist Theology*, London, SCM, 1983, pp. 252f.
80. Gutiérrez, *A Theology of Liberation*, p. 177 (cf. p. 217 and *The Power of the Poor in History*, p. 61); Jürgen Moltmann, *Theology of Hope*, London, SCM, 1967, p. 18.
81. Fierro, *The Militant Gospel*, p. 290.

82. Löwy, 'Marxism and Religion', p. 95.

83. Rowland, *Radical Christianity*, p. 100.

84. Moltmann, *Theology of Hope*, p. 16. It should be noted that in *The Crucified God*, London, SCM, 1974, Moltmann is concerned to show how 'the God of hope who contradicts suffering' also 'enters the sufferings of the present and takes them upon himself'; see Richard Bauckham, *Moltmann: Messianic Theology in the Making*, Basingstoke, Marshall, Morgan & Scott, 1987, p. 81.

85. John Gerassi, ed., *Revolutionary Priest: The Complete Writings and Messages of Camilo Torres*, London, Jonathan Cape, 1971, p. 330.

86. A good starting-point would be Stephen J. Casey, 'Nonviolence – A Christian Absolute?', in Thomas M. McFadden, ed., *Liberation, Revolution, and Freedom: Theological Perspectives*, NY, Seabury Press, 1975, pp. 139ff., and J. G. Davies, *Christians, Politics and Violent Revolution*, London, SCM, 1976.

87. Ruether, *To Change the World*, p. 29.

88. Davies, *Christians, Politics and Violent Revolution*, pp. 129–30.

89. Phillip Berryman, *The Religious Roots of Rebellion*, London, SCM, 1984, p. 314.

90. Pope Paul VI, *Populorum Progressio*, London, Catholic Truth Society, 1967, para. 31.

91. Míguez Bonino, *Toward a Christian Political Ethics*, p. 107. On Míguez Bonino and violence see Rebecca S. Chopp, *The Praxis of Suffering*, NY, Orbis, 1986, pp. 92ff.

92. Albert Nolan, *Taking Sides*, London, Catholic Institute for International Relations/Catholic Truth Society, n/d, p. 5.

93. *The Kairos Document*, London, Catholic Institute for International Relations, 2nd rev. edn, 1986, p. 10.

94. Hélder Câmara, *Church and Colonialism*, London, Sheed & Ward, 1969, pp. 109–10.

95. Denys Turner, 'Gerrard Winstanley', *New Blackfriars*, 62, 1981, p. 507.

96. Míguez Bonino, *Christians and Marxists*, pp. 129–30; cf. the views of Herbert Marcuse in Davies, *Christians, Politics and Violent Revolution*, p. 175.

97. In a private communication.

98. Jon Sobrino, *Christology at the Crossroads*, London, SCM, 1978, p. 370; cf. Jorge Pixley and Clodovis Boff, *The Bible, the Church and the Poor*, Tunbridge Wells, Burns & Oates, 1989, p. 135.

99. Herbert McCabe, 'The Class Struggle and Christian Love', in Rex

Ambler and David Haslam, eds, *Agenda for Prophets*, London, Bowerdean, 1980, p. 168.

100. McCabe, cited in Wicker, *First the Political Kingdom*, p. 130.
101. McCabe, 'The Class Struggle and Christian Love', p. 168.
102. Cited in J. Andrew Kirk, 'Attitudes to Violence Amongst Liberation Theologians', *Shaft*, 28, 1980, III.2; cf. the concept of *intellectus amoris* which has surfaced in recent debates about a possible 'paradigm shift' in liberation theology.
103. A commitment to exposing the ideological function of religion and to its 'deprivatization' is of course the foundation for all political theology: see for example J. B. Metz, *Theology of the World*, NY, Herder & Herder, 1969; Dorothee Sölle, *Political Theology*, NY, Fortress Press 1974; and the useful introduction in Chopp, *The Praxis of Suffering*, pp. 28ff.
104. Assmann, *Practical Theology of Liberation*, p. 139.
105. Míguez Bonino, *Christians and Marxists*, p. 126.
106. Jürgen Moltmann, *Religion, Revolution, and the Future*, NY, Scribners, 1969, p. 133.
107. Johann Baptist Metz, *Faith in History and Society*, London, Burns & Oates, 1980, pp. 184ff.; cf. Gutiérrez, *The Power of the Poor in History*, pp. 12, 80; Rowland and Corner, *Liberating Exegesis*, pp. 145–6; Milbank, *Theology and Social Theory*, pp. 238f.; Charles Davis, *Theology and Political Society*, Cambridge, Cambridge University Press, 1980, pp. 149f. In many contexts ownership of a Bible has been considered deeply subversive by the authorities.
108. Cited in Duncan B. Forrester, *Beliefs, Values and Policies*, Oxford, Oxford University Press, 1989, p. 29.
109. Mary Grey, 'Liberation Theology and the Bearers of Dangerous Memory', *New Blackfriars*, 75, 1994, pp. 514–16; see also *idem, Redeeming the Dream*, London, SPCK, 1989, pp. 93f.
110. Ivan Vallier, *Catholicism, Social Control, and Modernization in Latin America*, New Jersey, Prentice-Hall, 1970, pp. 124–5. On Nicaragua see for example Phillip Berryman, *The Religious Roots of Rebellion* and *Stubborn Hope: Religion, Politics and Revolution in Central America*, NY, Orbis, 1994, and my *Saints and Sandinistas*, London, Epworth Press, 1987. Some profoundly revolutionary reinterpreting of the gospels went on in the base community at Solentiname, Nicaragua, in the 1960s and 1970s; see Ernesto Cardenal, *The Gospel in Solentiname*, 4 vols, NY, Orbis, 1976–82.
111. Assmann, *Practical Theology of Liberation*, p. 140, and Feuer, *Marx and Engels: Basic Writings*, pp. 436–7.

112. Míguez Bonino, *Christians and Marxists*, p. 27.
113. Harry E. Vanden and Gary Prevost, *Democracy and Socialism in Sandinista Nicaragua*, Boulder, Colorado, & London, Lynne Rienner Publishers, 1993, p. 42; cf. Duncan B. Forrester, 'Priorities for Social Theology Today', in Michael S. Northcott, ed., *Vision and Prophecy: The Tasks of Social Theology Today*, Edinburgh, Centre for Theology and Public Issues, 1991, p. 32.
114. Alistair Kee, *Domination or Liberation: The Place of Religion in Social Conflict*, London, SCM, 1986, pp. 41, 35.
115. ibid., p. 39.
116. Míguez Bonino, *Christians and Marxists*, pp. 138, 140.
117. Moltmann, *Religion, Revolution, and the Future*, p. 146.
118. Míguez Bonino, *Christians and Marxists*, p. 140.
119. Lash, *A Matter of Hope*, p. 269; cf. idem, *Theology on the Way to Emmaus*, London, SCM, 1986, p. 207.
120. Klugmann, 'Communism – the Future', pp. 186–7; cf. Lash, *Theology on the Way to Emmaus*, p. 214.
121. James Bentley, *Between Marx and Christ: The Dialogue in German-Speaking Europe 1870–1970*, London, Verso, 1982, p. 95; cf. David McLellan, 'The Legacy of Marx', in Andrew R. Morton, ed., *After Socialism: The Future of Radical Christianity*, Edinburgh, Centre for Theology and Public Issues, 1994, pp. 16–17.
122. Assmann, *Practical Theology of Liberation*, p. 144; cf. Joseph Ratzinger, *Church, Ecumenism and Politics*, Slough, St Paul, 1988, p. 273. Critiques of Marx from an evangelical perspective also point to his failure to explore the real root cause of human alienation, estrangement from God through sin; see for example David Lyon, *Karl Marx*, Tring, Lion, 1979, pp. 43ff. On God's commitment to life see Gustavo Gutiérrez, *The God of Life*, London, SCM, 1991.
123. Eagleton, 'Faith and Revolution', pp. 161–3.
124. Moltmann, *Religion, Revolution, and the Future*, p. 146.

FURTHER READING

Ambler, R., & Haslam, D., *Agenda for Prophets*, Bowerdean, 1980.

Assmann, H., *Practical Theology of Liberation*, Search Press, 1975.

Berryman, P., *Stubborn Hope: Religion, Politics and Revolution in Central America*, Orbis, 1994.

Berryman, P., *The Religious Roots of Rebellion*, SCM, 1984.

Bradstock, A., *Saints and Sandinistas*, Epworth, 1987.

Davies, J. G., *Christians, Politics and Violent Revolution*, SCM, 1976.

Ellul, J., *The Presence of the Kingdom*, Helmers Howard, 1967.

Fierro, A., *The Militant Gospel*, SCM, 1977.

Gerassi, J., ed., *Revolutionary Priest: The Complete Writings and Messages of Camilo Torres*, Jonathan Cape, 1971

Goertz, H-J., *Thomas Müntzer: Apocalyptic Mystic and Revolutionary*, T. & T. Clark, 1993.

Gutiérrez, G., *The Power of the Poor in History*, SCM, 1983.

Gutiérrez, G., *A Theology of Liberation*, SCM, 1974.

Harries, R., *Should a Christian Support Guerillas?*, Lutterworth, 1982.

Hill, C., *The Religion of Gerrard Winstanley*, The Past and Present Society, 1978.

Hill, C., ed., *Winstanley: The Law of Freedom and other Writings*, Penguin, 1973.

Hopton, A., ed., *Gerrard Winstanley: Selected Writings*, London, Aporia Press, 1989.

Kee, A., *Domination or Liberation: The Place of Religion in Social Conflict*, SCM, 1986.

Kirk, J. A., *Theology Encounters Revolution*, IVP, 1980.

Lash, N., *A Matter of Hope*, Darton, Longman & Todd, 1981.

Lehmann, P., *The Transfiguration of Politics*, SCM, 1975.

Löwy, M. *The War of Gods: Religion and Politics in Latin America*, Verso, 1996.

Marsden, J., *Marxian and Christian Utopianism: Toward a Socialist Political Theology*, Monthly Review Press, 1991.

Matheson, P., ed., *The Collected Works of Thomas Müntzer*, T. & T. Clark, 1988.

McLellan, D., *Unto Caesar*, Notre Dame, 1993.

McLellan, D., *Marxism and Religion*, Macmillan, 1987.

Metz, J. B., *Theology of the World*, Herder & Herder, 1969.

Míguez Bonino, J., *Toward a Christian Political Ethics*, SCM, 1983.

Míguez Bonino, J., *Christians and Marxists: The Mutual Challenge to Revolution*, Hodder & Stoughton, 1976.

Míguez Bonino, J., *Doing Theology in a Revolutionary Situation*, Fortress, 1975.

Milbank, J., *Theology and Social Theory: Beyond Secular Reason*, Blackwell, 1990.

Moltmann, J., *Religion, Revolution, and the Future*, Scribners, 1969.

Moltmann, J., *Theology of Hope*, SCM, 1967.

O'Donovan, O., *The Desire of the Nations: Rediscovering the Roots of Political Theology*, Cambridge University Press, 1996.

Petegorsky, D. W., *Left-Wing Democracy in the English Civil War*, Alan Sutton, 1995.

Pixley, J. & Boff, C., *The Bible, the Church and the Poor*, Burns & Oates, 1989.

Radford Ruether, R., *To Change the World*, SCM, 1981.

Rowland, C., & Corner, M., *Liberating Exegesis: The Challenge of Liberation Theology to Biblical Studies*, SPCK, 1990.

Rowland, C., *Radical Christianity: A Reading of Recovery*, Polity Press, 1988.

Sabine, G. H., ed., *The Works of Gerrard Winstanley*, Russell & Russell, 1965.

Scott, T., *Thomas Müntzer: Theology and Revolution in the German Reformation*, Macmillan, 1989.

Sölle, D., *Political Theology*, NY, Fortress Press 1974.

Turner, D., *Marxism and Christianity*, Blackwell, 1983.

Winstanley can also be found on the Internet at
www.webcom.com/enoble/diggers/digg–eb.html

INDEX

Aesticampianus, Johannes Rhagius 5
Alsop, James D. 69, 78, 79, 80, 81, 183,
    184, 185
Althusser, Louis 142, 160
Alves, Rubem 150, 196 n.42
Antichrist 27, 34, 36–9, 44, 53, 62, 89,
    92, 114
Apocalyptic, apocalypticism 26, 64, 90,
    92
    Müntzer and 13, 24, 28, 32–60, 62,
    65, 180 n.23, 181 n.26
    Winstanley and 112, 113, 115, 119,
    122
Armytage, W. H. G. 95
Ashley, Maurice 85
Assmann, Hugo 140, 152, 167–8, 170,
    173, 194 n.2
Augustine of Hippo 6, 156, 181 n.25
Aylmer G. E. 76, 94, 104, 183 n.13

Bailey, Richard 34–5, 37, 52
Barth, Karl 158–9, 198 n.72
Bauckham, Richard 33, 199 n.84
Benjamin, Walter 168
Bernstein, Eduard 85, 186 n.9
Betto, Frei 197 n.51
Black Power 171
Blake, William 186 n.9
Bloch, Ernst 59–60, 146, 177 n.6
Bloch, Joseph 170
Boff, Clodovis 155, 194 n.11, 199 n.98
Boff, Leonardo 155
Bräuer, Siegfried 27, 65
Brugnoli, Pietro 140
Bubenheimer, Ulrich 4, 181 n.34
Burgess, John P. 180 n.20, 187 n.24,
    188 n.29
Burroughs, Edward 80

Calvin, John 3, 16, 97–8, 132
Câmara, Archbishop Hélder 164–5
Cardenal, Fernando 142
Carrión, Luís 170
Charles I xii, 101–2, 104, 113, 122, 189
    n.48

Charles II 80
'Christians for Socialism' 141
Clarkson, Lawrence 77, 79
Cleage, Albert 170–1
Cohn, Norman 109–10
Cone, James 170
Corner, Mark 110
Cox, Harvey 140, 155
Croatto, Severino 167
Cromwell, Oliver 78, 84, 91, 102, 104,
    117, 120

Dalton, R. J. 78, 79, 183 n.8, 185 n.21
'Dangerous memory' 168
Davies, J. G. 163, 199 n.86
Davies, Lady Eleanor, see Douglas
Davis, J. C. 84, 125–7, 193 n.48
Dawson, David 116
Denys the Areopagite 14
Diggers 72–80, 85, 87, 91, 95, 102–6,
    113, 118, 120, 127, 130, 166, 183
    n.11, 186 n.8
Douglas, Lady Eleanor (also Davies) 77,
    79, 184 n.15
Drake, Francis 72, 76

Eagleton, Terry 125, 156–8, 173–4
Eccleshall, R. 132
Eck, Johann 6
Eckhart, Meister 16
Edwards, Thomas 115
Elliger, Walter 17, 178 n.20
Elliott, Charles 178 n.13
Elmen, Paul 83, 90–1, 189 n.47
Engels, Friedrich 93, 119, 124, 146–9,
    161, 170, 195 n.28
Ernst of Mansfield, Count 8, 11, 28–9,
    47, 53, 55, 181 n.30
Eschatology x, 33, 110, 171
    in Müntzer xi–xii, 30, 33–5, 37, 39,
    45, 58, 59, 66, 180 n.23, 182
    n.10
    in Winstanley 93, 105, 107, 122,
    124–5, 162, 180

in contemporary revolutionary discourse 144–61, 167, 173, 174–5

Eternal Evangel, the; Eternal Gospel, the, see Everlasting Gospel

Eusebius of Caesarea 6, 56

Evans, Arise 190 n.16

Everard, William 74

Everlasting Gospel, the 34, 114, 118

Fairfax, General Sir Thomas (later Lord) 74–6, 105, 118, 129

Fell, Margaret 80

Feminist theology 171

Fierro, Alfredo 140, 142, 159–60

'Fifth monarchy' 35–6, 56

Fifth Monarchy Movement 85, 86, 115

Franz, Günther 36

Frederick the Wise, Elector of Saxony 8, 9, 26, 44, 46

Freire, Paulo, 150, 155, 169

Friends, Society of, see Quakers

'Friends of God' 15, 16, 18, 53

Friesen, Abraham 35, 195 n.28

Garaudy, Roger 172

Gater, Sarah 71

Gater, William 71

George, C. H. 94

George, Duke 12

Gersen, Ottilie von 7, 12

Gladman, Captain John 74

Goertz, Hans-Jürgen 3–4, 13, 24, 30, 59, 178 n.20

'Golden Age' xi, 97, 109, 128–32, 193 n.54

Government

   Müntzer on 25–6, 28

   Winstanley on 92, 95, 119, 120, 121, 129, 131

Graham, John K. 118, 185 n.1

Grey, Mary 169, 176 n.1

Gritsch, Eric 46–7

Guevara, Ernesto (Che) 153, 165, 170

Günther, Franz 6

Gutiérrez, Gustavo 141, 150–1, 153, 159, 160

Haferitz, Simon 8

Hardacre, Paul H. 184 n.15, 184 n.16

Hauerwas, Stanley 142

Hausmann, Nicholas 36, 37, 38, 48, 56

Hayes, T. Wilson 80, 112, 116, 122, 130

Heaton, Andrée 176 n.1

Hegesippus 6, 56

Herrgott, Johann 35

Hicks, Giles 79

Hill, Christopher 69, 70, 80, 85, 86, 87, 94, 95, 106, 114, 116, 120, 128–9, 147, 149, 187 n.18, 188 n.29, 193 n.47, 193 n.50

Hobbes, Thomas 98, 131, 188 n.37

Holstun, James 89, 184 n.20, 193 n.47

Hudson, Winthrop S. 102, 185 n.5

Hus, Jan; Hussites 7, 86

James, Margaret 186 n.12

Jerome 6

Joachim of Fiore 33–6, 39, 46, 114–15, 118, 123

John, Duke of Saxony 9, 10, 46

John Frederick, Prince 9

Juretic, George 84, 117–19, 191 n.32

Kairos Document 164

Kairos moment 30–1, 56, 59, 122, 154, 161

Karlstadt, Andreas Bodenstein von 6, 38, 182 n.43

Kee, Alistair 157, 170–1

Kendrick, Christopher 129, 186 n.8, 192 n.42

Kenyon, Timothy 83

King, Martin Luther 165

King, Susan (Winstanley) 71, 78

King, William 72, 78–9

Kingdom (reign) of God ix, x, xii, 65, 86, 109–10, 124–5, 196 n.38, 198 n.76

   Müntzer and xii, 24, 29, 30, 39, 43–4, 50, 56

   Winstanley and xii, 111, 116

   in contemporary revolutionary discourse 139–75

   defined 176 n.1

and utopia 196 n.48
Klugmann, James 157, 160, 172
Knott, James 96, 102
Kumar, Krishan 126, 190 n.20, 192 n.46

Lash, Nicholas 141, 152, 155–6, 172, 198
    n.70
Lebacqz, Karen 168
Lenin, V. I.; Leninism 153, 166, 198 n.72
Lenthall, William 190 n.16
Levellers 99–100, 117
Liberation theology 86, 140–3, 149–
    52, 154–5, 194 n.2, 196 n.35, 200
    n.102
Lilburne, John 99–100
Lindsey, William D. 129–30, 193 n.54
Lollards, see Wyclif, John
Löwy, Michael 148, 160, 196 n.35
Luther, Martin 3, 5–6, 14–15, 47, 51, 93
    and Müntzer 9–10, 16–17, 18, 20,
        25, 44, 45, 46, 48, 62–3, 180
        n.13, 180 n.14, 181 n.25
    on government and politics 25, 182
        n.40
Lyon, David 202 n.122

McCabe, Herbert 157, 166–7
McLellan, David 152, 155
Maguire, John 93, 147, 148
Mannheim, Karl 110, 122, 125–6
Marcuse, Herbert 199 n.96
Maron, Gottfried 180 n.23
Marsden, John 157
Marx, Karl; Marxism 66, 85, 93, 123,
    141–2, 145, 147, 151–3, 157–8,
    159, 160, 168, 170, 171, 172–3,
    201 n.122
Mary (mother of Jesus) xiii, 8, 45, 54
Matheson, Peter 17, 27, 44–5
Mede, Joseph 115
Meinhard, Christopher 50
Melanchthon, Phillip 6, 38, 44
Metz, Johann Baptist 168, 200 n.103
Míguez Bonino, José 60, 66, 141–2,
    150–1, 155, 164, 165, 168, 172,
    199 n.91
Milbank, John 142–3, 195 n.16

Millennium, millenarianism 144, 154,
    192 n.46
    Müntzer and 146–8, 149
    Winstanley and 84, 90–4, 109–27,
        131, 133, 149, 186 n.8
    defined 109–10
Miranda, José P. 153, 159, 198 n.76
Moltmann, Jürgen 150, 151, 159–61,
    168, 172, 174, 181 n.29, 199 n.84
More, Sir Thomas 126
Mulder, David 187 n.23, 188 n.29, 188
    n.36
Mulligan, Lotte 118, 185 n.1
Müntzer, Thomas x, xi, 70, 86, 93, 108,
    114, 122, 129, 139, 144, 154, 161,
    167, 171
    childhood and education 3–5
    ordination 5
    at Wittenberg 5–6, 15
    at Zwickau 6–7
    at Prague 7
    at Allstedt 7–10, 41
    marriage, family 7, 12
    at Mühlhausen 10–11, 28, 30, 51,
        58
    and the Peasants' War 10–12, 27–32,
        37, 45, 51–2, 57–9, 145, 146
    death 12
    on Antichrist 27, 34, 36–9, 44, 53,
        62
    apocalyptic thinking of xi–xii, 13, 24,
        26, 28, 32–60, 62, 64, 65, 122,
        180 n.23, 181 n.26
    on the Bible 17, 20–2, 24–5, 26, 34,
        36, 39, 42, 45, 53, 61, 144, 181
        n.25
    on the church 30, 35, 40–1, 52, 56–9,
        64–6, 146
    and communism 29, 146–7
    covenants/leagues 9–12, 28, 43, 49,
        51, 52
    as Daniel 9, 49, 50
    on the elect 7, 9, 10, 15, 22, 23, 26,
        27, 29–30, 37, 38, 39, 40, 42,
        50–4, 56–7, 59, 62–6
    as Elijah 48–50
    as Gideon 47–50, 57–8

on the 'godless' 8, 10, 22, 24, 26, 28, 40, 42, 43, 47, 50–1, 52–3, 55, 57, 66, 180 n.17, 180 n.21
on governments 25–6, 28
as Jehu 49–50
as John the Baptist 47–50
as Josiah 9, 49
and Luther 9–10, 16–17, 18, 20, 44, 45, 46, 48, 62–63, 180 n.13, 180 n.14, 181 n.25
and mysticism xi, 5–7, 13–24, 32, 54, 64, 65–6, 177 n.8, 179 n.12
on the *ordo rerum* xi, 5, 29–30, 46, 55, 60–6
on revolution xi, 25, 30, 32, 32–66, 145–9
on true faith 5–8, 10, 15–25, 33, 39, 42, 45, 46, 49, 51, 52–5, 61, 64, 66
utopian ideas of xi, 60–6
Protestation or Proposition 8
On Counterfeit Faith 8, 15, 18, 63
'Sermon to the Princes' 9, 19, 21, 26, 27, 35, 40, 42–3, 48, 49, 55, 56
A Manifest Exposé 10, 22, 24–5, 41, 42, 47, 48, 49, 51, 56, 61, 64, 65, 180 n.17, 180 n.21
Vindication and Refutation 10, 27, 35, 44, 48, 61, 63, 180 n.14
'Prague Manifesto' 4, 7, 15, 29–30, 37, 38, 40, 41, 44, 46–7, 48, 55, 56, 61, 63, 64–5, 180 n.18
Murphy, Walter F. 102, 192 n.39

New Model Army 131
Newton, Sir Isaac 115
Nicaragua xiii, 142, 144, 162, 169, 196 n.38, 200 n.110
Nicholas of Cusa 63
Nipperdey, Thomas 65
Nolan, Albert 164

O'Donovan, Oliver 142–3
Olson, Theodore 110, 125, 130
Ozment, Steven E. 181 n.34

Paul (of Tarsus) 21, 24, 26, 46, 63, 110, 153, 159, 172
Paul VI, Pope 163
Peasants' War 10–12, 27–32, 37, 45, 51–2, 57–9, 93, 146
Petegorsky, David 85, 94, 95, 120, 131, 192 n.30, 194 n.57
Pfeiffer (Schwertfeger, Heinrich) 10–12
Plato 5, 29, 63, 126
Platt, Parson John 76–7, 113
Poole, Matthew 114, 190 n.18
Populorum Progressio 163
'Preferential option for the poor' 169

Quakers 80–1, 86
Quintilian 5, 60

Rahner, Karl 151
Rainborough, Colonel Thomas 99
Ranters 76, 77, 86
Reay, Barry 80
Reeves, Marjorie 34, 36, 65
Resurrection xii–xiii, 14, 59–60, 109, 111, 116–17, 160, 171–4, 191 n.29
Rich, Arthur 157
Richards, Judith 118, 185 n.1
Richardson, R. C. 183 n.2
Romero, Archbishop Oscar 163
Rowland, Christopher 20, 33, 110, 155–6, 161, 166, 179 n.3, 187 n.16, 196 n.38
Ruether, Rosemary Radford 153, 163
Rupp, Gordon 15, 23, 29, 47, 63, 182 n.42

Sabine, George H. 70, 72, 77, 83, 91, 105, 123, 133, 190 n.15, 191 n.24
Sandinistas 144, 162, 170
Schwarz, Reinhard 19, 61, 63, 65–6
Scott, Peter 194 n.14
Scott, Tom 3, 30, 50, 178 n.20, 177 n.9
Scott Luckens, Carola 184 n.15
Segundo, Juan Luís 140–1
Selby, Peter 176 n.1
Shaull, Richard 158

Shulman, George M. 104, 184 n.19, 188
   n.37, 189 n.44, 189 n.48
Sobrino, Jon 166
South Africa xiii, 164
Spalatin, George 8
'Specific Christian contribution' ix-x,
   xiii, 32, 66, 127, 139–43, 157, 165,
   173
Stalin, Joseph 157
Staupitz, Johannes von ' 18
Stayer, James M. 17, 52, 178 n.20, 180
   n.15
Storch, Nicholas 7
Strobel, Georg Theodor 3, 15
Suso, Henry 13, 16

Taborites 33
Tauler, Johannes 6, 13, 15–16
Tertullian 38, 48, 62–3
Theologia Germanica 14–16
Thomas, Sir Keith 184 n.14, 191 n.23
Torres, Camilo 144, 162–3, 165, 169, 195
   n.24
Trigo, Pedro 198 n.65
Trotsky, Leon 157
Turner, Denys 93, 124, 142, 145, 154,
   165, 188 n.30, 189 n.44, 192 n.42

Utopia, utopianism 159, 171, 192 n.46,
   196 n.42, 196 n.48
   in Müntzer xi, 37, 60–6
   in Winstanley xi, 83, 109, 122, 126–
     30, 131, 133, 193 n.46, 193
     n.54
   in contemporary revolutionary
     discourse x-xi, xiii, 149–55
   defined 125–6

Vallier, Ivan 169
Vann, Richard 78–9, 184 n.16
Violence (and non-violence) ix, 59, 97,
   143, 162–7, 199 n.86, 199 n.91,
   200 n.102
   Müntzer and xi, 9, 25, 28, 59
   Winstanley and 103–5, 130–1, 134,
     189 n.48
Vogler, Günter 29

Wicker, Brian 158
William I (the Conqueror) 96, 100–1,
   104, 129
Williams, George H. 35–6
Wink, Walter 176 n.1
Winstanley, Edward 69, 183 n.1, 183 n.2
Winstanley, Gerrard x, xi, 139, 154, 156,
   161, 164, 167
   childhood and education 69–71
   moves to London 71–2
   marriages, family 71–2, 78, 80
   moves to Cobham 72
   and digging project 73–7
   on Antichrist 89, 92
   on the Bible 82, 85, 94, 112, 118–
     19, 144, 180 n.20
   on the church and clergy 69–71, 80,
     86, 87–8, 89–90, 92, 100–1,
     102, 113, 115, 133, 134, 183
     n.4, 183 n.11
   on communism and community
     xi, 77, 79, 82, 83, 89, 90, 91,
     96, 98, 100, 105, 108, 109, 115,
     116–17, 121, 122–3, 124, 127,
     129, 130, 133–4, 145, 147, 162
   on government 92, 95, 119, 120, 121,
     129, 131
   on human nature 97–8, 109, 127,
     130–5, 161–2, 166
   on the land 74–5, 87, 91, 95–100,
     102, 104, 105–7, 134, 188 n.34
   millenarianism of xi-xii, 84, 89, 90–4,
     109–24, 127, 131, 133, 144–5,
     147–9, 186 n.8
   and non-violence 103–5, 130–1, 134,
     162, 165, 166, 189 n.18
   and 'Reason' 86–7, 89–90, 96, 98,
     105, 115, 118, 120, 123, 127,
     131, 132–4, 162, 166, 187 n.19
   on revolution 82, 85, 92, 93, 95f., 100,
     102–4, 106–7, 108–35, 144–5
   utopian ideas of xi, 83, 109, 122, 125–
     30, 131, 133
   The Mysterie of God 69, 73, 111, 112
   The Breaking of the Day of God 73,
     112, 116, 123, 191 n.25

The Saints Paradice 73, 116, 185 n.3, 191 n.24

Truth Lifting up its Head above Scandals 70, 73, 96, 114

The New Law of Righteousnes 69, 70, 72, 73, 91, 98, 102, 106, 115, 116, 118, 127

The True Levellers Standard Advanced 74, 84, 90, 91, 105, 106, 117, 118, 127

A Declaration from the Poor Oppressed People of England 75, 97, 112, 118

Letters to Lord Fairfax 75, 76, 105, 118–19, 129

The Bloudie and Unchristian Acting of William Star and John Taylor 75

An Appeal to the House of Commons 75, 104

A Watch-word to the City of London and the Armie 71, 72, 75, 102, 103

A New-Yeers Gift 70, 76, 119

A Vindication 76

An Appeale to all Englishmen 76, 104

An Humble Request 77, 97, 104, 113, 119

Fire in the Bush 76, 96–7, 113, 118, 119, 128, 132, 184 n.14

The Law of Freedom in a Platform 77, 78, 79, 83–4, 85, 89, 90, 91, 95, 100, 102, 104, 117, 119, 120–1, 126, 127, 131, 148, 185 n.21, 193 n.47, 193 n.48

Winstanley, Susan, *see* King

Wolgast, Eike 25–6, 178 n.20, 182 n.40

Worsley, Peter 110

Wyclif, John; Lollards 7, 86

Zagorin, Perez 84–7, 90, 148

Zeiss, John 33, 34, 49, 62, 63, 64, 65

BIBLE REFERENCES

Genesis
1 61
3.15 112, 113, 118, 119
5.24 180 n.22
18.18 111

Deuteronomy
7 57

2 Kings
9 50

Psalms
2.9 43
3.6 48
19 61
35 51
39 51
98.1 44
98.6 44
98.9 44
118 63

Isaiah
11 61

Jeremiah
23.29 47
50.16 42

Ezekiel
34 45
39 45

Daniel
2 9, 27, 35, 36, 43
7 8, 26, 27, 36
7.25 37, 114

7.27 26, 28
12.7 114

Joel
2.28 22
3.13 42

Amos
9.1 190 n.16

Malachi
4.5 48

Matthew
9.37–38 39
13.24–30 39
13.36 40
24 38, 45
24.9 56
24.14 56
24.32–3 43
25.31f. 181 n.26

Luke
1.46f. xiii, 45
1.52 55
21.29–31 43

John
4.35f. 39
15.13 59
21.22–3 65

Acts
20.29 24

Romans
8.22 110

13 9, 10, 25, 26, 158
13.1 25, 26
13.3 25, 26

2 Corinthians
11.13 63

Colossians
1 63

Hebrews
11.5 180 n.22

Jude
18–19 44
24 180 n.22

Revelation
1.7 56
11 48
11.2 37, 114
11.3 37, 114
11.13 65
12.6 37
12.7–10 112
12.14 37, 114
13 118
13.1 190 n.17
13.5 37
13.16–17 190 n.15
13.17 113, 119
14.14f. 41
16 39
18 44
19 44
19.11–16 44
19.15 43, 44
20.4–6 109